Library of
Davidson College

THE EGALITARIAN CITY

THE EGALITARIAN CITY

Issues of Rights,
Distribution,
Access, and Power

Edited by
Janet K. Boles

PRAEGER SPECIAL STUDIES • PRAEGER SCIENTIFIC

New York • Philadelphia • Eastbourne, UK
Toronto • Hong Kong • Tokyo • Sydney

305
E28

Library of Congress Cataloging-in-Publication Data
Main entry under title:

The Egalitarian city.

  Bibliography: p.
  1. Equality. 2. Cities and towns—United States.
3. Social status—United States. I. Boles, Janet,
1944–
HT151.E36 1986   305   85-22371
ISBN 0-03-000157-9 (alk. paper)

Published and Distributed by the
Praeger Publishers Division
(ISBN Prefix 0-275)
of Greenwood Press, Inc.,
Westport, Connecticut

Published in 1986 by Praeger Publishers
CBS Educational and Professional Publishing, a Division of CBS Inc.
521 Fifth Avenue, New York, NY 10175 USA

© 1986 by Praeger Publishers

All rights reserved

6789 052 987654321

Printed in the United States of America on acid-free paper

INTERNATIONAL OFFICES

Orders from outside the United States should be sent to the appropriate address listed below. Orders from areas not listed below should be placed through CBS International Publishing, 383 Madison Ave., New York, NY 10175 USA

Australia, New Zealand
Holt Saunders, Pty, Ltd., 9 Waltham St., Artarmon, N.S.W. 2064, Sydney, Australia

Canada
Holt, Rinehart & Winston of Canada, 55 Horner Ave., Toronto, Ontario, Canada M8Z 4X6

Europe, the Middle East, & Africa
Holt Saunders, Ltd., 1 St. Anne's Road, Eastbourne, East Sussex, England BN21 3UN

Japan
Holt Saunders, Ltd., Ichibancho Central Building, 22-1 Ichibancho, 3rd Floor, Chiyodaku, Tokyo, Japan

Hong Kong, Southeast Asia
Holt Saunders Asia, Ltd., 10 Fl, Intercontinental Plaza, 94 Granville Road, Tsim Sha Tsui East, Kowloon, Hong Kong

Manuscript submissions should be sent to the Editorial Director, Praeger Publishers, 521 Fifth Avenue, New York, NY 10175 USA

PREFACE AND ACKNOWLEDGMENTS

John Kenneth Galbraith observed in 1958 that "inequality has ceased to preoccupy men's minds." This book of original essays on urban equality grew out of a concern that this may be no less true today. This shift in national priorities was brought into sharp focus for me when the publisher of a widely adopted textbook on American government, in planning for an updated edition, suggested to reviewers that perhaps the chapter on equality should be eliminated. That the chapter has thus far survived a second revision is only somewhat reassuring given numerous countertrends in the larger society: the attack on affirmative action; the *Grove City* decision; the middle-class tax revolt; the antibusing movement; the reduction in redistributive social spending; the reconstituted U.S. Civil Rights Commission; *ad infinitum*.

Indisputably, there are indications that there has been a rise in both fiscal and social conservatism in the late 1970s and early 1980s, a trend encapsulated in President Jimmy Carter's pithy statement that "life is unfair." And traditionally demands for equality have tended to covary with fiscal surplus, a bad omen in an age of retrenchment. Even so, historians have noted that eras of conservative reaction to egalitarian change are part of a well-established cyclical pattern in U.S. politics. The conservative 1920s and 1950s, it should be remembered, were each followed by more than a decade of extensive liberal reforms.

The underlying theme of this collection is that equality is not only a concept of enduring relevance for social science but also a requisite for our survival as an urban society. More specifically, the book had its genesis in a panel, "Visions for an Egalitarian City," at the 1983 American Political Science Association meetings. The chapters in this volume by Salem and Stone are revisions of papers originally presented at that panel. De la Garza and MacManus, each of whom presented papers at the APSA panel, later decided to contribute different papers in collaboration with others. Button, the discussant for that panel, too has written a chapter, again with a coauthor. The other contributors were selected as scholars known for their research on groups that have traditionally had problems attaining equality in the city. Both the panel participants and these other contributors were asked to consider what a more egalitarian city would look like, what barriers to equality must be surmounted, and what policy issues need to be addressed.

I am, of course, deeply indebted to all who accepted my invitation to participate in this project. Without the cooperation, hard work, and, most of all, patience of these authors, there would have been no book. I am also grateful to the Department of Political Science, Marquette University, for its support during the preparation of this manuscript. Henry Alcala and Josephine G. Morstatter stayed in good humor throughout the tedium of word processing. My research assistant,

Len Wojciechowicz, added the perspicacity of a graduate student to the editing of the manuscript. The assistance of Frances S. Johannes, a consultant with Computer Services, Marquette University, is deeply appreciated as well. Finally, I would like to thank Dorothy Breitbart of Praeger for her faith in the continuing importance of urban equality, even during a period between "egalitarian revolutions."

Janet K. Boles

CONTENTS

PREFACE AND ACKNOWLEDGMENTS	v
LIST OF TABLES	xiii
LIST OF FIGURES	xiv
PART I: INTRODUCTION	1

Chapter
1	Urban Equality: Definitions and Demands Janet K. Boles	3
	The Dimensions of Equality	3
	Cities, Groups, and Equality	5
	Equality Under the Law	6
	Urban Services and Equality	9
	The Problem of Access	10
	Power and Equality	12
	Urban Coalitions and Equality	12
	References	13

PART II: JURIDICAL EQUALITY	15

2	Mexican-American Political Clout in Small Urban Jurisdictions: Conditions for Maximizing Influence Susan A. MacManus and Charles S. Bullock, III	17
	Registration Rates	18
	Turnout Rates	19
	The Turnout Gap in 1972–74	19
	The Turnout Gap in 1983–84	20
	Candidacy and Candidacy Success Rates	21
	Candidacy/Candidacy Success Rates: School Board	22
	Candidacy/Candidacy Success Rates: City Elections	23
	Factors Affecting Mexican-American Candidacy/ Candidacy Success Rates	23
	Conclusion	24
	Notes	24
	References	25

3	The Gay Quest for Equality in San Francisco David J. Thomas	27
	The Gay Difference	28

The Right to Exist	30
Equal Security	31
Economic Equality	32
Political Equality	33
New Issues	37
Conclusion	39
Notes	41
References	41

4 The Voteless Constituency: Children and Child Care   42
   Jill Norgren

Children: Society's Precitizens	42
Child Care: Policy for the Young Child	45
The Need	46
Current Arrangements and Policy	47
Day Care in New York	48
Conclusion	53
Notes	56
References	56

PART III: DISTRIBUTIVE EQUALITY   59

5 Native Americans and the Unheavenly City:
   A Study in Inequality   61
   Joyotpaul Chaudhuri

Socioeconomic Characteristics of Urban Indians	62
Access to General Urban Services	65
Urban Indian Centers	66
The Survey	66
Findings	67
Funding Sources, Equity and Need	67
The Ruiz Case and Its Aftermath	69
Barriers to Equality	70
Urban Indian Political Participation	71
Conclusion	72
Notes	73
References	73

6 New Participants, Old Issues: Mexican-American
   Urban Policy Priorities   75
   Rodolfo O. de la Garza and Janet Weaver

Voting Rights	75
Methodology	77
Patterns of Political Efficacy	81

	Public Policy Concerns	83
	Mexican Americans and Anglos in San Antonio	83
	Mexican Americans in Three Cities	87
	Conclusion	87
	Notes	90
	References	90
7	Seeking Equality: The Role of Activist Women in Cities Joyce Gelb and Marilyn Gittell	93
	Traditional Urban Services	95
	Changes in Structured Delivery of Services	96
	Feminism and the Creation of Alternative Public Services in the City	99
	Health Care	99
	Violence Against Women	100
	Community Education	102
	Women in City Government	103
	The Challenge of the 1980s	105
	Conclusion	107
	References	108
8	An Exchange Approach to Community Politics: A Case Study of White Ethnic Activism in Staten Island, New York Irene J. Dabrowski, Anthony L. Haynor, and Robert F. Cuervo	110
	A Model of Community Politics	110
	Principal Categories of Actors in Urban Politics	111
	Goals or Interests of Actors	111
	Relationships Among Goals and Interests	112
	Decisions, Strategies, Tactics, and Resources	112
	Outcomes and Feedback Processes	113
	Exchange Processes in Selected White Ethnic Communities	114
	Identification of Actors	114
	Specification of Goals and Interests	114
	The Relationship Between Goals or Interests	116
	Decisions, Strategies, Resources, and Power	119
	Outcomes and Feedback Processes	123
	Conclusion	123
	Notes	125
	References	126

PART IV: EQUALITY OF ACCESS   129

9   Housing Assistance Programs For America's Urban Poor:
An Analysis of Political Choices Versus Social Reality   131
Byran O. Jackson

	Federally Assisted Housing for the Urban Poor	131
	Johnson's Housing Assistance Policy Initiatives	132
	Review and Critique of the Johnson Policy Initiatives	133
	The Nixon-Ford Era	134
	Review and Critique of the Nixon-Ford Policy Initiatives	135
	Carter's Urban Reform Package	136
	The Reagan Administration's Commission on Housing	137
	Measuring Changes in Housing Assistance Programs	138
	Changes in the Rental Housing Market, 1973–83	141
	Housing Quality	142
	Affordability	144
	Neighborhood Quality	144
	Conclusion	149
	Notes	150
	References	151
10	Gender Equity and the Urban Environment	152
	Greta Salem	
	Working Women and the Urban Environment	154
	An Equal Opportunity Environment	156
	Power, Values, and the Built Environment	158
	References	160
11	Access to the City Means More Than Curb Cuts: The Disabled	162
	Roberta Ann Johnson	
	The Berkeley Story	163
	Civil Rights for the Disabled	165
	The City Resists	166
	Implementation	170
	Conclusion	172
	Notes	173
	References	174

PART V: EQUALITY OF INFLUENCE, POWER, AND CONTROL   177

12	Is There a "Gray Peril"? The Aging's Impact Upon Sunbelt Community Taxing and Spending	179
	James W. Button and Walter A. Rosenbaum	
	The Political Importance of the "Other" Sunbelt	180
	Is There a Politics of Age? The "Gray Peril" Issue	181
	The Political Mobilization Controversy	182
	The "Gray Peril" and City Hall	183

Methodology	183
The Determinants of Taxing and Spending	184
Characterizing the Aging Population	186
The Local Governmental Budget	186
The Communities	187
The Longitudinal Dimension	187
Statistical Procedure	188
Findings	188
Conclusion	196
References	198
13 Race, Power, and Political Change	**200**
Clarence N. Stone	
Competing Schools of Thought	200
Pluralism	200
Coalitional Bias	202
Race and Class	203
Race and Political Change in Atlanta	206
Coalitional Bias Before the Civil Rights "Revolution"	206
The Civil Rights Movement as an Attack on Coalitional Bias	208
Atlanta and Neighborhood Activism	210
Atlanta: The Recent Period	212
Atlanta Then and Now: A Comparison	218
Race, Class, and Coalitional Bias	219
References	222
ABOUT THE EDITOR AND THE CONTRIBUTORS	**224**

TABLES AND FIGURES

LIST OF TABLES

Table		Page
2.1	Voter Registration by Ethnicity, 1980–84	19
2.2	Voter Turnout by Ethnicity, 1972 and 1974 Elections	20
2.3	Voter Turnout by Ethnicity, 1983 and 1984 School Board Elections	21
2.4	Candidate Success Rates in School Board Elections, 1970–83	22
6.1	Socioeconomic Characteristics of Respondents, by City and Ethnicity	78
6.2	Political Efficacy of Respondents, by City and Ethnicity	82
6.3	Most Important Problem Facing Mexican Americans and Anglos in San Antonio	86
6.4	Most Important Problem Facing Mexican Americans, by City	88
8.1	A Typology of Grass-Roots Activities	121
9.1	Substandard Rental Housing Stock, 1973–81	143
9.2	Renters Paying More Than 30 Percent of Income for Housing, 1973–81	145
9.3	Changes in Neighborhood Quality, 1976–81: Physical Attributes	147
9.4	Changes in Neighborhood Quality, 1976–81: Services	148
12.1	Inventory of Independent and Dependent Variables and Data Sources Used in Statistical Analysis	185
12.2	Significant Bivariate Correlates and Beta Coefficients for Community and Aging Variables, City Taxing and Spending, 1972–73	189
12.3	Significant Bivariate Correlates and Beta Coefficients for Community and Aging Variables, City Taxing and Spending, 1976–77	191
12.4	Significant Bivariate Correlates and Beta Coefficients for Community and Aging Variables, City Taxing and Spending, 1981–82	193

LIST OF FIGURES

Figure		Page
9.1	Total Units Reserved, by Presidential Administration	139
9.2	Units Reserved: 1965–1983	140
9.3	Federal Low Income Housing Assistance Annual Budget Outlays: 1957–1983	141

PART I
INTRODUCTION

1

URBAN EQUALITY: DEFINITIONS AND DEMANDS

Janet K. Boles

The U.S. political system has long tolerated a major societal paradox: the doctrine of egalitarianism remains one of the most popular and powerful in the political culture in spite of pervasive inequalities among the population. This gap between ideology and outcomes, however, has increasingly become the source of demands for equity policies and practices (Weale 1978). Not only do U.S. citizens favor egalitarian policies, but also the norm of equality may be essential to national cohesiveness, domestic tranquility, and basic social functioning (Gans 1973, p. xii; Grimes 1964, p. ix). Although social theorists have long recognized the potential for conflict between equality and some other value such as freedom (Wilhoit 1979) or efficiency (Okun 1975), the trend in the twentieth century United States has been to frequently favor equality in policy terms when one norm must take precedence.

THE DIMENSIONS OF EQUALITY

Despite this relatively recent competitive advantage for equality-based policies, a significant barrier to an egalitarian United States remains. While there is widespread societal agreement on the fairness and basic goodness of equality—as an abstract concept, equality is a simple affirmation of the worth of the individual—there is less agreement on the characteristics of and criteria for a political system based on equality. Scholars have devoted much attention to explicating the various meanings of equality (Rae 1981; Gutmann 1980; Rawls 1971). At a minimum, the following comprise the essential dimensions of equality as defined by contemporary social science usage:

1. *Political equality*, in policy terms, requires universal and equal suffrage in free elections; freedom of speech, association, and petition; equal representation; and equal access to public office.

2. *Social equality* refers to the distribution of prestige and social status within the larger society.
3. *Juridical equality* mandates equality before the law. Substantively, individuals must receive equal treatment from government through a system of state and federal courts dedicated to impartial adjudication and enforcement of legal equality.
4. *Economic equality* denotes equality of income, job security, and personal autonomy in the workplace.
5. *Distributive equality* requires that apportionment of goods and services be based on the principle of equal parts or some other standard of justice and equity.
6. *Equality of access* implies the absence of differential physical, political, juridical, and economic barriers to approaching, entering, obtaining, or making use of the full range of goods and services in society.
7. *Equality of influence, power, and control* refers to the pattern of agenda building, office holding, and decision making in society. Again, the principle of equality should be the controlling factor in these processes.

In addition to choosing among these various definitions of equality, the advocate of an egalitarian society also must decide whether "equality of opportunity" or "equality of results" is the ultimate goal. Many now argue that formal equality of opportunity (most commonly conferred by political and juridical equality) is insufficient to achieve equality of outcomes or results. In fact, making the rules the same for all may actually lead to greater inequalities of results for some groups and classes, handicapped in this now-fair competition by the effects of previous discriminatory policies. Instead, far more intrusive and coercive government action will be necessary for effective equality. Here policies governing income, status, distribution, and political influence are most relevant.

Further, a decision must be made as to whether individual or group equality is the policy goal. Although a focus on equality between individuals would, in theory, be most compatible with the U.S. tradition of individualism, in pragmatic political terms, group-based equality is more likely to become an agenda issue. Groups that have traditionally had problems attaining equality share common traits that facilitate group consciousness and political mobilization.

Finally, it is possible that such conscious choices of definitions and goals are not necessary. Perhaps equality should not be viewed as a series of unrelated end-states but instead as a process forming a developmental continuum of social change, ranging from political and juridical equality to equality of power and control. Wilhoit (1979, p. 126) has suggested that there probably is such a continuum. The poor, before receiving the vote and equal protection of the law, lack the political and judicial clout for acquiring a larger share of the national income. But he also concedes that the relationship works the opposite way as well: expanding equality in other realms is both the result and cause of advances made in the legal and political spheres.

CITIES, GROUPS, AND EQUALITY

Observers of the U.S. scene as far back as de Tocqueville have argued that United States citizens in general view equality as part of the natural order. However, it is no coincidence that egalitarianism gained ascendency as a norm for policy making during a period of rapid urbanization. Immigration from abroad and the rural South not only brought religious and racial heterogeneity to urban areas, it also created concrete demands based on the abstract value of equality. Until urbanization and industrialization gave rise to densely populated residential areas, the poor in the United States could live decently (and invisibly) through subsistence farming. With the emergence of a culturally and racially heterogeneous urban poor, the cities were forced to become forerunners in equity policies and practices in order to preserve domestic tranquility. Late nineteenth century cities gave relief through direct charity, almshouses, and home-based programs ("outdoor relief"). They established an extensive array of what would now be termed "in-kind services": public education, moral counseling, and job training. This resulted in an urban constituency that generally has been the leading force for equality in U.S. politics.

The questions and research topics that have most interested urban scholars also are, at root, issues of equity. Community control, racial disorders, service delivery and distribution patterns, social stratification, community power structures, electoral systems and office holding, agenda control—all deal with some specific concern or demand for equality in the city. Thus the focus of this book on urban equality is unique only in that it examines the diverse meanings of equality, links these meanings to concrete policy demands, and includes a multiplicity of urban constituency groups. Constraints of length mandated that not every urban interest group could be included here. However, virtually all of the groups that have traditionally had problems attaining equality in the city are represented.

Equality is treated here as a characteristic of groups, rather than individuals. Peterson (1981, pp. 116-28) has argued that "local politics is groupless politics." According to this view, urban constituency groups have little control or even significant impact in policy making. Reasons for this include low levels of organization and participation; the dominance of bureaucratically determined norms imposed in a relatively closed decision-making process; and the lower salience of local issues. Seen from a different perspective, however, urban areas suffer from overorganization, not underorganization (Yates 1977, pp. 23-25). A single city block may have two or three community organizations to articulate very specific demands for urban services.

Although not all groups discussed here are geographically based (and thus affected by the divisibility of such services), most (for example blacks, Mexican Americans, the elderly, the poor, homosexuals, and community groups) are. As for the rest (for example Native Americans, women, children, the disabled), geographic dispersal is viewed as a political liability. And however unsuccessful these groups may be in effecting change, theirs constitute the strongest and most frequently heard voices in urban politics. Thus, it is the demand side of urban policy making that is the focus of many chapters here, rather than the responsiveness of urban decisionmakers.

The view of the urban policy process emerging may closely resemble that of Yates' (1977) "street-fighting pluralism." That is, the many different constituency groups in the city reflect the diversity, variability, and complexity of urban interests. Black civil rights groups, for example, may fear being displaced by newer and more vital organizations representing environmentalists, consumers, gays, the disabled, and feminists (see Gill 1980). Even so, because these groups vary in their definitions of and problems with equality, the model of a multilateral conflict culminating in a zero-sum game may be inappropriate. Equality, as an ethical standard, should recognize group diversity and permit legitimate differentiation so long as invidious discrimination is not present.

Finally, even though seven dimensions of equality were identified earlier, only five are used here to structure this study of urban equality. Political and juridical equality are considered together because of their traditional association with equality of opportunity. The two are further linked in that political equality has most frequently been granted and guaranteed through the legislative and judicial systems. Economic and social equality have been dropped from this analysis, at least in terms of a focused study. Social equality is not easily addressed by either interest groups or public policymakers (although the lack of an established aristocracy in the United States and the U.S. penchant for informality in interpersonal relations makes ours one of the most socially egalitarian societies today). And although inequality of income often is the underpinning for all other types of inequality—access to the courts and political power are both a function of economic status in many instances—U.S. policy to redress these differences has been rare, ameliorative, and of uncertain impact. Economic inequality is essentially the product of a capitalist market economy that is strongly supported in both public and elite opinion (see Verba and Orren 1985). Furthermore, those economic redistributive policies that have been enacted by government have primarily originated at the national level (see Peterson 1981).

EQUALITY UNDER THE LAW

By most measures, the United States ranks high in its commitment to policies that maximize political and legal forms of equality. White male suffrage and representative institutions were creatures of the U.S. Constitution, and each, in turn, played a major role in the rise of the urban political machines of the nineteenth century. Even immigrants lacking most other political resources possessed the votes needed by brokers ("bosses") to maintain control of the political institutions of the city.

It was the Progressive-led urban reform movement of the late nineteenth and early twentieth centuries, however, that put U.S. cities in the forefront of efforts to maximize the political influence and equality of citizens. Their championing of laws requiring voter registration and making it illegal for a person to vote more than once in the same election made the Progressives early advocates of the modern principle of "one person, one vote." The direct primary and the initiative, referendum, and recall were two other equity legacies of that movement. Although, by some accounts, the Progressive reformers, enamored of the business corporation analogy as it applied to municipal government, wanted to restrict participation in city elections to property owners, they were aware that the trend nationally was in the direction of expansion of the electorate, not contraction. Thus, at the height of the campaign for woman suffrage, the Progressives embraced women voters as a force for urban reform coequal with such structural reforms as at-large elections, nonpartisan ballots, and council-manager government.

It is generally recognized today that several of these Progressive reforms in fact exacerbated inequalities among groups in the city. Earlier restrictive rules for voter registration reduced lower-class and minority participation, as did the preferred structures of reform government. Ironically, it was only after the reapportionment battles of the 1960s were settled in favor of underrepresented cities (again, under the rule of "one person, one vote") that these inequities began to be addressed. The poll tax was ruled unconstitutional and outlawed by constitutional amendment. Voter registration became less of a barrier to participation as residency requirements were eased and other rules regarding deadlines, sites, and registrars were liberalized. Most significantly, as the principle of population equality among electoral districts has been universally adopted, the legal and political controversy has shifted from that of avoiding gross population disparities to one of safeguarding against misrepresentation of ethnic and racial minorities.

The federal courts, since the passage of the Voting Rights Act of 1965, have heard a flood of cases challenging the discriminatory effects of at-large districting systems and racial gerrymanders that either divide a black or Hispanic community or "waste" minority votes by creating a minimum number of districts with huge majorities of racial or ethnic members. The Supreme Court, in these cases, has established and reaffirmed the concept of representation of groups, not of individuals, and the responsibility of the state to ensure that certain groups be guaranteed a proportionate share of seats in a legislative body.

As spokespersons for the nation's largest racial minority, black civil rights groups have, to date, been most active in seeking equality of representation in voting and office holding. However, if current demographic patterns continue, by the twenty-first century Hispanics will be the dominant minority group in the

United States. In particular, the future of politics in the Southwest is highly dependent upon the rate of increase of political participation by Mexican Americans and the ability of traditional political institutions to respond to their demands (See Bloomberg and Martinez-Sandoval 1982). The chapter by MacManus and Bullock in Section Two examines the accessibility of an urban political system in the Southwest to its Mexican American constituents, as measured by their rates of registration, voting, office seeking and office holding.

The remaining chapters in this section primarily focus on another dimension of juridical equality: equality of rights and opportunity as guaranteed by law and the "equal protection clause" of the Fourteenth Amendment. The decades of the 1960s and 1970s constituted a revolution of such rights for many claimant groups. The protection of the Fourteenth Amendment, passed as one of the post-Civil War responses to black inequality, was applied to several other forms of discrimination for the first time. The list of "protected categories" covered under national civil rights legislation expanded beyond "race, creed, or color" to include women, the elderly, and the disabled. And this rights revolution came to the cities in the form of the War on Poverty. Programs such as Head Start, Neighborhood Job Corps, Job Corps, job training, and counseling were designed to manipulate and open the urban opportunity structure. The Legal Services Corporation was established to assure equal access to the court system. Yet, as the chapters by Thomas and Norgren show, not all urban groups benefited equally during this period. Although the general policy trend has been to support equal rights for all, not all citizens, because of group characteristics, have been able to use these rights equally nor is there societal consensus that these groups should have equality of rights in all areas.

As Norgren notes, children as precitizens have no vote, hold no offices, have limited political resources, and are only rarely polled on matters of public policy. Instead of being represented by a constituency-based group in pluralistic politics, children are presumed to be adequately and accurately represented by self-declared advocates, parents, and court-appointed guardians. Assigned a special (and thus, by definition, unequal) legal status, children are "planned for" in a myriad of urban programs but are essentially "planned without." Using child care policy as a case in point, Norgren concludes that children's unique legal and political status has led to an inequitable response to their needs.

The legal and political demands of urban gays are not easily subsumed into a traditional model of equality either. On the one hand, many equity demands are quite conventional: local office holding; equitable treatment by the courts and the urban police; inclusion as a "protected category" under existing civil rights legislation on housing, employment, and public accommodations. By this view, it is easy to foresee gays being treated as "just another ethnic group," with the mayor as routinely marching in a "Gay Pride" parade as in one noting St. Patrick's or Columbus Day. Yet there is, as Thomas argues, "a gay difference" because of the unique centrality of sexual conduct to group identity. Gays, unlike other groups, assign a high priority to social equality, yet the incongruity of such demands with elite and societal values is greatest here.

Even so, the politics of San Francisco, the setting of Thomas' study, has proven conducive for pursuing gay equality. As described by Castells and Murphy (1982), gays there constitute a highly visible and mobilized community, with autonomous social institutions and a powerful political organization based on spatial concentration. Because of their lesser problems with economic inequalities—many gays are young professionals and small businessmen—the homosexual community and gay elected officials have made major contributions to urban revitalization and the housing market generally. Without the barriers of class-based discrimination, gays in San Francisco have been successful in gaining major advances in legal and political equality.

URBAN SERVICES AND EQUALITY

Issues of juridical equality in the city are rooted in national values and are closely linked with national policies. A concern for distributive equality, conversely, is one of the distinctive characteristics of urban areas. City government and its politics largely revolve around the design, allocation, and delivery of services. Because of the locality- or person-specific nature of this delivery system, the quality and quantity of services to a group or neighborhood provides a rough measure of standing in the community.

Those studying the distribution of municipal public services have explicitly defined distributive equality in terms of "equal shares." While some have found patterns of inequality of specific services based on race (Button 1982) or economic growth (Jones 1982), the preponderance of the evidence points to "unpatterned inequality" (for example Lineberry 1977; Jones 1980). That is, few, if any, services are distributed strictly on the principle of "equal shares." Instead, a group or community receiving more of one service is likely to receive less of another service. These "unpatterned inequalities" appear to be a function of bureaucratic decision rules based on demand, professional norms, need, equality, or reaction to political pressure (Lineberry 1977, p. 156).

It follows, then, that attempts to explain service distribution purely on the basis of the differential distribution or exercise of political power have been unsuccessful. Jones (1980), for example, found little sustained activity by community groups in the service delivery process in Detroit, nor did he find that the poor used the vote to get better services (but see Button 1982). Even so, some groups can and do exploit the bureaucratic "Adam Smith" rule more effectively than others. To the extent that urban governments do respond to service demands, most often in ward or competitive systems, vocal groups can gain an advantage.

However, as Rich (1982, p. 7) has written, "any study that examines only the distribution of services cities actually deliver can provide only a highly limited basis for judging the equity of service distribution." Equally important, given the variation in individual and group needs for urban services, is which services the city will produce and at what level. Here equality as "differences without discrimination" is most appropriate. Distributive equality may best be defined in terms of distributive justice or equity rather than "equal shares." Each of the four chapters in Section Three adopts this latter definition.

Chaudhuri examines a little-studied urban constituency group, the Native American. His survey of the directors of community-based Urban Indian Centers found a high level of perceived inequality of service distribution, which was attributed primarily to the lack of political mobilization of urban Indians vis-a-vis other groups in the city.

The chapters by Chaudhuri and de la Garza and Weaver (on Mexican Americans in three large Southwestern communities) each provide additional evidence that the policy agendas of racial and ethnic minorities differ in significant ways from that of Anglos. The lower level of satisfaction with urban services found by previous researchers among these groups may reflect the city's failure to provide desired programs rather than merely "equal shares" of available services.

Gelb and Gittell recount the experience of urban women mobilized through groups and informal networks for distributive equality. As Gittell and Shtob (1981) earlier chronicled, women since the 1820s have effectively used voluntary associations as an outlet when excluded from mainstream politics and, in fact, have been central to many urban movements for reform. Women historically have demanded and shaped new urban services and delivery systems. And, in the modern era, when thwarted by city government, they have created the alternative services for women required for distributive justice.

Dabrowski, Haynor, and Cuervo too look at group activity directed toward distributive equality: in this case, attempts by white ethnic community activists to obtain, avoid, retain, and dispose of urban goods and services in accordance with their definition of equity. As others have observed, community activism is crisis-based and reactive (that is, the city budget and other urban policies are not shaped by neighborhood groups during the decision process) yet is surprisingly effective. The authors also provide a model of community politics based on an exchange approach; through adaptation the community's goal of distributive justice and the urban bureaucracy's search for politically acceptable decision rules for allocation can both be accommodated.

THE PROBLEM OF ACCESS

At least in principle, equality of access is accorded a favored position similar to that of juridical and distributive equality. Constitutional guarantees of free speech, association, and petition are closely linked to the concept that all have the right to have their voices heard in U.S. politics. Recent attempts to place ceilings on campaign spending and private donations are predicated on the belief that more affluent citizens should not be allowed to purchase greater access to the political system.

In the urban context, traditional modes of access (for example elections, political parties, interest groups) are supplemented by direct contacts between government and citizens concerned about a specific urban service or issue. Because of the class bias inherent in both—the traditional linkage institutions are used more effectively as social class increases, while citizen-initiated direct contacts appear to be most frequently used by those of working-class and lower-middle-class status—two other modes are also of importance in the city: protest and mandated citizen participation. For those without stable political resources, protest can be a means of gaining access for issue-specific grievances. And government, in order to equalize access to public decisionmaking, has required that citizens be given a formal voice in certain programs through open hearings, advisory or governing boards, referenda, or comment periods.

With recent advances in juridical equality, however, political and legal barriers to equality of access have become less important than economic and physical impediments. Questions of supply and affordability still structure access to a full life in the city. And even the most equitable pattern of distribution cannot address problems rooted in the basic design of urban communities and services. The chapters in Section Four consider these latter restrictions on equality of access.

The chapter by Jackson looks at the history of urban housing subsidies designed to benefit the poor. Housing is perhaps the crucial mediator of access to many other social values in the city such as public services, education, commerce, and companionship. Jackson concludes that standard and affordable housing in good neighborhoods exists but that it is maldistributed in terms of equality of access.

Salem examines the barriers presented by the urban "built" environment to the economic equality of working women. She argues that urban spatial structure, with its characteristic separation of commercial, workplace, and household activity, is dysfunctional for women. Urban services (for example transit) and the lack of certain services (for example child care) in effect deny full access to women in the city.

The chapter by Johnson deals with the disabled, the group that is most conventionally viewed as having problems with physical access to the city. She recounts the experience of Berkeley in implementing Section 504 of the national Vocational Rehabilitation Act of 1973, which prohibited discrimination on the basis of handicap. Despite a supportive political culture and a sizable, visible, and mobilized disabled population, the process was not smooth. Early on it became obvious that equality of access for the disabled involved more than removal of physical and environmental constraints; the attitudes of nondisabled citizens and the diversity of disabilities posed additional barriers.

POWER AND EQUALITY

Of all the dimensions of equality considered in this collection, equality of influence, power, and control is the most problematic. The ideal is that citizens, acting within or outside groups, should have equal influence over governmental decisionmakers. And, in general, everyone's vote is equally powerful. Yet the three terms are inherently inegalitarian in that some other must be influenced, controlled, and hence less powerful. A concern for the distribution of power in the city has fueled the decades-long debate over community power structures and, more recently, the changes, if any, that will follow from the rise of new urban claimant groups (for example blacks, Hispanics, women, and, in some Sunbelt retirement communities, the elderly).

Economically disadvantaged groups have traditionally sought greater political power in order to pursue policies advantageous to the group from positions within government. Political control, however, is not necessarily accompanied by agenda management. Both chapters in the concluding Section Five investigate the relationship between electoral power and agenda control.

Button and Rosenbaum examine the budgetary impacts of the rising older populations on local government taxing and spending in Florida cities over the past decade. Concomitantly, they provide an empirical test of the "Gray Peril" hypothesis: to wit, that a growing and politically active aging population will successfully demand programs and services important to the elderly, while forcing reductions in other crucial services not impinging on their interests.

Stone, in looking at political developments in Atlanta since the end of World War II, found that neither the political equality imposed by district elections nor the dominant electoral power of blacks there has displaced business influence in Atlanta politics, especially in controlling economic development decisions. Governing is different from winning elections and black public officials are predisposed to seek the cooperation of those with greater economic resources.

URBAN COALITIONS AND EQUALITY

In a period between egalitarian revolutions, such as the current one, it is imperative that equity concerns be regularly placed on the public agenda. One factor in successful agenda building is the extent to which ties and alliances are formed with other groups and key individuals of compatible interests. Nearly all governmental decisionmakers will be hesitant to disregard the demands of a strong coalition of groups.

A common concern for economic equality unites virtually all of the urban groups considered here. Beyond that, their priorities differ and even conflict. And, it must be remembered, demands for equality are most effectively driven by group-based self-interest, not egalitarian ideology, powerful though these values may be.

Of the ten urban constituency groups discussed in this book, only four (the old, the young, the poor, and Native Americans) have yet to define political equality in terms of actual representation in local elective office. For women and the disabled, however, an at-large electoral system may be preferable to a ward system once a sense of entitlement for these two groups is generally accepted in the city.

The implementation of job training programs and affirmative action have also been accompanied by sharp competition among new claimant groups for participation and special consideration. (Women and Hispanic males, however, have been allies in challenging the job-relatedness of height and weight requirements of public safety jobs.) Community-based organizations have clashed over the allocation of federal block grants within the city. Long-lived organizations seek to retain existing funding; the newly mobilized struggle to gain initial support for their programs.

All groups seek, or at least welcome, the support of others in pressing their demands for equality. But some face obvious disadvantages. Programs for the urban young have often been viewed as a means to another group-based end (for example job creation, maternal employment). The aging, once viewed as economically disadvantaged, are now suspect as a group that is successfully pursuing economic and distributional equality at others' expense. Gays and women, both of whom pursue equity goals at variance with the prevailing values of some important sectors in society, also face difficulties in being accepted as desirable coalition partners.

A final difficulty facing a broad-based urban coalition of the disadvantaged is the constant-sum nature of many aspects of urban equality. Even if equity demands formed a neat Maslowian hierarchy, those needs, once fulfilled, are not automatically retained for all time. Though the situation is not quite so conflictive as the concept of "street-fighting pluralism" would imply, neither is an alliance of equality-oriented urban groups a likelihood. Instead, a number of movements for urban equality, each based on group distinctions, is most likely to mark urban politics in the future.

REFERENCES

Bloomberg, Warner and Rodrigo Martinez-Sandoval. 1982. "This Hispanic-American Urban Order: A Border Perspective." In *Cities in the 21st Century*, edited by Gary Gappert and Richard V. Knight, pp. 112–32. Beverly Hills: Sage.

Button, James W. 1982. "Political Strategies and Public-Service Patterns: The Impact of the Black Civil Rights Movement on Municipal- Service Distributions." In *The Politics of Urban Public Services*, edited by Richard C. Rich, pp. 69–82. Lexington, Mass.: Lexington.

Castells, Manuel and Karen Murphy. 1982. "Cultural Identity and Urban Structure: The Spatial Organization of San Francisco's Gay Community." In *Urban Policy Under Capitalism*, edited by Norman I. Fainstein and Susan S. Fainstein, pp. 237–59. Beverly Hills: Sage.

Gans, Herbert J. 1973. *More Equality*. New York: Pantheon.

Gill, Gerald R. 1980. *Meanness Mania: The Changed Mood*. Washington, D.C.: Howard University Press.

Gittell, Marilyn and Teresa Shtob. 1981. "Changing Women's Roles in Political Volunteerism and Reform of the City." In *Women and the American City*, edited by Catharine R. Stimpson et al., pp. 64–75. Chicago: University of Chicago Press.

Grimes, Alan P. 1964. *Equality in America: Religion, Race, and the Urban Majority*. New York: Oxford University Press.

Gutmann, Amy. 1980. *Liberal Equality*. New York: Cambridge University Press.

Jones, Bryan D. 1980. *Service Delivery in the City: Citizen Demand and Bureaucratic Rules*. New York: Longman.

Jones, E. Terrance. 1982. "The Distribution of Urban Services in a Declining City." In *The Politics of Urban Public Services*, edited by Richard C. Rich, pp. 103–12. Lexington, Mass.: Lexington.

Lineberry, Robert L. 1977. *Equality and Urban Policy: The Distribution of Municipal Public Services*. Beverly Hills: Sage.

Okun, Arthur. 1975. *Equality Versus Efficiency: The Big Tradeoff*. Washington, D.C.: Brookings.

Peterson, Paul E. 1981. *City Limits*. Chicago: University of Chicago Press.

Rae, Douglas. 1981. *Equalities*. Cambridge, Mass.: Harvard University Press.

Rawls, John. 1971. *A Theory of Justice*. Cambridge, Mass.: Harvard University Press.

Rich, Richard C. 1982. "The Political Economy of Urban-Service Distribution." In *The Politics of Urban Public Services*, edited by Richard C. Rich, pp. 1–16. Lexington, Mass.: Lexington.

Verba, Sidney and Gary R. Orren. 1985. *Equality in America: The View From the Top*. Cambridge, Mass.: Harvard University Press.

Weale, Albert. 1978. *Equality and Social Policy*. London: Routledge and Kegan Paul.

Wilhoit, Francis M. 1979. *The Quest for Equality in Freedom*. New Brunswick: Transaction.

Yates, Douglas. 1977. *The Ungovernable City*. Cambridge, Mass.: MIT Press.

PART II
JURIDICAL EQUALITY

2

MEXICAN-AMERICAN POLITICAL CLOUT IN SMALL URBAN JURISDICTIONS: CONDITIONS FOR MAXIMIZING INFLUENCE

Susan A. MacManus and Charles S. Bullock, III

One of the key equity issues confronting urban governments today is the accessibility of their political systems to minority constituents. As a consequence of the Voting Rights Act, a great deal of litigation has been focused on the degree to which minorities have participated in the political process as voters, candidates, and officeholders. Most of this attention has been on blacks, but the rapid growth rate of the Hispanic population, especially in the Southwest, has highlighted the need for more studies of this group's political participation.

Mexican Americans have gradually become more politically active and influential (Brischetto and de la Garza 1983). Historically, Hispanic participation and electoral success rates have lagged behind those of Anglos and blacks (McCleskey and Nimmo 1968; Grebler, Moore, and Guzman 1970; Shinn 1971; McCleskey and Merrill 1973; Antunes and Gaitz 1975; MacManus 1978; Taebel 1978; Karnig and Welch 1979; MacManus and Cassel 1982; Welch and Hibbing 1984; Wrinkle and Miller 1984). To date, few studies have examined how much and under what conditions the traditional participation and electoral success gaps between Hispanics and other racial and ethnic groups have closed.

The few studies which have addressed the narrowing of the political participation gap (in terms of registration and turnout) have focused on state-level contests (Wrinkle and Miller 1984) or on local contests in large urban settings (Garcia 1979). Likewise, studies of the comparative electoral influence and success rates of Mexican Americans, Anglos, and/or blacks have focused on national and state contests (Cain and Kiewiet 1984; Welch and Hibbing 1984) or on local contests in large urban settings for school board (Garcia 1979) or city council races (MacManus 1978; Taebel 1978; Karnig and Welch 1979). All of the studies are time-bound. Most of them are based on data collected during the early and mid 1970s. In fact, the bulk of the literature on Mexican-American political participation appeared during this period (cf. Ambrecht and Panchon 1974; Baird 1977; Burma 1970; Castro 1974; Foley 1977; Garcia 1974; Garcia and de la Garza

1977; Moore 1970; Steiner 1968; Vigil 1978). Only one contains post-1980 data and, even here, the analysis is limited to a single Congressional race in 1982 (Cain and Kiewiet 1984).

In this study, we focus on political participation and electoral success rates of Mexican Americans during the first half of the 1980s in contests for the county commission, school board, and city council. The setting is West Texas County with a population of slightly more than 5,000. Hispanics make up 40 percent of the county and school district population. (The county and school district boundaries are coterminous.) The largest city in the county, the one examined in this study, contains 75 percent of the county's population and 65 percent of the county's Hispanics. Hispanics make up 34 percent of the city's population. Hispanics constitute 30–40 percent of each jurisdiction (county, school district, city), a level at which Hispanic influence and success are hypothesized to become significant (Garcia 1979, p. 181). While the primary focus is on the closing of the gap during the 1980s, when data are available, we extend our analyses back into the 1970s. Specifically, we compare registration, turnout, candidacy, and electoral success rates of Mexican Americans and Anglos[1] in county, school board, and municipal elections. We also include some state-level contests in which a Mexican-American candidate competed against an Anglo.

REGISTRATION RATES

Registration rates for West Texas County for 1980–84 are reported in Table 2.1. There has been a gradual increase (from 31 percent to 35 percent) in the share of the registrant population who are Mexican American, even as the overall registration figures have declined. The drop in registration coincides with a population decline in response to an ailing petrochemical industry. Registration rates (registered voters as a percent of the voting age population) among Hispanics increased between 1980 and 1984 from 62.6 percent to 64.0 percent while registration rates of Anglos decreased from 81.5 percent to 69.6 percent. Thus Mexican-American registration is almost proportionate with Mexican-American voting age population (36.9 percent). Mexican-American registration in West Texas County is much higher than Spanish surname registration generally in the United States. In only four years the gap in Mexican American-Anglo registration rates closed considerably: from 18.9 percentage points in 1980 to 5.6 points in 1984. The Mexican-American registration rate in West Texas County in 1984 was only 7 percent less than that reported by Wrinkle and Miller (1984, p. 312) for Hildalgo County—a border county in southern Texas with twice the Hispanic population (81 percent). This suggests that Hispanic-Anglo gaps are closing throughout the Southwest at a similar pace.

There are at least three possible explanations for the closing of the gap. One is predominantly legal. Increased Hispanic registration rates may result from the

TABLE 2.1. Voter Registration by Ethnicity, 1980-84

Year	Total Registered Voters — Mexican American	Anglo	Total Number
1980	31%	69%	2,522
1981	31	69	2,517
1982	32	68	2,707
1984	35	65	2,287

Source: Compiled by the authors from voter registration lists supplied by the County Clerk's Office. Data for 1983 were not available.

elimination of the poll tax and annual registration requirements coupled with the provision of bilingual registration and election materials (Wrinkle and Miller 1984). Evidence of growing Mexican-American registration in the 1980s suggests a delayed reaction to changes in legal conditions surrounding elections. A related explanation may be the massive voter registration efforts of groups like the Southwest Voter Registration and Education Project (de la Garza and Brischetto 1983b). Age may provide yet another explanation. As noted by de la Garza and Brischetto (1983a), younger Mexican Americans (the fastest growing cohort of the Hispanic population) face fewer discriminatory obstacles, are better educated, have higher status jobs and higher incomes, and are less likely to be language-bound (monolingual) than the older generations. As a consequence, younger Mexican Americans currently are more likely to be politically involved than their ancestors.

TURNOUT RATES

Traditionally, turnout rates among Mexican-American voters have lagged behind Anglo turnout rates. It is difficult to determine the ethnicity of voters in Texas since neither registration nor turnout is reported by race. Therefore, to determine ethnic turnout rates we inspected voter sign-in sheets and classified voters as Anglo or Mexican American. We were able to get sign-in sheets for two distinct time periods: 1972-74 and 1983-84.[2] Ethnic differences in turnout were far less in 1983-84 than a decade earlier.

The Turnout Gap in 1972-74

Table 2.2 shows that the Mexican-American–Anglo turnout gap of a decade ago was quite wide. The mean figures show Anglos voting at more than twice

TABLE 2.2. Voter Turnout by Ethnicity, 1972 and 1974 Elections

Election	Mexican American %	Anglo %
1972 Primary	20.5%	46.7%
1972 Runoff (2d Primary)	18.2	38.3
1972 General	43.2	65.8
1974 Primary	13.6	43.0
1974 Runoff (2d Primary)	13.6	31.4
1974 General	15.9	44.6
Mean	20.8%	45.0%
N in 1972	44	120
N in 1974	44	121

Source: Compiled by the authors from voter sign-in sheets supplied by the County Clerk's Office. Turnout figures were based on a 10 percent sample.

the rate of Mexican Americans (45 percent and 21 percent, respectively). In the 1974 primary, Anglo turnout was three times greater than the Hispanic turnout rate.

The Turnout Gap in 1983-84

In contrast, ethnic turnout differentials in the 1980s were less. (See Table 2.3.) The voter sign-in sheets from the spring 1983 school board elections revealed a gap of only three percentage points. The Anglo turnout rate was 21.3 percent; the Mexican-American turnout rate, 18.5 percent.[3]

In the 1984 school board contest, Anglo and Mexican-American turnout rates remained fairly similar (56 percent and 48 percent, respectively). However, the gap was wider in a local referendum. In the October 1983 school bond election called to finance a new high school, the turnout rate was 49.7 percent for Anglos but for Mexican Americans, it was only 30.9 percent. The interesting point is that the bond election turnout rate for both groups was nearly double that for the school board election. At first blush, this may seem unusual since historically bond elections are low turnout elections. On the other hand, interest in school policy, particularly among Mexican Americans, has intensified in recent years (Garcia 1979; San Miguel 1982). As noted by Garcia (1979, p. 168), Mexican Americans have criticized education systems on a number of grounds

TABLE 2.3. Voter Turnout by Ethnicity, 1983 and 1984 School Board Elections

Election	Mexican American %	Anglo %	Mexican-American Turnout as a Ratio of Anglo Turnout
April 1983 (Candidate Election)			
Precinct 1	17.6%	6.5%	.873
Precinct 2	22.6	21.9	
Total	18.5	21.3	
October 1983 (Bond Election)			
Precinct 1	27.6	40.8	.622
Precinct 2	52.3	55.5	
Total	30.9	49.7	
April, 1984 (Candidate Election)	47.6	56.2	.847

Notes: Turnout was calculated by dividing the number of Anglos/Mexican Americans voting by the number of Anglos/Mexican Americans registered. All absentee ballots were credited to Precinct 2 in the official canvas. The effect of this is to increase the apparent turnout in Precinct 2 at the expense of Precinct 1.

Source: Compiled by the authors from registration data provided by the Secretary of State's Office and from voter sign-in sheets supplied by the County Clerk's Office.

including monolingual-monocultural curricula, lack of policy representation, and inferior facilities. Consequently, the high interest in the high school bond election is not nearly as unusual as it might otherwise have appeared.

The higher participation in the bond election by both races should not blind us to the magnitude of the ethnic turnout gap. Without a Mexican-American candidacy, the turnout gap in the bond referendum was similar to some of those a decade earlier. Thus it appears that the content of the vote is a critical variable in explaining Anglo–Mexican-American turnout differentials. Mexican-American turnout rates are more nearly equal to Anglo turnout rates in candidate-based, rather than issue-based, elections.

CANDIDACY AND CANDIDACY SUCCESS RATES

Obviously candidacy success is contingent upon running for office. To date, there have been no studies of Mexican-American candidacy rates. However, on the basis of the registration and turnout figures, we expect that candidacy and candidacy success rate gaps between Mexican Americans and Anglos in these West Texas County jurisdictions have narrowed. To provide a comparative, longitudinal perspective, we focused on school board and city elections.

Candidacy/Candidacy Success Rates: School Board

Table 2.4 reports the number of candidates in each ethnic group that sought election to the school board and the number that won. Over the 14-year period examined (1970-83), the number of Anglo candidates (52) greatly exceeded the number of Mexican-American candidates (15). However, 1980-83, the candidacy rate gap narrowed (15 Anglos; 7 Mexican Americans), although Anglos still outnumbered Mexican Americans two to one. Narrowing of the gap in candidacy rates may be due to the victorious Mexican-American candidacies in 1978 and 1981. As reported in Table 2.4, Anglos have been far more successful at getting elected than Mexican Americans, with 61.5 percent of those who sought election winning as compared with a success rate of only 13.3 percent among Hispanics.

TABLE 2.4. Candidate Success Rates in School Board Elections, 1970-83

Year	Mexican American # Candidates	# Won	Anglo # Candidates	# Won
1970	1	0	2	2
1971	1	0	4	3
1972	0	-	5	2
1973	1	0	6	2
1974	1	0	4	3
1975	1	0	3	2
1976	2	0	3	2
1977	0	-	3	3
1978	1	1	5	1
1979	0	-	3	2
1980	2	0	3	3
1981	4	1	5	2
1982	0	-	4	2
1983	1	0	3	3
Totals	15	2	52	32
Rate of Success[1]		13.3%		61.5%

Source: Compiled by the authors from election returns.

[1] Rate of success was calculated by dividing the number of elections won (# won) by the number of candidates (# candidates).

(Both victories by Mexican Americans were registered by the same individual.) However, some of this candidacy success rate differential might be explained by the incumbency factor.

Since incumbents almost invariably win when they seek reelection to the West Texas County School Board, we investigated the election rates for the two ethnic groups in contests in which there was not an incumbent. Our results show that in open seat contests, 44.4 percent of the Anglo candidates won versus only 14.3 percent of the Mexican-American candidates. Except for one race (when the Mexican-American school board member won his first term), unsuccessful Anglos lost to fellow Anglos. Still, the proportion of Anglos who won remains 30 percentage points higher than the success rate for Hispanics.

Candidacy/Candidacy Success Rates: City Elections

A candidacy rate gap has also characterized municipal elections. The gap over the 14 years was even wider (36 Anglos; 7 Mexican Americans) than in school board races. However, the success rate of Mexican Americans who run for city council is high (71.4 percent) and even exceeds that of Anglos (66.7 percent). Again, there is evidence of the incumbency factor at work, even for Mexican-American candidates. All of the Hispanic candidacy successes have accrued to one individual who has enjoyed a long tenure on the council.

Factors Affecting Mexican-American Candidacy/Candidacy Success Rates

This analysis of candidacy and candidacy success rates has suggested that incumbency and historically poor electoral success rates as well as lower socioeconomic characteristics have depressed Mexican-American candidacy rates, making them lower than either their proportional makeup of the voting age population or registered voters would suggest. The inability to achieve proportional representation on local governing bodies has led some Hispanic leaders to litigate and force changes in the method of electing county commissioners and school board members.

The creation of a single member district system for the County Commission as a result of litigation resulted in the creation of one heavily Hispanic district from which the first Mexican American to serve on the commission was elected in 1977. After the post-1980 Census redistricting, a second Hispanic was elected in 1982 from a less heavily Hispanic district. In the case of the school board, a recently agreed upon switch to a mixed system (four district; three at-large), once implemented, is likely to yield two or three Mexican-American school board members. Undoubtedly, Mexican Americans in West Texas County will push for similar alterations in the city election system. It should be noted that successful leveraging for change is much more effective when the size of a minority population is significant, as it was here (Garcia 1979). Also, changes to district-based representational systems are most effective when minority group members are geographically concentrated (MacManus and Cassel 1982), as was the case here.[4]

CONCLUSION

In this study, we found that the gap between Anglo and Mexican-American registration and turnout rates has narrowed tremendously since the early 1970s, so that by 1983 they were almost equal (except in issue-oriented elections). Factors that have helped narrow the gap in registration rates have probably been legal, political, and socioeconomic in nature. More specifically, these have included elimination of legal barriers to registration and mandated bilingual registration materials, among others. Active registration efforts of politically oriented Hispanic organizations have also increased the Mexican-American voter rolls. Finally, the age structure of the Hispanic population, namely the large, high growth young cohort, politically and economically socialized in the post-Voting Rights Act period, has stimulated registration among Mexican Americans. In terms of turnout rates, we found the narrowing of Anglo–Mexican-American differentials to be most evident in open seat contests.

Our analysis of candidacy and candidacy success rate differentials showed that a significant gap still exists but that the gap has narrowed considerably between 1970 and 1983. Possible factors that deterred Mexican-American candidacies were incumbency and historically poor success rates. Dissatisfaction with Mexican-American presence on local governing bodies has led Hispanic leaders to litigate on behalf of their increasingly participatory group to force changes in the electoral system. These changes may produce more Mexican-American representation on local legislative bodies which may then impact on decision making and service distribution. The policy consequences of more Mexican-American representation in West Texas County will depend upon the nature of the accommodation reached between Mexican-American and Anglo representatives, since Anglos are likely to continue to hold a majority of the seats on these collegial bodies.

NOTES

1. Blacks make up less than 0.1 percent of the county, school district, and city populations.

2. Turnout figures for 1972–74 were based on a 10 percent sample while a full enumeration was done for 1983 and 1984.

3. While it appears the Mexican-American turnout rate dropped since 1974 (21 percent to 18 percent), it must be noted that the earlier figures were based on traditionally high-turnout, partisan contests for higher offices, whereas the 1983 figure was based on a nonpartisan local school board

race. At any rate, the focus here is on the closing of the gap between Anglo and Mexican-American participation rates, which is clearly documented in the 1983 figure.

4. A district-based system does not always result in increased minority representation.

REFERENCES

Ambrecht, Biliana C.S. and Harry P. Panchon. 1974. "Ethnic Mobilization in a Mexican American Community: An Exploratory Study of East Los Angeles 1965-1972." *Western Political Quarterly* 27 (September): 500-19.
Antunes, George and Charles M. Gaitz. 1975. "Ethnicity and Participation: A Study of Mexican-Americans, Blacks, and Whites." *American Journal of Sociology* 80 (March): 1192-211.
Baird, Frank L., ed. 1977. *Mexican Americans: Political Power Influence or Resource?* Lubbock: Texas Tech Press.
Brischetto, Robert R. and Rodolfo O. de la Garza. 1983. *The Mexican American Electorate: Political Participation and Ideology.* Occasional Paper No. 3. The Mexican American Electorate Series. San Antonio: Southwest Voter Registration Education Project and Austin: Center for Mexican American Studies, University of Texas.
Burma, John, ed. 1970. *Mexican Americans in the United States.* Cambridge, Mass.: Schenkman.
Cain, Bruce E. and D. Roderick Kiewiet. 1984. "Ethnicity and Electoral Choice: Mexican American Voting Behavior in the California 30th Congressional District." *Social Science Quarterly* 65 (June): 315-27.
Castro, Tony. 1974. *Chicano Power: The Emergence of Mexican America.* New York: Saturday Review Press.
de la Garza, Rodolfo O. and Robert R. Brischetto. 1983a. *The Mexican American Electorate: A Demographic Profile.* Occasional Paper No. 1. The Mexican American Electorate Series. San Antonio: Southwest Voter Registration Education Project and Austin: Center for Mexican American Studies, University of Texas.
———. 1983b. *The Mexican American Electorate: An Exploration of Their Opinions and Behavior.* Occasional Paper No. 4. The Mexican American Electorate Series. San Antonio: Southwest Voter Registration Education Project and Austin: Center for Mexican American Studies, University of Texas.
Foley, Douglas E. et al. 1977. *From Peones to Politics: Ethnic Relations in a South Texas Town, 1900-1977.* Austin: University of Texas Press.
Garcia, F. Chris, ed. 1974. *La Causa Politica: A Chicano Politics Reader.* Notre Dame: University of Notre Dame Press.
———. and Rudolph O. de la Garza. 1977. *The Chicano Political Experience.* North Scituate, Mass.: Duxbury.
Garcia, John A. 1979. "An Analysis of Chicano and Anglo Electoral Patterns in School Board Elections." *Ethnicity* 6 (June): 168-83.
Grebler, Leo, Joan Moore, and Ralph C. Guzman. 1970. *The Mexican American People.* New York: Free Press.
Karnig, Albert K. and Susan Welch. 1979. "Sex and Ethnicity in Municipal Representation." *Social Science Quarterly* 60 (December): 465-81.
MacManus, Susan A. 1978. "City Council Election Procedures and Minority

Representation: Are They Related?" *Social Science Quarterly* 59 (June): 153-61.
_____. and Carol A. Cassel. 1982. "Mexican Americans in City Politics: Participation, Representation, and Policy Preferences." *The Urban Interest* 4 (Spring): 57-69.
McCleskey, Clifton and Bruce Merrill. 1973. "Mexican American Political Behavior in Texas." *Social Science Quarterly* 53 (March): 785-98.
_____. and Dan Nimmo. 1968. "Differences Between Potential, Registered, and Actual Voters: The Houston Metropolitan Area in 1964." *Social Science Quarterly* 49 (June): 103-14.
Moore, Dan with Alfredo Cuellar. 1970. *Mexican Americans*. Englewood Cliffs: Prentice Hall.
San Miguel, Guadalupe, Jr. 1982. "Mexican American Organizations and the Changing Politics of School Desegregation in Texas, 1945 to 1980." *Social Science Quarterly* 63 (December): 701-15.
Shinn, Allen M. 1971. "A Note on Voter Registration and Turnout in Texas, 1960-1970." *Journal of Politics* 33 (November): 1120-29.
Steiner, Stan. 1968. *LaRaza: The Mexican Americans*. New York: Harper and Row.
Taebel, Delbert. 1978. "Minority Representation on City Councils: The Impact of Structure on Blacks and Hispanics." *Social Science Quarterly* 39 (June): 142-52.
Vigil, Maurilio. 1978. *Chicano Politics*. Washington, D.C.: University Press of America.
Welch, Susan and John R. Hibbing. 1984. "Hispanic Representation in the U.S. Congress." *Social Science Quarterly* 65 (June): 328-35.
Wrinkle, Robert D. and Lawrence W. Miller. 1984. "A Note on Mexican American Voter Registration and Turnout." *Social Science Quarterly* 65 (June): 308-12.

3

THE GAY QUEST FOR EQUALITY IN SAN FRANCISCO

David J. Thomas

Every idea originates through equating the unequal—
Nietzsche, *The Will To Power*

A marked feature of our era is the public assertion of claims to equality and the political struggle to attain them by numerous minority groups, previously oppressed, exploited, and even invisible. Blacks, Hispanics, women, the disabled—the list is increasingly familiar, the categorizations well underway. Equality before the law, equal rights and entitlements, and political equality have been sought and partially attained. A startling addition to this list is that of gays, or lesbians and gays.[1] Would anyone writing 35 years ago have predicted the modern gay movement, its rapid growth, its modest successes? Consider a few landmarks in San Francisco gay history (see D'Emilio 1981; D'Emilio 1983, pp. 176-95).

In September 1955, eight women gathered secretly in San Francisco to form a discreet lesbian social club, obscurely but appropriately named the Daughters of Bilitis. Though the Daughters soon split, members of the main group continued to seek through education "to fight for understanding of the homophile minority" and to promote the adjustment of the "variant" to society (Martin and Lyon 1983, pp. 210-15).

On New Years' Eve 1964, the newly formed Council on Religion and the Homosexual, consisting of concerned liberal Protestant ministers and homophile leaders, gave a ball at California Hall. Despite prior assurances of police cooperation, the hall was surrounded by squad cars, police demanded admittance, and each of the more than 600 guests was photographed as they entered and left the hall. In response, the ministers called a press conference and publicly denounced the police deceit and misconduct, and the American Civil Liberties Union (ACLU) defended those arrested. At the trial, the judge directed a verdict of not guilty and chastised the astonished officers. One gay lawyer arrested that night is now Municipal Judge Herb Donaldson.

In January 1978, bold, exuberant Harvey Milk, his lover next to him, was sworn in as Supervisor of the City and County of San Francisco while cheered by hundreds of gay supporters from his home turf in the Castro. He was the first openly gay elected official in a U.S. city. Among his accomplishments while in office was the enactment of a comprehensive gay rights ordinance. Eleven months after his election he was shot and killed along with the liberal mayor of San Francisco, George Moscone, a supporter of gay claims, by a former colleague on the board, Dan White.

On July 15, 1984, 100,000 lesbians and gays marched for their rights down Market Street. Two days later the Democratic Party, meeting in San Francisco for its presidential nominating convention, adopted a broad gay rights plank in its platform. Specific provisions included amendment of the 1964 Civil Rights Act to include "sexual orientation" as a protected category; a ban on discrimination against gays in employment, housing, and public services; a reform of immigration law to prohibit the exclusion of homosexuals; increased funding for AIDS research and patient care; and even federal action to end discrimination against lesbians and gay men in the military.

While gay life exists and even flourishes in some small towns and rural areas, large cities are at the center of the movement. Since the 1950s, Los Angeles, New York, and San Francisco have been recognized as the "Big Three." The movement was born in Los Angeles in 1950. New York was the scene of the dramatic Stonewall Riots of 1969 that sparked the current mass movement. Although both cities have larger gay populations, it is San Francisco that has become the American "gay mecca." Its gay population is more concentrated, move visible, and more influential than that of any other U.S. city. Its marches and parades are the biggest and its political impact is greatest. Its leader in the 1970s, Harvey Milk, was the movement's most dramatic. His slaying gave gays their most vivid martyr, and the White Night Riot which erupted in response to the lenient verdict for his killer was the largest gay riot in known history. What happens in San Francisco affects gay politics everywhere.

THE GAY DIFFERENCE

The San Francisco story is an extraordinary one: from timid, supplicatory education efforts to vindication in court to electoral victory to acknowledged legitimacy by a major political party. There are parallels and similarities with other traditionally disadvantaged groups that have struggled for equality in our epoch. These other groups have influenced the gay movement at times, both as models and, less frequently, as allies. Yet despite some common patterns and similar activities, the gay movement differs significantly from the others.

Gays, and thus their movement, are distinctive in three ways. There is the striking oddity of a politics rooted in the intimate recesses of self and its personal relations. At least as much as the women's movement, the lesbian and gay movement has proclaimed that the personal is the political. This confounds deep prevailing assumptions about the division between the public and the private as well as conventions of normal sexual and social conduct. It confuses gays as well as their opponents. It pushes political debate and sometimes action into unfamiliar territory. That the personal is the political has become true, but it is not the whole truth.

Second, the membership of the gay "community," actual and potential, is impossible to determine. While the boundaries of other groups are interestingly fuzzy, like blacks who used to "pass" or quarter-blood Indians, the boundaries of gays simply disappear. Who is gay or homosexual or lesbian? Do gays and lesbians constitute one or two groups? Are desires, private acts, or public affirmations the decisive criterion? Or is it an identity, consciously chosen or imputed, ascribed or achieved, and what sort of identity is it? There are those who see no difference between gays and nongays, except for what they do in bed, and those who see every difference between gays and others, apart from what they do in bed.

These are not just academic questions, though they are that too; they are central politically. Membership is a crucial political issue whether we speak of community or interest group, participation or representation. If it is unclear as to who counts as a member of the gay community—and it is, to gays as well as to others—much else is thrown in doubt.

Visibility is part of what matters. Most gays, even those who identify as gay, can choose to remain invisible, closeted. To choose to be visible, to "come out" is a political choice, the most important many gay people will ever make. It necessarily moves the issue from private to public. The choice can be harrowing. It requires courage and it is seldom to one's simple advantage. Nor is coming out an all-or-nothing or-once-and-for-all matter. It is not even a necessary series of stages. For example, one can be "out" to friends but not to family, or "out" socially but not at work, or "out" at work but shun political activity except for (secret) voting. To participate openly in the gay movement, uncloseted to gays and nongays alike, is to choose full visibility. Only a fraction of those who act homosexually make this choice.

What it means to be gay, and therefore who is gay, has become the central question of the movement, though the question is not always asked. How it is answered shapes concrete demands for equality. For whom do movement leaders speak? Equality for publicly identified, upfront gays is not the same as for closeted ones.

Third, gays may be "the last minority," as Senator Christopher Dodd (D.-Conn.) called them (though students of Tocqueville should doubt it). Homosexuals also may be the most oppressed people in the society, as Huey Newton said to the Black Panthers in 1970. Unlike other minority groups today, however, gay claims to recognition, acceptance, inclusion, legitimacy, and equality are vigorously and self-confidently denied, resisted, and fought by significant elements of U.S. society. This is not to minimize past or present opposition to blacks and others of color, to women, and to Jews and other religious groups nor to suggest that their claims have been met. It is, though, no longer politically acceptable or expedient to openly reject the grievances of these others. Many Republicans oppose the Equal Rights Amendment (ERA), but President Ronald Reagan talks about remedial legislation and appoints some women to office. People oppose quotas or busing but no longer publicly defame blacks. Taxpayers grouse at the cost of refitting public buildings to make them handicapped-accessible, but they do not deny the desirability of ramps.

Opponents of gays range from punks and teenage gangs through public officials to archbishops and rabbis. Assassinations, murders, beatings, imprisonment, shock therapy, evictions, firings, exclusion, and denial are all part of gay experience. Opposition to many forms of equality for gays is religiously based or rationalized in Judaism and Christianity with the claim of biblical warranty. Others insist on the unnaturalness of gay sexuality. Thus both God and Nature are invoked by opponents. This gives the conflict its aspect of intractability. The issue of equality for gay men is not primarily an economic one—it is more so for lesbians—and cannot readily be bargained over nor the difference split. Of no other group which plausibly aspires to legitimacy and equal treatment is a central defining feature of the group itself a criminal activity. Before 1962, sexual behavior between consenting adults of the same sex was a criminal offense in all states; it is still illegal in 23 of them. The nature of this opposition shapes the gay struggle for equality.

To summarize: the unconventional linkage of the personal and the political, the vexed nature of membership in the gay community with the attendant issue of visibility, and the uncompromising virulence of the opposition distinguish the gay movement from other movements for equality.

On July 3, 1968, two dozen lesbians and gay men demonstrated at the Federal Building in downtown San Francisco and called "for the completion of the American Revolution"; they sought "to extend the principles of the Declaration of Independence to all Americans" (*Advocate* 1968, p.3). That such appeals had often been sounded before made this one neither banal nor clear. To claim equality is common but to clarify it is not. Equality of opportunity is not equality of condition; treating equal cases equally is not political equality. The ambiguity of gayness is matched by the elusiveness of equality. Few oppose equality now but all interpret. Gays in San Francisco have claimed equalities of different kinds in several areas. This chapter examines gay efforts to gain the (legal) right to exist, equal security, economic equality, and political equality.

THE RIGHT TO EXIST

Existence precedes equality as well as essence. Prior to 1976 in California, sexual behavior between persons of the same sex was illegal, a criminal felony offense referred to as sodomy or the crime against nature (Boggan et al. 1975, pp. 166–67). The long-standing existence of such a statute shows how the personal had been politicized by the opposition long before gays reacted. Although the statute was seldom enforced, the stigma was unique among all modern groups seeking equality. As long as even adult, private, consenting homosexual conduct was criminal, ready arguments were available to reject any other gay claims.

The issue also raises the paradox of one kind of gay politics. Once the state has proscribed a certain form of conduct, even one which many believe to be profoundly private, public mobilization is necessary to repeal it. This is the minimal case for gay politics. Yet to mobilize requires of gays that they become visible. Is it plausible that people who are safely invisible will take on the challenge of visibility solely in order to become legitimately invisible?

Repeal of the law was, of course, a state matter. Yet it was San Francisco's Assemblyman (later Speaker) Willie Brown and Senator (later Mayor) George Moscone who recognized the growing gay clout in their city and sponsored the bill.

EQUAL SECURITY

Thomas Hobbes was not wrong to stress the fear of violent death as crucial to politics. For identifiable gay men and for all lesbians, it is an ongoing concern even in a city as seemingly benign as San Francisco. Harrassment (verbal and physical), beatings, even murder are regular features of urban gay life. A demand for equal security is one of the oldest of gay concerns. Opponents create the issue but it becomes more salient as gays become more visible. Community United Against Violence (CUAV), a gay, community-based, city-funded group that monitors antigay violence, received reports of 332 attacks against lesbians and gay men in 1983. Of these 35 percent involved the use of weapons and an equal number required medical attention (*Bay Area Reporter* 1984). Reports in 1984 were even higher.

A dilemma common to many oppressed groups is particularly sharp for gays: how can they turn to the authorized public agency for providing security, the police, when the police are among their most ardent harassers? When rowdy off-duty male cops crashed a lesbian bar, Peg's Place, in 1979 and caused a ruckus, someone shouted, "Let's get the cops." The revelers, who injured several patrons, replied, "We *are* the cops!" (Hoffman 1979). Gay-police relations have long been tense, and the tension did not end with the passage of the consenting adults bill.

For years bars were almost the only havens for gays. Efforts to close gay bars were endemic. Mayor George Christopher, embarrassed by election charges in 1959 that he had allowed San Francisco to become "the national headquarters of homosexuals in the United States," launched a crackdown against the bars. After the California Supreme Court affirmed the right of homosexuals to gather in taverns, several emboldened bar owners reported that they had been subject to shakedowns from the police and the state liquor board. The upshot of the "Gayola" scandal was that all but the two officers who pleaded guilty were acquitted, and each of the bars was eventually forced to close (D'Emilio 1981, pp. 85-89).

In addition to bar harassment, periodic raids on parks were made. Under Mayor Joseph Alioto, by 1971 police were arresting an average of about 2,800 gay men each year on public sex charges; the same year, only 63 such arrests were made in all of New York City (Shilts 1982, p.62). Things changed for the better with liberal Mayor Moscone's election and his appointment of a remarkably progressive police chief, Charles Gain. Gain met regularly with gay groups, supported a controversial drive to recruit gay officers, and restrained his men initially during the White Night Riot of 1979. Yet Dan White, the killer of Moscone and Milk, was a former cop and was widely believed to have covert police sympathy. After the riot at City Hall, the police savagely attacked gay men in the Castro bars.

To gain equal security from the police, gays struggled for over 30 years: to change laws and to make the police lawful; to recruit lesbians and gays to the force; to win the appointment of an openly gay member of the Police Commission; and to establish more effective civilian review. These were accomplished by 1982. Some gays denounced this liberal agenda as cooptation, a sell-out to the pigs, the enemy.

Another strategy emerged concurrently, that of direct community self-protection. The Butterfly Brigade, founded in 1977 and succeeded by CUAV, organized patrols, distributed whistles to be blown at signs of physical danger, conducted workshops on self-protection, and regularly reported on and publicized continuing antigay violence. This dual pattern of both seeking equal access to and consideration from established institutions became characteristic in the 1970s.

ECONOMIC EQUALITY

If elemental survival concerns, existence and security, are met, others come to the fore. In the economic arena gays have most resembled other minority groups in pursuing equality. Here the difference between lesbians and gay men is probably sharpest, for lesbians usually face the double discrimination visited upon those both female and queer, while white gay males often are not economically disadvantaged. Yet for visible, openly gay men this is relatively recent. Job discrimination against gays has a long history. While legal remedies have been pursued, groups of gay-owned and operated businesses such as the Tavern Guild and the Golden Gate Business Association have also banded together for mutual protection and support.

The first step in legal job protection came in 1972 when "sexual orientation" was added to the list of classes protected against discrimination. This, however, applied only to contractors with the city of San Francisco. In 1975, the school board extended protection to teachers. Then in 1978, the board of supervisors gave newly elected Harvey Milk one of his biggest victories; it enacted by a vote of 10-1 a comprehensive gay rights ordinance banning discrimination throughout San Francisco in employment, housing, and public accommodations. The Human Rights Commission is empowered to investigate, mediate, and enforce the ordinance. In 1982-83, 87 complaints were filed. Of these, 63 percent concerned employment (San Francisco 1984).

Even here in this most familiar of civil rights' strategies there was a distinctive gay twist. Harvey Milk in a television interview later used in the 1984 documentary film, *The Times of Harvey Milk*, said that the ordinance was intended less to protect those gays who were already "out" than to allow others to "come out" without fear of losing their jobs. Its purpose, thus, was in part to increase the visible membership of the gay community.

Decriminalization, physical security, nondiscrimination in employment and housing—these represent a minimum agenda of equality within the context of a liberal system. Their adoption shows a minimal recognition of the basic claims of gay persons, a modest public acknowledgment of equal worth. Each of these rights applies to individuals. Were they to be fully enforced by the state, the gay issue might disappear. For some, this would be ideal: a polity blind to sexual orientation. Yet there is a countercurrent, one that insists that the personal is the political and seeks to strengthen the visible gay community. Equality is slippery. What seems simply economic may become political. Claims once made lead to further ones; they spill over.

POLITICAL EQUALITY

Consider the important court decision in the case of *Gay Law Students Association* v. *Pacific Telephone and Telegraph Company*, first tried in Superior Court in San Francisco and ultimately decided by the California Supreme Court. The class action suit alleged discriminatory employment practices and sought appropriate relief. That this company refused to hire open, "upfront" gays was a long-standing complaint in the community, one that Milk often made. The case involved numerous issues and was of limited value in establishing precedent since the public utility, as a government regulated entity, was held to standards stricter than those for private employers. Nonetheless, Justice Tobriner, writing in 1979 for a 4-3 majority, found that the company could not, under both state and federal equal protection clauses, arbitrarily discriminate against homosexuals as a class in hiring, firing, and promoting employees.

This is familiar legal reasoning, but the court went further. It found that a political right, a right to political activity on the part of homosexuals, was violated, if the alleged facts were correct, under the state labor code. Remarkably, the decision stated:

> A principal barrier to homosexual equality is the common feeling that homosexuality is an affliction which the homosexual worker must conceal from his employer and his fellow workers. Consequently one important aspect of the struggle for equal rights is to induce homosexual individuals to "come out of the closet," acknowledge their sexual preferences, and to associate with others in working for equal rights (*Gay Law Students Assn.* v. *Pacific Telephone and Telegraph Company* 1979, p.32).

Politics is the nub. Without a gay political movement the justices could not have reached such a finding. Without a gay political movement the consenting adults bill would not have passed, nor minimum security been attained, nor the comprehensive city nondiscrimination ordinance enacted. A gay politics was necessary and instrumental to attaining equal rights, juridical equality. Gay politics in San Francisco, though, has become more than instrumental. It has also become expressive, an end in itself, seeking to shape an ongoing collective life, increasingly in concert with other groups. These different ends are often mixed.

Chris Perry, a founder of the San Francisco (later Harvey Milk) Lesbian and Gay Democratic Club, wrote in the first issue of *GAYVOTE* in 1978:

> We felt it was time for gay people to quit courting favors from "tolerant" politicians and to start forming coalitions with other minorities struggling for equality.... We wanted to work within the electoral process as equal partners with labor, women, and environmental groups.... It's time for San Francisco's lesbians and gay men to claim that to which our 125,000 votes entitle us. No decisions which affect our lives should be made without the gay voice having been heard. We want our fair share of city services. We want openly gay people appointed and elected to city offices.... We want the schools of San Francisco to provide full exposure to and positive appreciation of gay lifestyles (Perry 1978, p.2).

Proportionate entitlements, distributive equality in services, representational equality, equality with other groups, equal cultural recognition, a movement from requests for recognition of claimed rights to active, public self-determination—all these are present in Perry's revealing statement. It was made on the occasion of Harvey Milk's swearing-in as supervisor. That victory had been a long time coming.

The first openly gay candidate to run for office was the legendary Jose Sarria, a gutsy, flamboyant, drag impresario at the Black Cat bar. His Sunday afternoon campy opera spoofs were widely admired as was his insistence that all who attended afterward stand, put their arms around each other, and sing "God Save Us Nelly Queens." Sarria collected enough signatures to run for supervisor in 1961. As he explained, "I was trying to prove to my gay audience that I had the right, being as gay and notorious as I was, to run for public office, because people in those days didn't believe you had any rights" (D'Emilio 1983, pp.187–88). He received 6,000 votes during this period of heavy police oppression. Winning was not the objective; helping to instill self-respect in the gay community was.

During the 1960s, gays cautiously edged into city politics. Small groups held candidates nights and made endorsements. A few politicians advertised in gay publications, and some, like Willie Brown, took up gay causes. The explosion of gay activity, consciousness, visibility, and assertiveness that followed the June 1969 Stonewall Riots in New York quickly surfaced in San Francisco. The Bay Area, as a national center of radical politics and countercultural experimentation in the 1960s, was more receptive than most places, both to "sexual migrants" and to their new politics. A number of new radical groups emerged but they were short-lived. Longer lasting were emergent separate lesbian institutions and gay Democratic clubs. The oldest, the Alice B. Toklas Club, was founded in 1971. Its style was to work for reformist goals through established Democratic Party figures.

In the 1970s ever more gay men and lesbians poured into San Francisco. For economic, security, and social reasons the men in particular concentrated in the geographically central area of the city, the region around Castro Street. Lesbians were more dispersed and less visible. Castells (1983, pp.407–8) has estimated that by 1980 there were between 110,000 and 120,000 gays (two-thirds male, one-third lesbian) out of a total population of 678,974. These new migrants were usually young, active, and much more assertive than the gays of previous decades.

Even so, a crucial change in San Francisco's political structure was necessary before Milk could be elected. In 1976 neighborhood activists accomplished their long sought goal of electing supervisors by district rather than at-large. The new District 5, which encompassed the Castro, the Haight-Ashbury, and Noe Valley, was the ideal turf for a gay supervisor (Castells 1983, pp.145–63). Campaigns not dependent on downtown money now had a chance of success. On his third try for office, Milk was elected in 1977.

Brash and canny, Harvey Milk catalyzed this potentially strong but still inchoate population into the strongest assertion yet of urban gay equality. As the first openly gay elected official in the country, he became a major mover in San Francisco politics in the brief 11 months that he served as supervisor. Milk's significance, though, goes far beyond his election and short legislative record. By his presence, his message, and his actions, he insisted on gay equality in a fuller sense than anyone before, and he stimulated others to do the same. He both realized and raised the aspirations of many gay people. He demanded that they overcome their self-oppression, come out, stand up, and claim not only equal rights and equal entitlements, but equal political participation. He even suggested that to do so, despite the dangers, was joyful. It was not enough for gays to receive a fair distribution of public resources from the hands of nongay politicians and administrators—not that that had ever happened. Gays were to be, in Milk's view, fully equal participants in the political process itself.

With Milk working on so many fronts at once this shift was not always apparent, but it was decisive. Some kind of equal political participation was necessary to insure any kind of equal distribution, but what was beyond that was crucial. Equal self-respect too required equal citizenship, and equal citizenship meant not just periodic voting but a continuing, active, collective self-determination of the gay community.[2] This meant assuming new responsibility. In an exchange captured in the 1980 CBS television documentary "Gay Power, Gay Politics: The San Francisco Experience," Mayor Dianne Feinstein criticized the gay community for "its lack of standards." Cleve Jones, a prominent aide to Milk, tartly replied, "The gay community will set its own standards." This is not just a rejection of the mayor's moralizing, it acknowledges a new community task.

Yet San Francisco gays, though by now a sizable presence in the city, were and would remain a minority. Many were more conventional and conservative than Milk. Since he rejected the separatist politics which some advocated, the alternative was coalition. Milk was remarkably successful in promoting coalitions between gays and such improbable groups as the Chinese-American Democrats, the Teamsters, and the Firemen's Union (Thomas 1982b). He showed that gays were desirable coequal partners. Never an ideologue, Milk had a gut loyalty to underdogs and an antipathy to the Establishment. For a time the prospect for a broad progressive coalition of the oppressed and dispossessed seemed bright. This historical opportunity opened by Milk and his supporters has been pursued, under less promising conditions, by Supervisor Harry Britt, Milk's successor. Britt has emphasized women's concerns much more than did Milk and has actively worked with tenants, the disabled, and the elderly. In 1980, a second openly gay official, Tim Wolfred, was elected to the Community College Board. He too pursues coalition politics.

In a sense the brief period of Harvey Milk's ascendancy was the high point of gay equality in San Francisco. The personal had been dramatically politicized by gays and not just by their opponents; the community was more visible and stronger than ever before. Gay politics had moved from a focus on rights to one of coalition. Substantial juridical equality was attained with the rights ordinance, advances were made in distribution of city services and appointments, and gays were recognized as a group whose concerns must be recognized along with more established groups. Milk symbolized and demonstrated political equality, rooted in his own community, reaching to city hall and beyond.

These achievements were not secure. In Milk's last months, in fall 1978, he devoted much of his time to combatting California Proposition 6 (the Briggs

Initiative), which would have barred openly gay teachers from the public schools. During the previous year city-council-enacted gay rights ordinances had been repealed by popular vote in Miami, St. Paul, Wichita, even the university town of Eugene, Oregon. Prospects and spirits were low in California; in September the first statewide poll on Proposition 6 showed public opinion favoring it 61 to 31 percent (Shilts 1982, p.242). In the November election, however, the initiative was handily defeated statewide, and in San Francisco it lost by a decisive margin of 75 to 25 percent. This reflected not only the gay vote but also the opposition of most of the city electorate to blatant, stigmatizing discrimination.

After the assassinations of Milk and Moscone on November 27, 1978, there was slippage and regression. The police appeared released from previous constraints. The new mayor, Dianne Feinstein, a rival of Moscone and a self-proclaimed centrist, had supported gay rights ordinances, but she was seen as prissy and uncomprehending of gays' real concerns. Initially, for instance, she declined to repeat Moscone's crucial pledge to appoint a gay police commissioner.

Then on May 21, 1979, the jury in the Dan White murder trial returned a verdict of voluntary manslaughter, the lightest possible conviction and one which would give the killer freedom in little more than five years. This astonishing verdict was universally seen in the gay community, and by many nongays as well, as blatant injustice, a violation of the most elementary requirement of equality before the law.

The White Night Riot, which erupted that night at City Hall and elsewhere, involved thousands of demonstrators and several hundred thousand dollars in property damage. Records indicate that 129 persons were treated for injuries. It called on that most primitive form of moral equality—revenge. Though nongays were also involved, it was the largest riot in known gay history. The riot showed visibility and outrage, a new kind of gay strength. The unleashed fury of White Night was matched by controlled powerful emotion at the long-planned public Harvey Milk Birthday Party on Castro Street the following night. San Francisco was on notice that its gay population could be pushed only so far (Shilts 1982, pp.324-39; Thomas 1982a).

NEW ISSUES

In the years since the riot, survival issues have returned to the fore. Violence against gay men and lesbians has not abated—in summer 1984 it rose dramatically—and complaints about police abuse continue, even as more gay police are recruited and trained.

The acquired immune deficiency syndrome (AIDS) crisis confronted the gay male community with anguish, fear, and death without precedent. It raises issues which go far beyond the compass of equality. Opponents of gays have sinister new arguments and slogans. The question of membership in the gay community takes a new urgent turn as those who engage in homosexual conduct but do not identify themselves as gay (and therefore do not get the best gay health advice) may be at greatest risk to the deadly disease. The personal links not only with the political but also with the medical. Gays had largely escaped a medical model (Weeks 1981, pp.99-107) and were struggling to become a political minority. They are now threatened with intellectual remedicalization and popular perceptions as a public health menace.

A revealing new issue of equality is that of spousal rights or "domestic partners legislation," as it is called in San Francisco. Such legislation would require the city to "use domestic partnership in the same way" as it now uses marriage for such matters as bereavement leave and health insurance. This would apply to the partners of lovers of (necessarily) unmarried gay men and women. For many this is a clear case of removing a discriminatory economic inequality, a plain and simple matter of justice. To others, though, this is a definitive example of gays pushing too far, to the point of officially denigrating marriage and the family. Opposition ranges from sarcastic inquiries if one's dog could qualify, to objections over cost and practicability, to vigorous rejection by Catholic, Jewish, and conservative Protestant leaders.

That the legislation carries strong symbolic meaning was acknowledged by active supporter Supervisor Harry Britt: "This legislation has one purpose in mind—to recognize that the relationships of gay people and straight people who are not married are as meaningful as those of people who marry" (San Francisco *Examiner* 1982a). The *Examiner* (1982b) had earlier editorialized that "the notion that an unmarried relationship is the equivalent of marriage is an attack upon social norms." San Francisco Catholic Archbishop John Quinn too described the measure as "severely inimical to marriage and the family, which are the foundations of society." It would, he charged, "further erode the moral foundations of civilized society" (Rannels 1982). The proposal, however, was approved by the Board of Supervisors on November 22, 1982, by an 8-3 vote. But even though a poll (Cole 1982) showed that 57 percent of San Francisco residents supported it, it was vetoed by Mayor Feinstein on December 9.

The issue raised fierce emotions and contentious accusations. It showed how the continuing logic of liberal equality could lead to policies abhorrent to people who had supported earlier gay claims. It showed that the public symbolic recognition of ongoing gay relationships as having parity with traditional marriage was far more important than the economic issue of "equal access to fringe benefits." It also divided gays. The most vocal supported official recognition of gay "families," while both radicals and conservatives rejected the idea. The matter of treating gay relationships equitably is far more troubling than that of extending equality to individuals.

CONCLUSION

The gay quest for equality in San Francisco has been an extraordinary one. There have been parallel developments in other U.S. cities involving immigration, geographical concentration, creation of community-based institutions, visibility, political assertion, and political influence. Los Angeles, Boston, Minneapolis, Washington, D.C., Houston, New York—each in some ways resembles San Francisco, but, despite Washington's larger number of openly gay commissioners and Los Angeles' remarkable fund-raising capacity, San Francisco's gay politics is the most intense.

Gay men and women have been denied equality in virtually every area of their lives: security, housing, employment, criminal justice, recognition, participation. Each matters, but the struggle for equality in these areas has also been a means to attain the social bases of self-respect, without which there can be no equal moral worth (See Rawls 1971, pp.440-46). This is the source of much pathos and misunderstanding. Yet neither simple equality nor full equality can be attained, because equality is neither a simple nor a complete notion. While the tide of egalitarian discourse flows on, we must think of equalities. Conceptions and realities of equality clash. The primitive though powerful "equalling out" in the vengeance of the White Night Riot, the equal opportunity sought through nondiscrimination ordinances, the idea that the gay community is on a par with other minorities and should have equal say in self- and city government—these equalities are related, yet there is tension between them. The tension is not always recognized by those who pursue equality. The stigma of denial is so great that equality of almost any sort is prized.

The most important contrast has, on one side, a focus on persons and seeks equality of opportunity, rights, and entitlements irrespective of the past or present stigma of homosexuality. The upshot of this tendency is to eliminate homosexuality as a relevant public matter, to consign it to the private realm, to negate its political significance. Ironically, this can happen only through the assertion of political power, for only through such power can employers, landlords, the police, public service agencies, and others with power and resources be constrained from discrimination against gay people.

The contrary tendency is to emphasize the community, with all the attendant ambiguities of that notion, and the equal legitimacy of its needs, claims, and interests with those of others. This extends from parade permits to AIDS funding to claims for proportionate representation in city offices. It raises deep questions as to who speaks for the gay community. What does membership mean? Since self-identification for gays is at least partially chosen, visibility usually so, and the kind of participation fully, the issue is profoundly political. The aspiration for some kind of collective self-determination on the part of gays readily provokes the question of how gays, as a permanent minority, are to relate to other groups, to the majority. One response to this is a strategy of seeking a populist coalition of the dispossessed, the strategy of Harvey Milk and Harry Britt.

It is easiest for the system to accommodate claims for nondiscrimination ("equal rights") against individuals. Discrimination is demonstrable, organized gays demand its elimination, it is hard to defend, the basic logic of the U.S. political tradition opposes it, and nondiscrimination ultimately offends few interests other than some churches. Much more awkward to handle is the claim for some kind of group or community equality, particularly when that community is at once recently visible, deeply offensive to some, and has the most obscure boundaries. To acknowledge group claims is to confer a kind of legitimacy entirely different from holding homosexuality irrelevant for employment or housing. Yet even here, the peculiar U.S. tradition of gradually accommodating minority groups has proven serviceable. That the Irish-descended Sheriff of San Francisco, Mike Hennessey, can refer to the city's lesbians and gay men as "another ethnic group," may startle but it is politically apt. Distributing offices, appointments, and city services among an amalgam of politically significant groups is hardly unprecedented in American urban history.

Still intractable, though, is the issue of establishng a sanctioned public equality for gay relationships. The economic aspect here is much easier to treat than the symbolic. Relations between persons, other than contractual or traditionally sacramental, can be ill accommodated by either liberalism or the churches. Voting against a Certificate of Honor recognizing lesbian leaders Phyllis Lyon and Dell Martin for their 25 years of partnership and service to the community, Supervisor Quentin Kopp said, "toleration yes, glorification no" (Jetter 1984, p.9).

Lesbians and gay men do not seek glorification. Many do seek to move from being tolerated to being fully accepted in city life. Archbishop John Quinn responds, "That's their agenda, and that's where we can never have any agreement. That will always be impossible, for the Catholic Church to accept that agenda" (San Francisco *Chronicle* 1983).

Behind the many specific equalities, some contradictory, that gay men and lesbians have sought and sometimes obtained in San Francisco, is a deep aspiration for equal respect. To the extent it has been gained, it has required changes in gays themselves as much as in others or in laws. Viewed from 30 years ago, the movement toward that end is astonishing. Viewed as a supporter of Harvey Milk, or by a gay man on the street subject to regular gay-baiting and in danger of fag-bashing, or as a lesbian denied custody of her child, or a gay Catholic seeking full welcome from the Church—that goal seems remote. Deep structures of ideology and power remain opposed to gay equality. They would not have yielded to the extent they have nor will they retreat further without the active, political effort of gay people themselves.

NOTES

1. There is no satisfactory solution to the naming of this chapter's subject. In general I use gay as both noun and adjective and use it, in accord with early 1970s gay liberation usage, to include women. When I wish to emphasize the distinction, I use gay men and lesbians.
2. Radical critics might claim that this could not happen through representative electoral politics nor under capitalism or patriarchy, but their voices were weak in these years.

REFERENCES

Advocate. 1968. "News Briefs." July 10.
Bay Area Reporter. 1984. Letter from Assemblyman Art Agnos. September 20.
Boggan, E, Carrington et al. 1975. *The Rights of Gay People*. New York: Avon.
Castells, Manuel. 1983. *The City and the Grassroots: A Cross-Cultural Theory of Urban Social Movements*. Berkeley: University of California Press.
Cole, David M. 1982. "57% of Residents Back 'Domestic Partner' Plan." San Francisco *Examiner*, November 29.
D'Emilio, John. 1983. *Sexual Politics, Sexual Communities: The Making of a Homosexual Minority in the United States, 1940–1970*. Chicago: University of Chicago Press.
———. 1981. "Gay Politics, Gay Community: San Francisco's Experience." *Socialist Review* 11 (January-February):77–104.
Gay Law Students Assn. v. Pacific Telephone and Telegraph Company, 156 California Reporter (Sup. Ct. 1979).
Hoffman, Judith. 1979. "Police Punished for Peg's." *GAYVOTE*, August, p.1.
Jetter, Alexis. 1984. "The Fight for City Hall 1984 Style." *Coming Up!* 6 (November):p.9.
Martin, Dell and Phyllis Lyon. 1983. *Lesbian Woman*. rev. ed. New York: Bantam.
Perry, Chris. 1978. "SF Gay Politics: A Style for 1978." *GAYVOTE*, January, p.2.
Rannels, Jackson. 1982. "Archbishop Urges Veto of Live-in Lovers Benefits." San Francisco *Chronicle*, December 8.
Rawls, John. 1971. *A Theory of Justice*. Cambridge, Mass.: Harvard University Press.
San Francisco, California (city and county). 1984. Statement by the Human Rights Commission dated July 1.
San Francisco *Chronicle*. 1983. "An Interview with the Archbishop." May 30.
San Francisco *Examiner*. 1982a. Letter from Supervisor Harvey Milk. November 24.
San Francisco *Examiner*. 1982b. "Defeat the Britt Proposal." November 21.
Shilts, Randy. 1982. *The Mayor of Castro Street: The Life and Times of Harvey Milk*. New York: St. Martin's Press.
Thomas, David. 1982a. "San Francisco's 1979 White Night Riot: Injustice, Vengeance, and Beyond." In *Homosexuality: Social, Psychological, and Biological Issues*, edited by William Paul, pp.337–50. Beverly Hills: Sage.
———. 1982b. "An Interview with Randy Shilts." *Christopher Street*. 6:31–32.
Weeks, Jeffrey. 1981. *Sex, Politics, and Society: The Regulation of Sexuality Since 1800*. New York: Longman.

4

THE VOTELESS CONSTITUENCY: CHILDREN AND CHILD CARE

Jill Norgren

People have long debated whether cities are healthy places for children. Far from grandma, fresh air, green grass, and trees to climb, urban life for children is often described in terms of deprivation. It is thought, for example, that primary social relations weaken in the city and that children lose sight of their identity or roots. Worthy, traditional values are described as dissolving before the onslaught of Sodom and Gommorah-like urban influences. Yet, as President Theodore Roosevelt's 1908 Country Life Commission reported, rural life has never been all milk and honey; drudgery, barrenness, and heavy drinking, the commissioners wrote, characterized rural regions (Richardson 1972, p.374). And, indeed, despite unrelenting rhetoric in praise of the sweet, freer country life, young people have long been abandoning the "paradise garden" of rural regions to seek their fortunes in the city, for cities are where money is to be made (Richardson 1972, p.371). The city is, in Jane Jacobs' (1961, p.447) words, a place of "diverse opportunities and productivity."

In fact, we know very little empirically about whether cities are good or bad places for children. The terms—good and bad—are themselves heavily value laden. All cities, too, are not alike. And, finally, all residents of any one city do not experience that place in the same way. Urban life is mediated by a prism of class, health, previous experience, and personality.

This does not mean, however, that certain questions cannot be asked about the nature and distribution of public resources and rights for children living in cities. And, indeed, these are essential questions to ask within a study on the promise of equality—for of the United States' total population of 220 million, 64 million are children, most of whom live in urban areas.[1]

CHILDREN: SOCIETY'S PRECITIZENS

In terms of both their numerical size and their role as the generation of the future, children constitute a formidable constituency. Yet, children have little, if any, authoritative involvement in the political process. Children as a political and social constituency face many barriers in the pursuit of policy serving their needs.

As minors children have no formal status as political actors in the system that determines who gets what, when, and how. Children, of course, cannot vote or hold public office. Furthermore, it is not until they are high-school age that the young command any of the other political resources—money, mobility, knowledge of the system, social connections—that Robert Dahl and others identify as complementing the vote as tools of political influence (Dahl 1961, pp.85, 271-75).

Americans may not think of children as a disadvantaged constituency. But in a republic where decisions are made in a maelstrom of interaction between voters, lobbyists, and representatives, any group without the resources of influence is politically unequal and, therefore, disadvantaged.

Admittedly, most Americans are not troubled by this lack of political equality for children. Although children are a voteless and virtually unorganized constituency, adults assume that other mechanisms properly function as authoritative, though not democratic, substitutes. Quite simply, the "children's cause," as Gilbert Steiner (1976) has termed it, depends upon a ward-guardian or fiduciary concept. As precitizens, children rely upon others—adults—to define and present their "case."

The potential pitfalls of this dependency are numerous. There is no guarantee that those we think of as children's guardians will take the fiduciary responsibility seriously. Or, for perfectly benign reasons, the guardian may not recognize a problem, even if articulated by the children, or may not perceive its intensity. Conversely, a guardian may understand the legitimacy of a particular children's cause but, as a third party, may weigh the relative importance of competing demands differently than children. It follows that the initial design of policy, the timing and the manner used by guardians to penetrate the political system, and the policies adopted might vary significantly from those preferred by children themselves.

There are several examples, real and speculative, that support this argument. One of the most painful has been the issue of child abuse, physical and sexual. Child abuse is not new. Although there is evidence that abuse is more prevalent today, adults have long engaged in such abuse and children have long asked for legal, economic, and social policies to brake and cushion this behavior (Family Service America 1984). Historically, however, parents, physicians, teachers, and judicial or legislative guardians have not acted in concert with the needs of children when weighing the competing problems of false testimony, legal suits, or the parental right to discipline. The historical fact of child abuse as a slighted issue on political agendas speaks directly to the dilemma of children as precitizens.

Similarly, adult politics and adult compromises have significantly affected the availability of day care in urban areas. Yet, logically, young children would not freely choose to be left home alone... to be "latch-key" children. Most would instead prefer adult companionship or adult guidance.

In other policy areas, how universal is the finding (Lynch 1977, p.55) that Australian urban planners and politicians developing new recreational facilities were "well ignorant of what the children do" and how they would plan play space? Would children approve "adults only" residential communities, accept cuts in food programs, or turn down public school budgets? To be sure, some might—it is naive to believe that children are a homogeneous group. But children have some common interests, such as the protection of the integrity of their bodies against abuse, in addition to interests that follow subgroupings such as race, class, and sex. Thus, it is equally simplistic to assert that guardians will always serve the interests of children as children would themselves. This often means that children's interests are not served at all.

There is one final case of third party guardianship which, like that of the parent, presents an especially grave problem for the children's cause. This is the issue of representation of children's interests by legislators. One popular theory of political representation holds that an elected representative should mirror the attitudes of his or her constituency. Aside from the issue of whether such officials consider children part of their constituency at all, since children do not qualify as voters, there is the practical problem of how such representatives could reflect the position of a youthful constituency. Children are not only unorganized, they are usually outside the probings of the pollsters.

Moreover, legislators at all levels of government are still predominantly white males. This means that these (adult) legislators remain outside the contemporary experience not only of youth but also of girls and minorities. And empathy is not always easy, as Washington *Post* journalist Richard Cohen (1984, p.75) has written in reference to two children's policy issues: "Day care—even child support—remains a coldly intellectual issue to lots of men, not because they cannot appreciate its importance, but because they cannot feel the importance of it."

This is not to say that urban policies and programs for children do not exist. In addition to basic policies for youth such as education and juvenile justice, urban communities generally provide a mix of children's programs. Traditionally, these have included playgrounds, sports teams, and children's programming at the public library, zoo, museum, and orchestra. Sometimes there is a summer youth jobs program. These and other programs like school breakfasts or vaccinations are consciously directed toward children. They are proposed and justified because of children. When such programs are introduced and when they fail or are eliminated, the impact on children is clear. This is not the case in other urban policy areas such as transportation. When policymakers choose to invest in highways rather than mass transit or increase mass transit fares, the needs of youth are not explicitly considered. Yet, the availability of public transportation—and its cost—very much influences the equality of the urban child's life. The cost and quality of transportation may determine what school a family can select for a son or daughter. Transportation determines the feasibility of a trip to the museum or downtown branch of the library, the location of after-school lessons, and the frequency of visits with friends. Transportation may also determine the nature of job opportunities open to teenagers. Thus, decisions about free transit passes, of half-fares, become very important to both children's independence and opportunities.

Mayors, city councils, and bureaucracies are clearly as important to the children of an urban community as to its adults. These government officials develop, maintain, and sometimes terminate or retrench, dozens of programs affecting the mental, cultural, and physical well-being of children. Policies for children, like those for adults, are vulnerable to the exigencies of local politics, intergovernmental relations, and larger social trends. Children then are clearly not ignored by urban decision makers. Yet, the process of initiating policies for children is fundamentally different because it is characterized by representation that is not necessarily direct, responsive, or accurate.

The remainder of this chapter considers child care policy. Child care represents a broad range of services, and their availability has a far-ranging impact on the "precitizen" child. Child care affects the physical, social and intellectual development of the young child at a critical age. Through an examination of child care policy, the needs of children and how they are met in the distribution of urban resources can be most economically considered.

CHILD CARE: POLICY FOR THE YOUNG CHILD

Child care policy is a term used to refer to a cluster of public programs and benefits offered variously by cities, states, and the national government to influence the care of children. In the largest sense, the list includes group and family day care, maternity and paternity leave, flexible parental work schedules, and tax credits.

In this country, the earliest ongoing child care programs (dating from the mid-1800s) consisted of day care centers for children of the working poor and those whose parents suffered social or physical pathologies. Most were in cities. Since World War II, and in particular since the late 1960s, parents who want to work have demanded public child care programs or public subsidies.

The development of child care policy in the United States has been intimately associated with the highly emotional and ideological issue of government intervention in family life. The rhetoric, though by no means the reality, of U.S. politics has long held that the family is in the private sphere—a haven from the long arm of the government. The prevailing myth is that a successful family is a self-sufficient family—resilient and independent. As Zigler and Muenchow (1983, p.92) have written, ". . . unlike many European countries, the United States has tended to believe that parents alone should finance the costs of bearing and raising children."

Opposition to public child care, fed by an undercurrent of belief that mothers—not government—should care for the very young, was encouraged by two other factors. One was the "dreary" character of early American day care centers. The second was the realization that mothers, receiving neither salaries not pension benefits, were vastly cheaper sources of care than any public program or subsidy. As a result, there was no significant, federally funded day care program after World War II until 1967.[2] Moreover, taking their cue from Washington, virtually no city or state government—with the notable exceptions of New York City and California—chose to establish major programs. Until the late 1960s, then, despite statistics clearly indicating a public need, government-sponsored or supported child care programs were almost nonexistent in most urban communities.

In the late 1960s, pressure built to create national, and urban, policy on child care. This challenge resulted from a constellation of changes in U.S. politics and demographics. First was the impact of the civil rights movement and the economic opportunity programs of the Johnson years. Using this supportive environment welfare families and the working poor pressed government at all levels for day care programs to replace their expensive, and often patched-together, child care arrangements. Their demands reflected an immediate need but also were linked to the U.S. promise of equality of opportunity. They argued that safe, inexpensive, and reliable day care was a prerequisite for parents who wanted to care properly for their children while at work or at an adult educational program.

Alone, it is not clear what policy changes these citizens might have affected. This became a moot issue, however, as the combined impact of rapidly spiraling inflation and the women's movement in the late 1960s encouraged an increasing number of women to go to work. Suddenly, child care policy was on the political agenda of the working and middle classes and new coalitions were born. In 1970, proponents spoke of a new era for U.S. day care policy. In fact, however, the only major national legislation in the 1970s to build upon the 1967 federal day care funding program was the 1976 child care income tax credit (see Norgren and Cole 1982; Nelson and Waring 1982). Aside from amending the tax credit to make it more equitable for working class families, Washington in the early 1980s has ignored issues of child care or turned them over to local government as part of President Reagan's "new federalism."

The Need

The social world experienced by U.S. children, in particular urban children, has changed dramatically over the past 30 years. Children today are more likely to live in a female-headed household and/or to have a working mother. Both situations have greatly increased the need for new child care policies.

Through death, divorce, out-of-wedlock birth, and choice, female-headed, single-parent families are created. Since at least 1960 there has been a steady increase in such female-headed families, primarily due to higher rates of divorce and a greater number of unmarried mothers. While the incidence of divorce has shown signs of leveling off in the 1980s after a 20-year surge, out-of-wedlock births—particularly in urban areas—have not. In 1983, for example, more than one of every three children born in New York City were born to unmarried women; this figure is triple that in the early 1960s. In Newark and Baltimore, the percentage of out-of-wedlock births approached 60 percent in the early 1980s (Berger 1984). As a result, although some of these mothers—as well as divorced mothers—eventually marry or remarry, over 20 percent of U.S. children now live in single-parent homes, a figure double that of 1960 (U.S. Department of Commerce 1980, p.11).

An even more dramatic revolution has occurred in the work patterns of children's mothers. Thirty years ago, only 12 percent of women with preschool children worked (U.S. Department of Commerce 1982, p.3). By 1983 over 50 percent did (U.S. Department of Commerce 1983a, pp.16-17). Currently more than eight million youngsters under six years of age, and 32 million children under eighteen, have working mothers. Moreover, researchers expect the number of preschool children with working mothers to exceed 10 million by 1990 (Grossman 1982).

These figures show that children—particularly in urban areas, where there are more working women and more female-headed households—need child care programs. Yet government at every level has been unresponsive to their needs. As a result, public child care is still neither available nor affordable for many families. The direction of policy in recent years, moreover, has made child care least available to those whose need is greatest: the working poor and those with very young children. And, finally, the lack of a national maternity, or parental, leave policy forces many families to seek child care although they would prefer not to. Viewed either from the perspective of equal distribution of society's material resources or of juridical rights to fundamental well-being[3], urban children must make do with incomplete and inadequate child care policies. Judged in this fashion, the promise of an egalitarian city eludes them.

Current Arrangements and Policy

Fifty years have elapsed since child care first came onto the public policy agenda as an issue of substantial concern during the Depression. Beginning with this federally funded Depression program, however, the provision of child care has been, in Boles'(1980, p.345) words, "rationalized not as an end in itself but as a tool for the achievement of other economic, political, and social goals." Ironically, the needs of children have always been secondary in the creation of child care legislation.

The first aspect of child care policy that confronts a newly born child in the United States is his or her lack of a right—juridical or statutory—to have a working parent remain at home. This is because—unlike most industrial nations of the world—there is no national law in this country guaranteeing parents or, more narrowly, mothers the right to maternity or child care leave with job protection after the birth of a baby (Kamerman, Kahn, and Kingston 1983; Norgren 1984).[4] With the exception of a handful of states that have mandated temporary maternity disability benefits, local government, too, has determined not to tread on the time-honored rhetoric—and myth—of the self-sufficient family (see Keniston 1977, pp.7-23; Norgren 1981, pp.138-9). Coping with a new child is very much viewed as a private parental responsibility, not a public concern.

The failure of public policy in the United States to provide child care leave places parents in a position of making tough decisions for themselves and their children. Some employed parents provide the child care themselves, either looking after the child while at work or working swing shifts. According to 1982 Census data (U.S. Department of Commerce 1983b, p.5) about 23 percent of employed mothers solved their child care problem in this fashion. But what of the remaining families? What happens in families where work and parental child care do not mix? One possibility is that a parent take unpaid leave—losing salary, health and pension benefits, and, perhaps, the job itself—and stay at home as childminder. Alternatively, parents can seek someone else to look after the child.

Traditionally, working parents have sought the help of the extended family. This network of relatives is especially important for unmarried working women with young children. In 1982, for example, nonparental care by relatives amounted to 40 percent of the principal child arrangement for unmarried mothers. By contrast, only 27 percent of married working women relied on the help of relatives (U.S. Department of Commerce 1983b, p.9).

Over the past two decades, however, the availability of relatives as childminders has declined significantly; today, children with working parents are likely to be in the care of a nonrelative, outside the home. One notable response has been the increased use of group day care. Three times the number of children, or 15 percent of the total needing child care, are now in group care as compared with the early 1960s. Enrollment in nursery schools—most of them private—doubled in the 1970s (Kamerman 1983, p.132). Black mothers and mothers with high incomes, good educations, and full-time jobs are particularly likely to use group care (U.S. Department of Commerce 1983b, p.1).

Day Care in New York

In the United States, virtually all contemporary urban day care programs began as a result of 1967 "workfare" child care legislation. This bill made federal day care funds available to local child care programs for "past, present, or future recipients" of Aid to Families with Dependent Children (AFDC) or those participating in the government's Work Incentive Program (WIN). Prior to this legislation, only in California and in New York City were there locally funded day care programs that had survived the temporary federal funding episodes of the Depression and World War II.

Public day care programs in New York City began as a direct result of the federal funds made available in the early 1930s from the Works Progress Administration. The city has maintained a publicly funded program of center and family care ever since. From 1942 until the passage of the 1967 congressional legislation, New York kept this program going on its own. It served children of poor and working class families. That a child care program continued in the city after the loss of federal funds in 1942 must be credited to the spirited, ongoing lobbying of a core group of child-oriented professionals and volunteer activists, most of whom were not service users (see Norgren 1974, chapters 3 and 4). To succeed, they had to overcome formidable opposition, including that of the popular mayor, Fiorello LaGuardia, who told these day care advocates he was reluctant to make the state the "father and mother of a child" and declared that the worst mother was better for a child than an institution (Norgren 1974, p.70).

As suggested above, children in other urban communities did not fare as well. Responding to rhetoric that mothers belonged at home and should not take jobs away from men, local officials all over the United States started closing down public day care programs following World War II. Chicago, for example, had 23 centers during the war, but by 1968 there were none in Illinois. Eighty centers operated in Detroit in the early 1940s; a decade later just three remained (Baxandall 1979, p.138). In these years, public centers only survived where, as in New York City and California, local government agreed to provide total funding.

Although day care continued in New York in the decades after World War II, only a small percentage of children actually in need of day care were served. Throughout this period, the number of working mothers constantly increased, as did the number of immigrant women coming to the city who needed child care in order to work or attend classes. Yet, as late as 1969, only 11,600 children could be enrolled in public group and family day care programs in New York (Lash, Sigal, and Dudzinski 1980, p.56).

That New York, like other urban areas, had a large, unsatisfied demand for public child care services was amply demonstrated as local governments started using the federal funds made available by the 1967 day care legislation. The New York program that had enrolled less than 12,000 children in 1969 expanded threefold in four years to an enrollment of 35,100 (Lash, Sigal, and Dudzinski 1980, p.56). Yet, considering estimates of 200,000 children under six with working mothers, there was still an unmet need for more public services (Brozan 1983). Some children, of course, were, and are, in private child care programs, but this is not necessarily out of choice as these programs are far more costly than publicly subsidized facilities.

The availability of these public programs to children is broadly limited by three factors: the level of public funding, fees, and family eligibility. Analyzed against either the perspective that free child care should be a social right of all families or, at a minimum, available at a cost to all working parents, even cities like New York have failed their children. And, defined even more narrowly as a program only for children of poor or working class families, cities fail to provide sufficient day care facilities. The level of funding since the 1967 legislation stimulated local programs has never been sufficient to serve even this latter group. Eligibility requirements and fees have further limited access to programs.

The day care program in New York is funded under a tripartite federal-state-city arrangement. In the early 1980s federal funds accounted for 66 percent of the city's day care budget (Lash et al. 1983, p.136). The state and the city contributed the remaining funds. The policies of the Reagan administration have had a significant negative effect on the program. The budget of the social services block grant has been cut further in response to the problems of a large national budget deficit. In fiscal year 1982, for example, the state of New York lost $60 million in Title XX (social services) funds (Lash et al. 1983, p. 137).

The implications of such federal funding cuts for state and city governments are clear: make proportional cuts in local program services or increase local funding. Initially in the early 1980s day care clients in New York City were shielded from a worst-case scenario by the state and the city. To offset the loss of federal funds, the state shifted several million dollars from the Low Income Energy Assistance Block Grant to the Social Services Block Grant. But it also passed along some funding reductions to local social service districts. In fiscal year 1982 to avoid having to close some day care centers, New York allocated $15.4 million from the city's reserve fund for child care (Lash et al. 1983, p.137). Funding bailouts of this kind, however, are not necessarily feasible over a long period, or possible in states with poor fiscal health. In New York, as in the nation, Reagan's "new federalism" has meant that local day care constituencies have had to vie more than ever before for nontargeted funds.

If federal funding continues to decrease, and the economy does not improve significantly, it is not likely that all state and local governments will be able to continue shifting funds in this ad hoc fashion. Their treasuries simply will not permit it. This is happening already in cities where, unlike New York, there is not a long tradition of public day care and a well-established, savvy child care lobby. And even in the state of New York, for example, there is a "grossly uneven level of service in areas outside of New York City" (Wallick 1984). This is because the state has no policy of child care for the working poor. The decision whether to have public day care is left to county social service directors. As a result, in 1983, 34 counties in New York had no child care for the working poor who receive no welfare. Moreover, in this state, as in many others, single parents (usually female) who work lose child care support when their income exceeds the public assistance level. And where state law does not mandate day care services, as is the case in the state of New York, fiscally hard-pressed counties simply stop child care subsidies.

Fees and eligibility requirements also limit access to public child care programs. Day care has never been available to families in the United States as a matter of social right. This is quite contrary to policy in many other industrial nations where—with varying fee schedules—child care is provided without an income test on the theory that society cannot say that it needs its population replenished, or that it needs parents to work, without also sharing in the responsibilities of childrearing.

Cities and states vary in their fees and eligibility policies. Traditionally, public child care has been a service only for those on welfare or the working poor. Almost universally today, a sliding scale of fees based on family income is used. Economically marginal families, in general, pay nothing. The budget cutbacks of the early 1980s, however, prompted local governments to offset lost Title XX funds by increasing day care fee schedules—thus shifting more of the cost of day care to the consumer. In New York City, until 1981, a child whose family income was below $11,410 received free care. In 1983, free care was only available to those children with family incomes under $9,041 (Lash et al. 1983, p.138-9). These, and other changes, apparently explain a decrease of more than 1,500 enrolled children in New York City day care between 1981 and 1983 (Lash et al. 1983, p.140). A 1982 Census Bureau survey (U.S. Department of Commerce 1983b, pp.2,16) confirms the relationship between fees, parental work, and use of child care: the study indicated that "among mothers of young children who were not in the labor force . . . 36 percent of those with family incomes under $15,000 responded that they would look for work if child care were available at a reasonable cost, compared with 13 percent of those with incomes of $25,000 or more." The problem of increased fees, according to one observer, can be easily stated: day care is in danger of being "gentrified" (National Council of Churches of Christ 1982a).

Affordability is clearly a critical child care issue. But so (still) is availability. Families who can only afford government subsidized child care programs apply and invariably, in every city in the United States, are told of lengthy waiting lists. Although there has been an expansion of both private for-profit and nonprofit programs, even these do not match demand. The number of public school kindergartens has expanded in the past decade but most of these programs are only half-day and, therefore, of limited help to the working parent. All-day (9 to 3) kindergarten programs have been initiated in cities like New York but guaranteed places in all-day programs are still not the rule. Early education experts have also publicly urged that schools begin taking children at three or four. Citing encouraging data from longitudinal studies, most notably the 20-year Perry Pre-School Project in Ypsilanti, Michigan, they argue that children benefit significantly from early education programs—and in ways that "pay for themselves in economic terms" (Fiske 1984, p.B15). Whether this message can be carried to weary taxpayers, particularly in fiscally hard-pressed urban communities, remains to be seen. Taxpayer resistance to higher school budgets makes the broad implementation of such policies unlikely, particularly in urban communities where they are most needed.

Availability of child care for infants and toddlers is a particularly critical problem. In most cities licensed group or family day care is virtually nonexistent for these young children—an ironic fact considering that mothers with children under three currently constitute the fastest growing segment of the labor force. A 1982 child care survey by the National Council of Churches of Christ (1982b), for example, indicates that more than half of such church programs (many receiving public funds) are for preschool (ages 3-5) youngsters exclusively. Only six percent enroll infants, and only 13 percent accept toddlers. At the other end of the age scale, after-school programs for elementary school children are similarly scarce despite unequivocal need of these still-young people for activities and supervision. This, too, is ironic given the profusion of words about the growth of crime in our society.

Critics of publicly subsidized child care argue that virtually all working parents do find child care. And, with the exception of latch-key children, this is true. But for a majority of children, this is care in an unlicensed program or in an unlicensed family care home. This means no publicly established and enforced standards regarding, for example, the caretaker's background (for example a history of drug addiction or abuse of children) and training, the number of children under one person's supervision, or health and safety regulations. It is a stunning contradiction that our society has chosen to protect school age children with public health and safety codes, as well as state academic accreditation, while it leaves the care of much younger children outside the protective arm of public scrutiny and regulation.

The lack of access to child care because of an insufficient supply of programs or high fees threatens the fundamental well-being of young urban children—in particular, children from economically marginal homes. First, opportunities for upward economic mobility are stifled. Where child care is not available, parents often have no choice but to stay, or to go, on welfare. A study carried out in New York City in the 1970s, for example, found public day care to be an important factor in helping low-income women and their children maintain self-sufficiency. When the city closed 77 day care centers, 40 percent of the affected low-income mothers experienced new problems with job punctuality, while 30 percent could not avoid increased absenteeism. Women previously considered good employees were fired. The authors of the study conclude that, lacking reliable, low-cost day care, these mothers had to create "elaborate schemes for survival" (McMurray and Kazanjian 1982, pp.ii,7,8,13).

Lack of child care also can mean that children are left unsupervised. Fearful of the law, parents do not report such practices. It is thus difficult to get an accurate count. Child care professionals know, however, that the number of latch-key children runs in the thousands in large cities (U.S. Department of Commerce 1982, p.6). Finally, as discussed above, children may not be left on their own but may be subjected to physically, socially, and/or educationally inferior child care. All of these outcomes are curious in a society that has endorsed both the rhetoric of child development and diminished use of welfare!

Viewed from the city, the possibilities of improved child care are uncertain and increasingly dependent upon local rather than national policy decisions. The optimistic discussions of the early 1970s—of broadly available, comprehensive child care programs—have been a memory for some time. A national policy of guaranteed maternity or parental leave has yet to be given a serious hearing. Flex-time and job-sharing programs are not widely available employee options. At the same time, the public debate has become more complicated. Policies that many observers thought secure such as the national child care tax credit (which spawned many similar state tax programs) are now spoken of as expendable. Under the Reagan administration's "new federalism," federal standards designed to provide a minimum quality of day care have been abandoned even though a number of states have no, or few, local regulations governing standards of care (U.S. Department of Health and Human Services 1981; Lindsey 1984).

Public child care has never been broadly available in U.S. cities. There have always been eligibility requirements, fees, and a shortage of facilities. But following the heightened national awareness of poverty in the 1960s, the success of Project Headstart, and the pressure of the women's movement, there did emerge a belief that public day care could be expanded and the working poor served equitably in terms of cost. Today, there seems little possibility of universal program expansion. As Washington falls back in its commitment, the fiscal health of state and local governments, along with their basic interest in child care programs, will determine how present policies are remedied to increase equity of services. The implementation of compulsory kindergarten attendance in a growing number of states, recent attempts to make all-day kindergarten available, and preliminary discussions of early education for all three- or four-year-olds suggest that local government can provide leadership in the child care field. It is, however, far too early to know if a large number of urban governments will take a more assertive role, or if this only will occur in cities like New York where there has been a long-standing commitment to programs for children.

CONCLUSION

As precitizens children stand in a unique relationship to their society. By themselves, they have no currency to trade in the market of politics save the much worn notion that America's future is its children. They must rely, therefore, on various guardians to win for them a fair share of society's resources.

In his book, *The Children's Cause*, policy analyst Gilbert Steiner (1976, p.242) observed that "the political system does not necessarily turn aside from children's issues though they are not voters or lobbyists." This chapter asks whether Steiner is correct. Using child care policy as the yardstick, it settles on the more guarded conclusion that children's dependence upon others has led to a less than fair resolution of their child care needs.

The child care policies developed at the national level, and by most local governments, have been stimulated by concern for adult labor problems, the size of welfare budgets, or the discontent of middle class working women. Because licensed, public child care programs have never been ample, children have been, and continue to be, placed in a variety of less than satisfactory arrangements that include being left home alone, sitting around a parent's workplace, or attending an unlicensed program.

Historically, children of the working poor have been confronted with tuition costs that burden them disproportionately, and thus, unequally. Certainly the passage of the child care tax credit in 1976, with its decidedly middle class bias, did nothing to inject greater fairness into the distribution of child care subsidies. More recent changes in local eligibility requirements and fees, which increase the cost of day care both to those on welfare and to the working poor, increase the inequity of child care costs for these client groups.

The contraction of funding for child care programs comes at a time when the number of single, female-headed households (many living in poverty) and the number of working women is increasing. Given such conditions, these new policies again demonstrate a striking disregard for the needs of children and their right to society's resources.

Finally, the failure of this society to have a policy of job-protected parental leave also speaks to the indifference of adults concerning the well-being of children. In this regard, it is interesting to compare the decision of U.S. policymakers to invest heavily in the medical care of the elderly (Medicare) at the same time that they have refused even to contemplate a nationally mandated policy of maternity or parental leave.

This comparison with Medicare and the elderly is not made innocently. Both children and the elderly are often described as dependents. Yet, as sociologist Samuel Preston (1984,p.44) has recently argued, despite significant growth in the number of elderly persons and the decrease in the number of children under 15, "the well-being of the elderly has improved greatly whereas that of the young has deteriorated." According to Preston, between 1960 and 1982, the number of children under 15 fell by seven percent, whereas from 1960 to 1980 the number of people 65 or older grew by 54 percent.

Logically, these relative states of well-being are not what we might expect.

> Fewer children should mean less competition for resources in the home and greater per capita availability of social services such as public schools. More

old people, on the other hand, should put great pressure on resources such as hospitals, nursing homes and social security funds (Preston 1984,p.44).

Preston's analysis of well-being relies upon four measures commonly used by social scientists: levels of income, health, educational achievement, and reports of satisfaction with life. In each, he reports the well-being of children has declined relative to the elderly. Using data describing monetary income and non-cash transfer payments (such as food stamps and Medicare), Preston reports that in 1982 four percent of the elderly lived in poverty compared with 17 percent of children. This is strikingly different from their relative poverty status in 1970. When asked about their life situation in a 1982 Gallup Poll, 71 percent of those 65 or older reported they were "highly satisfied with their standard of living" (quoted in Preston 1984, p.46). Health statistics show similar patterns in favor of older groups, while recent national and local studies show decreasing effectiveness of schooling, the area of largest expenditure for children.

These changes have occurred over several decades. During this time, the U.S. family experienced significant change—change that has affected its willingness and ability to care for dependents. The increase in female-headed families noted earlier means an ever larger number of children with absent fathers, a majority of whom contribute no financial support. Put simply, for many children in the United States today there are fewer family members to take care of them while they are dependents. This is also true for the elderly. But, as Preston argues, because families have relinquished responsibility for the elderly over a longer period of years and because the elderly have used this time to lobby for government support, they have felt the effects of recent structural changes in the family less than children.

Demographic factors have influenced political potential. The elderly have a high rate of voting; combined with their growing numbers, they have increasingly demanded, and won, attention from legislators. Children, of course, whatever their number, cannot vote. What of the guardians described at the beginning of this chapter? Preston argues that as more middle-aged people have living parents, and fewer children, their dependency concerns are shifting toward the elderly. This, plus the ability to contemplate their own old-age needs, makes many people not currently senior citizens politically supportive of policies for the elderly. "Most government programs for those more than 65 years old are to some extent perceived as a social contract enabling middle-aged adults to transfer resources to themselves later in life" (Preston 1984, p.47).

Demographics alone, however, do not explain this shift in relative well-being. The long-standing U.S. lack of interest in collective responsibilities for children also makes political action on behalf of children difficult. The common wisdom is that parents alone should finance the costs of bearing and raising children. This attitude is even more aggressively defended in this "free-choice" era of birth control. Although the United States has developed a welfare state in the twentieth century, it has done so begrudgingly, particularly with respect to children. With the exception of education, most public programs for children have a means test. In contrast, society no longer expects older people to be the responsibility of their families, regardless of the family's economic status. Medicare, for example, is not an income-related benefit.

Through Social Security and Medicare, senior citizens have become successful claimants to the collective responsibility of society. Children, through their guardians, have yet to duplicate this accomplishment and it appears that neither demography nor history is on their side. If we continue to deny an equitable allocation of resources to children and their parents, the result may be an equally mean-spirited assertion of selfishness. The future may find young adults refusing to have children until and unless society shares the costs of childrearing. Eventually the United States may realize that today's children are tomorrow's taxpayers and that, in the most pragmatic sense, there can be no future without children. If altruistic concern for children has failed as a motive of public policy, then lobbyists for the children's cause must move to a different position—one that will be perceived to be beneficial by many constituencies. In particular, this appeal should be made to citizens of middle-age, whose comfortable old age will depend on a growing cohort of children.

NOTES

1. In 1978, two-thirds of U.S. families lived in metropolitan areas. Children living in families maintained by women with no husband present were more likely not only to live in metropolitan areas but also, more specifically, in central cities. (See U.S. Department of Commerce, Bureau of the Census, 1980. *American Families and Living Arrangements*. Current Population Reports, Series P-23, No. 104, p. 18. Washington, D.C.: Government Printing Office.)

2. This legislation, passed as amendments to the Social Security Act, was meant to reduce dependence on public welfare. The eligibility requirements were so flexible and the initial funding so generous (the appropriation was open-ended) that publicly funded day care blossomed all over the United States. Economic need, caused by inflation and the Vietnam War, and the growing women's movement led many middle class women to push their way into these "Title IV" day care programs in the early 1970s. This, however, was not what Congress had intended.

3. A "juridical right to fundamental well-being" refers to so-called "fundamental rights" litigation. (See, for example: *Shapiro* v. *Thompson* 394 U.S. 618 [1969]; *Dandridge* v. *Williams* 397 U.S. 471 [1970]; *Goldberg* v. *Kelly* 397 U.S. 254 [1970]; *Lindsey* v. *Normet* 405 U.S. 56 [1972].)

4. The 1978 Pregnancy Disability Act requires that if income and job protection exists at a workplace for any disability, maternity disability must be covered in the same way. Since a majority of employers in this country provide no disability insurance, even minimal maternity disability leave is unavailable to most women.

REFERENCES

Baxandall, Rosalyn F. 1979. "Who Shall Care for Our Children? The History and Development of Day Care in the United States." In *Women: A Feminist*

Perspective, 2nd ed., edited by Jo Freeman, pp.134-49. Palo Alto: Mayfield.
Berger, Joseph. 1984. "Unwed Mothers Accounting for Third of New York Births." New York *Times*, August 13, p.1.
Boles, Janet K. 1980. "The Politics of Child Care." *Social Service Review* 54 (September): 344-62.
Brozan, Nadine. 1983. "Day Care in New York: A Growing Need." New York *Times*, July 20, p.C8.
Cohen, Richard. 1984. "Sharing." *Ms.* 13 (August): 74-75.
Dahl, Robert. 1961. *Who Governs?* New Haven:Yale University Press.
Family Service America. 1984. *The State of Families: 1984-85.* New York: Family Service America.
Fiske, Edward B. 1984. "Start of School at 4 Is Pressed." New York *Times*, December 17, pp. B1, 15.
Grossman, Allyson Sherman. 1982. "More Than Half of All Children Have Working Mothers." *Monthly Labor Review* 105 (February): 41-43.
Jacobs, Jane. 1961. *The Death and Life of Great American Cities.* New York: Vintage.
Kamerman, Sheila B. 1983. "The Child-Care Debate: Working Mothers vs. America." *Working Woman* 8 (November): 131-35.
_____, Alfred J. Kahn, and Paul Kingston. 1983. *Maternity Policies and Working Women.* New York: Columbia University Press.
Keniston, Kenneth. 1977. *All Our Children: The American Family Under Pressure.* New York: Harcourt, Brace, Jovanovich.
Lash, Trude W. et al. 1983. *Public Expenditures for Children 1980-1983 New York City: The Impact of Federal Policies on Services for Children:* New York: Foundation for Child Development.
_____, Heidi Sigal, and Deanna Dudzinski. 1980. *State of the Child: New York City II.* New York: Foundation for Child Development.
Lindsey, Robert. 1984. "Increased Demand for Day Care Prompts a Debate on Regulations." New York *Times*, September 2, pp. 1,52.
Lynch, Kevin (ed.) 1977. *Growing Up in Cities: Studies of the Spatial Environment of Adolescence in Cracow, Melbourne, Mexico City, Salta, Toluca, and Warszawa.* Cambridge, Mass.:MIT Press.
McMurray, Georgia L. and Dolores P. Kazanjian. 1982. *Day Care and the Working Poor.* New York: Community Service Society of New York.
National Council of Churches of Christ. 1982a. "Massive Day Care Survey Shows Impact of Federal Cuts." Press release dated November 5. Mimeographed. New York.
_____. 1982b. "Child Care Project-Fact Sheet 2." Mimeographed.
Nelson, John R. Jr. and Wendy E. Waring. 1982. "The Child Care Tax Deduction/Credit." In *Making Policies for Children: A Study of the Federal Process,* edited by Cheryl D. Hayes, pp.206-59. Washington, D.C.:National Academy Press.
Norgren, Jill. 1984. "Child Care." In *Women: A Feminist Perspective*, 3rd ed., edited by Jo Freeman, pp. 139-53. Palo Alto: Mayfield.
_____. 1981. "In Search Of A National Child Care Policy: Background and Prospects." *Western Political Quarterly* 34 (March): 127-42.
_____. 1974. "Political Mobilization and Policy Input in Urban Day Care: A Case Study of New York City." Ph.D. dissertation, University of Michigan.

———, and Sheila Cole. 1982. "Child-Care Tax Credit: Heaven Help the Working Mother." *Nation* 234 (January 23): 77-78.

Preston, Samuel H. 1984. "Children and the Elderly in the U.S." *Scientific American* 251 (December): 44-49.

Richardson, James F. 1972. *The American City: Historical Studies.* Waltham: Xerox College Publishing.

Steiner, Gilbert, 1976. *The Children's Cause.* Washington, D.C.: The Brookings Institution.

U.S. Department of Commerce. Bureau of the Census. 1983a. *American Women: Three Decades of Change.* Special Demographic Analyses CDS-80-8. Washington, D.C.: Government Printing Office.

———. 1983b. *Child Care Arrangements of Working Mothers: June 1982.* Current Population Reports, Series P-23, No. 129. Washington, D.C.: Government Printing Office.

———. 1982. *Trends in Child Care Arrangements of Working Mothers.* Current Population Reports, Series P-23. No. 117. Washington, D.C.: Government Printing Office.

———. 1980. *American Families and Living Arrangements.* Current Population Reports, Series P-23, No. 104. Washington, D.C.: Government Printing Office.

U.S. Department of Health and Human Services. Administration for Children, Youth and Families. Day Care Division. 1981. *Report to Congress: Summary Report of Current State Practices in Title XX-Funded Day Care Programs.* Washington, D.C.: Government Printing Office.

Wallick, Gloria. 1984. "Children Who Can't Wait for a State Day-Care Policy to Evolve." New York *Times*, May 8, p. A30.

Zigler, Edward and Susan Muenchow. 1983. "Infant Day Care and Infant-Care Leaves: A Policy Vacuum." *American Psychologist* 38 (January): 91-94.

PART III
DISTRIBUTIVE EQUALITY

5

NATIVE AMERICANS AND THE UNHEAVENLY CITY: A STUDY IN INEQUALITY

Joyotpaul Chaudhuri

Alexis de Tocqueville's two volume commentary on U.S. politics and culture evolved from his interest in the rise of mass democracies. Even though the Frenchman's writings were based on an 18-month visit to the United States in the 1830s, many of his insights remain part of contemporary intellectual discourse on politics and morals in the United States. Included in de Tocqueville's volumes was a considerable body of commentary on ethnic relations, including those affecting Indians. While de Tocqueville was clearly correct regarding the devastating effects of European culture on Indians, he clearly underestimated the ability of Indians to survive the march of "civilization" and urbanization.

De Tocqueville, correctly, stood in awe of the march of equality as a force in the United States and the world. He argued that while equality was a dominant force in U.S. political culture, it was not likely to have a long-run beneficial effect on American Indian tribes.

> I believe that the Indian nations of North America are doomed to perish and that whenever the Europeans shall be established on the shores of the Pacific Ocean, that race of men will have ceased to exist. The Indians had only the alternative of war or civilization; in other words, they must either destroy the Europeans or become their equals (de Tocqueville 1972, p. 343).

Despite his many insights, de Tocqueville was in error in his observation on the future of Indians. Indian nations did not perish; some tribes such as the Navajos are more numerous today than they were in de Tocqueville's time.

This study would not be possible without decades of contributions of my wife, Jean Chaudhuri, a full-blood Creek Indian who placed service before self as an Indian woman in facing the challenge of leadership in the delivery of urban services. The study also would not have been completed without the help of Judy Groves and Stephen Stribling of the Department of Government at New Mexico State University.

Despite the destruction of tribal governments and societies, Indians in the twentieth century continue to increase in numbers. Neither have the Indians achieved equality of opportunity, access, or result. Over half today live in urban areas, isolated from their tribal institutions and largely overlooked by urban elites and scholars of urban politics.[1]

De Tocqueville thus may well be correct in one of his other observations if we apply it to urban settings rather than to the 1830s: "Indians will perish in the same isolated condition in which they have lived, but the destiny of the Negroes is in some measure interwoven with that of the Europeans" (de Tocqueville 1972, p. 356).

The paradox of examining the issue of equality and urban Indian life is highlighted by two facts—one historical and the other demographic. Historically, Indians were guaranteed the advantages of positive inequality in the form of recognized aboriginal rights based on treaties, agreements, and the special provision in Article I of the Constitution whereby commerce with Indian nations was made a federal responsibility. Yet today the majority of Indians, who were the first beneficiaries of the rhetoric of affirmative action, live in urban areas because of a major shift in federal policy.

SOCIOECONOMIC CHARACTERISTICS OF URBAN INDIANS

The caveat in Indian studies about the dangers of generalizing about all American Indians holds for urban Indians as well. Urban Indians share some common experiences of deprivation in the area of governmental services. However, the differences are quite significant as well. The environment of an Oklahoma Seminole in Tulsa is quite different from that of an Oklahoma Seminole in Los Angeles. In Tulsa the tribal member is much closer to Indian churches, Indian stomp grounds (traditional Creek, Seminole, and Cherokee dance locations), and other similar institutions. One has to be quite careful to interpret urban Indian data in contextual and relative terms. This is true for both descriptive generalizations and moral questions.

Moral questions of relative well-being, for instance, should take into account the value systems of different Indian groups. Hopi drinking patterns tends to be more private and different from that of Navajos in places like Flagstaff and Phoenix. Arapaho drinking patterns in Oklahoma City, in turn, is often more public than that of Creeks. Public alcohol consumption data may therefore be misleading as indicators of Indian behavior unless tribal attitudes and patterns are taken into account.

When we move away from value-laden questions to the purely descriptive, serious problems remain. A good example would be the usage of census data for cross-tribal comparisons or even longitudinal comparisons for the same tribe. There has been much unintentional undercounting of urban Indians by the U.S.

Census Bureau in some areas (see Chaudhuri 1974, pp. 9–22). While the Census Bureau has been steadily improving its ethnic data collection methods, the urban Indian population remains one of the most elusive groups for purposes of demography. Cross-time comparisons of Indian data must take into account the quite different definitions of "Indian" used in different census years. Since 1970, the perceptions of respondents have been the only measure of Indian ethnicity; earlier, more objective or verifiable criteria, including tribal affiliation and blood quantum from Bureau of Indian Affairs records or tribal rolls, were used. Additional problems in the purity of the data stem from multiple tribal identifications and changing social attitudes. Thus the considerable increase in the number of Cherokees relative to Papagos, 1950–80, is partially due to the decline of social stigma in being identified as part Cherokee, since this tribe is generally regarded as more assimilated than Papagos or Apaches. Despite these methodological difficulties, census data can be instructive if one understands the limitations involved.

The 1980 census counted 1,364,033 American Indians, omitting Eskimos and Aleuts (U.S. Department of Commerce 1983, p. PC80-1B1; Taylor 1983). Of these, 52.7 percent lived in urban areas, compared to 43.5 percent in 1970 and 26.7 percent in 1960. While the majority of Indians live in urban areas, less than a third live on reservations. The balance are in nonreservation rural areas, particularly in rural Oklahoma and North Carolina. Roughly 37 percent live in urban areas of 50,000 or more population. Twenty-one percent reside in large central cities.

Regional concentrations of urban Indians are as follows: West, 347,371; South, including Oklahoma, 186,024; North Central, 130,692; and Northeast, 54,960. Among the states, California has the largest number of urban Indians (161,192), followed by Oklahoma (83,936).

The cities with the largest urban Indian populations remain relatively unchanged, 1970–80: Los Angeles, Tulsa, Oklahoma City, Phoenix, Seattle, Albuquerque, New York, Minneapolis, Tucson, Detroit, Chicago, Dallas, Denver, Washington D.C., and Portland, Oregon. Of these, the Washington D.C. area is a special case because of the location of Indian-related offices there.

This residential pattern is not primarily an accident of history, geography, or tribal choices. Indian migration to urban areas was shaped by the same economic forces as those of other minority and ethnic groups, but specific federal government decisions also played a major role in this population shift. For example, the removal of Indians to Oklahoma in the nineteenth century, combined with the loss of tribal governmental powers as a result of Oklahoma statehood, created the nascent conditions for the concentrations in Oklahoma City and Tulsa ultimately triggered by economic forces.

One of the most important factors shaping migration patterns of Indians to urban areas took place in the Eisenhower era of the 1950s. The administrative goal was rapid assimilation. One of the prongs of this force was "termination," the proposed phasing out of special Indian tribal status in several stages. Another prong was "relocation" of able, employable Indians to selected urban areas, such as Los Angeles, rather than aiding the reservation economies directly. Indians seeking employment in reservation and other rural areas in Indian country (and Oklahoma in particular) were counseled and directed toward migration to employment assistance programs in "destination cities" with special receiving and processing centers. By the 1960s, the majority of urban Indians were either direct participants in employment assistance programs or relatives and friends of participants.

Indians today continue to move into urban areas for some of the same reasons as other ethnic groups, including the search for employment. The federal urban relocation program for Indians, which stimulated the Indian migration patterns of the 1950s, has been slowed down, and there are now more economic development programs on the reservation. However, Bureau of Indian Affairs (B.I.A.) assistance programs still exist and many Indians are still encouraged by the federal bureaucracy to move to some of the same relocation areas as the designated destination cities of the 1950s. The lack of job opportunities on reservations is an additional factor in migration. According to 1980 census data, Indians, age 19 years and over, had the highest unemployment rate (13.2 percent) of all ethnic groups, including blacks (11.8 percent). However, rural Indians had, by far, the highest rate of unemployment (15 percent); in comparison, rural black unemployment was only 10.7 percent. In fact, among ethnic groups Indians make the greatest employment gains by urban migration. Therefore, the economic conditions on reservations and other nonreservation rural areas continue to be a driving force for urban relocation.

In both urban and rural areas Indians have the lowest mean age of all ethnic groups, except for Hispanics whose mean age is about a year lower. This is, in part, due to lower life expectancy, which in turn is related to available health care.

Rural Indians have the highest number of persons per family (4.21) among ethnic groups. However, in urban areas their family size (3.53) is slightly smaller than blacks (3.62) and Hispanics (3.85). Since an improved economic status often results in smaller family size, this suggests that even though urban Indian poverty is extensive, urban migration facilitates upward mobility for Indians.

These gains in income relative to reservation life are not without their costs. Reservation housing and easy access to the medical care provided by reservation hospitals are sacrificed. (One should not idealize Indian hospitals, however, since many of them deal only with primary care and do not have sufficient funds for extensive contracting for major medical services.) Another indicator of interethnic equity in urban life is public education. Among central city residents 16–17 years of age Indians trail all other ethnic groups in percentages enrolled in school in 1980. In rural areas Indians have a higher percentage of 16–17 year-olds in school, compared to other ethnic groups. In the crucial areas of employment, health (as indicated by life expectancy) and education, Indians appear to be more disadvantaged in most urban areas than are Hispanics and blacks.

ACCESS TO GENERAL URBAN SERVICES

As city residents, urban Indians are entitled to participate in the municipal programs and services that are generally available to all residents. There are several factors that lead to uneven administration and underutilization of these services by Indians (see Chaudhuri 1974). Unlike other ethnic minorities, Indians frequently do not cluster in dense ghettos or barrios. The relatively more scattered residential patterns found in Los Angeles and many other cities restrict access to targeted public services such as neighborhood centers. Further, because of a lower incidence of automobile ownership, Indians have greater difficulties in obtaining physical access in sprawling cities, such as Phoenix, that lack an extensive public transportation system. These factors, in combination with a weak sense of participation in the social contract and the lack of pan-tribal coalitions, often mean few demands are made on urban bureaucracies on behalf of Indians.

In cities such as Tucson and Phoenix interethnic coalitions for demanding social services have been attempted from time to time. But Indian constituents, while included in political rhetoric, end up being overlooked in recruitment for manpower programs and other services. Whether Indian demands for access are subordinated to those of black, Hispanic, or women's groups varies by context and location. A different or less effective process of political socialization makes many urban Indians less persistent and aggressive with urban administrators in comparison to blacks in Chicago or blacks and Mexican Americans in Tucson.

In many urban areas that are near reservations, Indians often have difficulties of access to hospital services because of ambiguous or inequitable eligibility requirements. Reservation programs may direct Indians to urban services, and urban service administrators will sometimes withhold services, expecting that the Indian will receive tribal services. Indians also face problems of eligibility because of demographic factors. Due to their lower life expectancies, the Indian "aged" are often younger than their white and black counterparts and are therefore ineligible for some senior citizens' programs.

Differential ethnic pathologies can also create problems for urban Indians. Indians are far more prone to tuberculosis and nonjuvenile diabetes than other ethnic groups. Yet, predominantly white medical personnel in large cities often lack the cross-cultural training needed for proper diagnosis and care of many of the hidden side effects and symptoms of diseases that occur frequently among Indians. The cutbacks in urban health care programs and the urban components of the Indian Health Service (a division of the U.S. Public Health Service) add to the severity of these problems.

URBAN INDIAN CENTERS

In the delivery of governmental services to urban Indians, an important set of values is provided by urban Indian centers and their primarily Indian managers. The need for Indian centers arose from the problems that Indians faced in communicating with social agencies serving the general public as well as those primarily serving other ethnic groups. While urban Indian agencies are not the exclusive vehicles of service delivery for Indians, they are important both as clearinghouses for service information and as service providers.

The bulk of urban Indian centers became institutionalized as part of the Great Society programs of the 1960s. A few had earlier modest beginnings under local church or private community leadership. In the 1960s and 1970s some of the Indian centers were encouraged by the "Indian desk" of several federal programs, particularly those within the Department of Health, Education, and Welfare (HEW). Little support was received from the Bureau of Indian Affairs. Other Indian centers were started by urban Indian activists in Minneapolis, Phoenix, and Tucson, among other places, in order to insure that manpower, health, counseling and educational services reached Indian groups.

Most Indian centers administer several programs. While there were and are specialized programs such as alcohol counseling, most combine employment assistance, counseling, limited health services, referrals, advocacy and recreation—all within the limits set by their financial and human resources.

The Indian centers often have had a checkered administrative history due to a variety of factors. These include: lack of community in urban areas; poor intertribal relations; lack of understanding of the roles of policy boards; job insecurity; funding fluctuations; administrative inexperience; and competition with the more developed organizations representing other groups.

THE SURVEY

Identifying urban Indian programs is not easy. Many have relatively short life spans or frequent changes in location, governing board composition, staff, and management. Some are innovative programs that serve as catalysts for local change, while others depend on standard federally funded and guided styles of service delivery.

The Indian Resource Development Institute of New Mexico State University obtained a list of urban Indian centers from the Bureau of Indian Affairs of the U.S. Department of Interior. The most current list, unfortunately, was compiled in May 1978. Although not comprehensive, it was the best available list of urban Indian agencies and thus provided a starting point for the first national survey of such programs. The survey was intended to measure the general attitudes of urban Indian managers and leaders and was not designed to test specific hypotheses.

The B.I.A. list of urban Indian centers provided the names and addresses of 48 urban Indian centers in the contiguous United States and Alaska. All 48 centers were sent a questionnaire, together with a cover letter explaining the nature of the study and asking that the top manager of each agency answer the 16-item survey. In the case of address changes, new addresses were obtained by mail or by phone and fresh questionnaires were again mailed out. Agencies that did not reply within three weeks were sent reminders. Five of the 48 agencies had either closed or could not otherwise be reached. This created a pool of 43 agencies. In a seven-week period, 20 agencies responded to the survey. One pointed out that theirs was really a university-based Indian studies program. The remaining 19 fully cooperated with the survey. The resulting return rate (45.2 percent) is respectable considering the instability of many urban Indian centers.

The responding agencies' service area (Indian) populations varied from 1,500 in Lincoln, Nebraska to 60,000 in the San Francisco area. The agencies were widely dispersed throughout the United States and included those in Spokane (Wash.), San Jose (Cal.), Winslow (Ariz.), San Francisco (2), Dallas (2), Baltimore, Philadelphia (2), Minneapolis, New York City, Lincoln (Neb.), Detroit, Omaha, Oklahoma City, Chicago (2), and Rapid City (S. Dak.). This geographical diversity provides a basis for comparing urban Indian programs in a variety of legal, cultural, political, and demographic contexts.

FINDINGS

Funding Sources, Equity and Need

For the overwhelming majority of agencies (78.9 percent), the federal government provided more than half of their funding. Only one agency had a private source of funding that matched federal contributions. This was the St. Augustine Center, which probably has a church affiliation. With only two exceptions, city funding for those centers receiving such support was less than seven percent. Baltimore provided nine percent of center funds, and Chicago provided 13% of the St. Augustine Center's budget. Four of the respondents reported that the county contributed two to ten percent of agency budgets. Eight listed some state support. Of these, three were located in California, which has the largest Indian (mostly urban) population. Not a single agency listed any of the Indian tribal governments as a source of funds. This is understandable since Indian tribal governments are resource poor in comparison to federal and state governments.

More interesting, however, was the response of the agency leaders to a question dealing with the relative sensitivity of five levels of government and the private sector to urban Indian problems. Asked to rank order the six from most to least sensitive, only two agency program heads or executive directors (10.5 percent) rated the tribes higher than third. Forty-seven percent ranked the tribes in fifth or sixth place. The federal government, on the other hand, was listed either first or second by 84.2 percent of the respondents. The percentages of respondents placing the private sector and the other levels of government in the top two positions were: private sector, 42.1 percent; local governments, 31.6 percent; states, 15.85 percent; and counties, 0 percent.

The responses clearly illustrate that off-reservation Indian institutions continue to have a special love-hate relationship with the federal government. While they are often critical of federal programs, Indians still perceive the federal government as being a greater source of equity than local or state governments. There are exceptions, to be sure, to this generalization. The leadership of several urban Indian organizations, including those of Chicago, Lincoln, and Minneapolis have been able to achieve some access to city support.

Local governments are generally perceived as being less than equitable in service delivery to Indians, compared to other ethnic groups. Over 84 percent of the agencies reported that Indians received proportionately fewer social services than other ethnic groups. Fully 68.4 percent of the respondents thought that Indians benefited least from local services compared to blacks, Hispanics, Anglos, and women. A similar percentage (63.2 percent) felt that Indians received less than other groups even on a per capita basis. And over half believed that recent program cuts had affected urban Indians more adversely than other ethnic groups.

A variety of barriers to equal treatment of Indians in urban areas were mentioned, but the most common was the level of political mobilization among the urban Indian population. A large majority (84 percent) agreed that interest activity has a significant impact on service delivery. Yet all characterized urban Indians as the least active of urban interest groups.

Several of the questionnaire items inquired about urban policies. Respondents were asked to rank order seven different types of programs according to their importance for urban Indians. These included: housing, health care, unemployment, training, counseling, transportation, and other benefits. Seventeen of the nineteen respondents listed unemployment as the most severe problem. Even so, the other programs were viewed as highly important by sizable numbers of the respondents.

The Indian program managers were also asked to "list the major kinds of generally available services that should be provided that are not provided readily for urban Indians." Housing, health, and counseling were most frequently listed.

These responses are particularly significant in that this was a national sample of Indian center administrators. While these centers, like other institutions, have vested interests and internal politics, they also directly and primarily deal with urban Indians and thus have unique vantage points on the urban Indian experience. The managers' beliefs that urban Indians are on the bottom of the urban totem pole corresponds with the more objective census data on urban Indians.

The Ruiz Case and Its Aftermath

Within the context of this relative inequality of access for urban Indians, continued dependence on federal programs has some inherent problems. For instance, there are many difficulties with B.I.A. services, a topic at issue in the U.S. Supreme Court case, *Morton, Secretary of the Interior* v. *Ruiz, et ux.* 415 U.S. 199 (1973). The case involved the proper interpretation of the 1921 Snyder Act, which originally outlined the responsibilities of the Bureau of Indian Affairs. In addition to other services, the B.I.A. provided health care until H.E.W. was formed during the Eisenhower administration. The Snyder Act stipulated that under the direction of the Secretary of Interior, the B.I.A.:

> shall direct, supervise, and expend such moneys as Congress may from time to time appropriate for the benefit, care, and assistance of Indians throughout the United States... (42 Stat. 208, 25 U.S.C. 13).

The evidence in the proceedings showed that while the B.I.A. included off-reservation Indians as part of their service population for obtaining appropriations, actual services to off-reservation Indians were minimal.

The plaintiff in the *Ruiz* case was a Papago named Ruiz who lived and worked in Ajo, Arizona, a few miles from the Papago reservation. Ruiz was unable to receive unemployment assistance after the mine where he worked was shut down by a strike. He faced the classic jurisdictional shuffle encountered by many urban Indians. The state authorities were unable to help him and referred him to the B.I.A., who in turn denied him assistance because he was living off the reservation. The U.S. Supreme Court appeared to take a middle of the road view in clarifying the meaning of "throughout the United States." The court ordered the extension of general assistance to include people like Ruiz who live near their reservation for the purposes of employment and who still maintain close ties with their cultural community. The Supreme Court remanded the case to district court for further definition of the B.I.A. rules in order to include people like Ruiz.

Ten years after the *Ruiz* case, there appears to be only very scattered and minor efforts by the B.I.A. to extend services to urban Indians, even though the majority of Indians live in urban areas. Almost 70 percent of the urban Indian administrators thought that the *Ruiz* decision had brought no significant increase in B.I.A. services to urban Indians. Two thought that there had been a slight increase; two others felt that there had been a moderate increase. Only one, in Oklahoma City, saw a significant increase.

This latter perception may reflect the unique context of Oklahoma Indians. The distinction drawn by the B.I.A. between Indians in tribal areas and off-reservation areas is most blurred in Oklahoma. Oklahoma does not have reservations, as conventionally defined, owing to the break up of Indian lands into individual allotments in the 1890s. The impact of Oklahoma statehood in 1907 on tribal governments was to diminish the autonomous features of tribal life. Further, despite the rise of Oklahoma City and Tulsa as major Indian urban settlements, some B.I.A. services are available in urban areas. Many urban Indians in turn use the minimal health, education, and training services available in areas other than Oklahoma City and Tulsa. Claremore, Okemah, Anadarko, and Muskogee are such service areas. Thus, an Indian from Tulsa does have access to the Indian Health Services hospital at Claremore, Oklahoma, though the hospital neither has the capability nor the contracting funds to provide much more than primary care.

BARRIERS TO EQUALITY

For equal access to urban governmental services by American Indians, several barriers must be removed. The written comments from the survey suggest that among these barriers are lack of understanding of Indian needs by people in power; lack of Indian understanding of the political system; lack of effective Indian mobilization; and insufficient tribal support of urban Indian needs.

Urban Indians constitute the most invisible minority in the urban political system. They are relatively small in number and not as visually distinctive as blacks. They often live in scattered residential patterns rather than concentrated Indian ghettos or barrios. Interracial and intertribal marriage patterns also give the superficial impression of social assimilation and acceptance. In matters of assimilation or adaptation, however, there are dangers of overgeneralization. In addition to adaptation being an individual and/or family matter, there are tribal differences as well. As applied anthropology literature confirms, some tribes find cultural accommodation much easier. For example, Creeks generally have made a more complete adaptation than the Sioux, and the Sioux in turn have adapted to a greater extent than the Navajos in Los Angeles (Price 1972).

When Indians are visible in urban areas, however, it is often because of socially marginal behavior (for example public drunkenness). Even here, there are tribal differences. Theodore Graves (1972) makes several observations based on a general literature review and his own extensive studies of Navajo adjustment to urban life in Denver. Among ethnic groups in the United States, the number of arrests per 100,000 population is the highest for Indians. The Indian arrest rate is about 2.5 times as high as that of blacks and 15 times that of Asian Americans. His study showed that 76 percent of these arrests of Indians were alcohol related, a figure 2.5 times greater than that for blacks. These figures apply not only to Denver but also to many other urban areas.

It is generally believed that alcohol pathology reflects the distance between dominant and minority groups. Graves argues persuasively that Indian drinking is part of an adaptive repertoire not based on Indian physiology or Indian culture.

Instead, he suggests that structural factors provide much of the explanation. In addition to genuine socioeconomic inequalities in urban areas, "relative deprivation" may be a factor here. For many Indians migration to urban areas had an economic motive. However, compared to their expectations of substantial economic gains, the differences between life in cities and on reservations fall far below expectations. Other ethnic groups have been better able to articulate their needs, and as the socioeconomic data suggest, urban Indians continue to face the highest rate of unemployment of any urban ethnic group.

URBAN INDIAN POLITICAL PARTICIPATION

General political apathy among urban Indians prevents their organization around questions of urban equality. Indian participation in tribal elections has markedly increased. But compared to other ethnic groups, Indian participation in municipal elections is low and largely invisible. The primacy of tribal identification as opposed to "Indian" identification, relatively small populations, dispersed residential patterns, and psychological distance from the notion of social contract—all are possible explanatory factors. Rather than electoral politics, some Indian groups have been more effective in executive and administrative lobbying for social services. Urban Indian coalitions in Phoenix, Arizona have enjoyed some success in the past (Chaudhuri 1974). However, in many other areas (for example, Tucson, Arizona), intertribal communication problems and Indian factionalism restrict access to city hall. Although a small but well-organized minority can be highly successful in interactions with city hall on specific aspects of redistributive politics, seldom have these tactics been utilized by urban Indian groups. Some of the most vocal Indians such as Dennis Banks and Vernon Bellecourt of the American Indian Movement (AIM) have come out of urban settings, but Indian political mobilization for urban programs lags considerably behind black and Hispanic mobilization in the same urban areas.

One of the reasons that urban Indian leaders concentrate on bureaucratic lobbying is the relatively uneven, sporadic, and weak voting participation by urban Indians. The literature on Indian voting patterns is also quite sparse (but see McCool 1982; Kunitz and Levy 1970; Ritt 1979; Davis 1983; National Indian Youth Council 1983). For example, one of the few studies of "national" Indian political behavior involved a sample of 151 Indians. However, the literature and field observations show certain trends that may be summarized.

Indians generally vote more heavily in their tribal elections than in state and national elections. As a matter of fact, some tribal elections, such as those of Navajos, have much higher turnouts than U.S. presidential elections. Urban Indians tend to have lower turnout than blacks and Hispanics in general elections. However, there are wide variations in this pattern. Indians in Oklahoma show levels of urban voting participation comparable to the general population. In contrast, urban Papago voting turnout in Tucson is much lower. It is interesting to note that the emergence of Indian protest in the 1970s not only occurred most frequently in urban areas but also that this protest was strongest in areas of low Indian voting participation, such as Minneapolis, and weakest in areas of greater conventional participation, such as Tulsa.

CONCLUSION

Indians clearly form a distinct socioeconomic class in urban areas. As a group they have higher unemployment rates than blacks or Hispanics. Indians have a higher arrest rate than other ethnic groups, and the arrests are more frequently alcohol related. Indians drop out of school earlier and at a higher rate. They have less political clout in city hall, which often means that they do not have equal access to urban manpower and other training and employment programs. Indians live in scattered fashion in urban areas and are less visible and less mobilized than other minority groups. Therefore, they usually have more difficulty in articulating their needs and obtaining equal access to public housing projects. Urban service programs are more likely to be designed in accordance with black or Hispanic needs because of the politically more experienced leadership of those groups.

In areas near reservations, urban Indians face an additional problem, the shifting of governmental responsibilities from one jurisdiction to another. Urban agencies try to refer the problems to tribal or federal agencies, while the latter often will try to punt the problem to the city, the county, or the state.

One of the great political ironies is that there is a clear discrepancy between public attitudes about Indians and the actual delivery of urban services. In most urban areas Indians are less likely to face overt racism than are blacks or Hispanics. Superficially, then, upward mobility should be easier for Indians. A "pedestal" effect seems to be involved here—a verbal romanticization of the first Americans, combined with actual neglect in urban programs.

Indian "problems" created by contacts between Indians and non-Indians were historically federal problems in the evolution of constitutional and statutory policy. Even where considerable state jurisdiction in Indian affairs has been traditional, including states such as Washington and Oklahoma, federal Indian policy (for example the heritage of Indian removal, creation of Indian reservations, transfer of jurisdiction to some states in the termination period of the 1950s and the Oklahoma Statehood Bill) has had major impact.

Since federal policy has in large part created the nature, direction, and size of the urban Indian migration, federal policymakers need to examine directly the impact of their "Indian policy" on urban Indians. To the extent that Indians have special rights, they might need to be protected in the same way that veterans' rights to employment, health, and education are protected—that is, make them portable. Thus, if by treaty or law an Indian is entitled to health care, he should have access to care at nearby federal facilities rather than in the Indian Health Service hospital in his tribal area.

The unequal and adverse impact of local government decisions on urban Indian communities also deserves special attention. It is commonplace in social science to maintain that social policies often have an unequal impact on groups. One of the major underlying thrusts of this chapter is that urban elites, policymakers, and social scientists are far more likely to examine the impact of urban inequality on blacks, Hispanics, and women than on urban Indians. This does not imply that Indians do not have responsibilities as well. When urban injustice or, at least, inequality is clearly there, political systems do respond to pressure and, as utilitarians know, intensity and tactics can make up for lack of numbers in interest group competition. We often get the government we deserve. This chapter, at a minimum, highlights the context for examining the issues of equality for native Americans in our contemporary city on the hill or, as it has been called, the unheavenly city.

NOTES

1. For example, Lineberry has a brief review of the literature of urban equality but limits his ethnic focus to Hispanics and blacks. (Robert L. Lineberry. 1977. *Equality and Urban Policy*. Beverly Hills: Sage.)

REFERENCES

Chaudhuri, Joyotpaul. 1974. *Urban Indians of Arizona*. Tucson: University of Arizona Press.
Davis, James A. 1983. "Native-Americans in Oklahoma: Political Attitudes and Behavior." Paper presented at the Annual Meeting of the American Political Science Association, September 1-4, Chicago.
de Tocqueville, Alexis. 1972. *Democracy in America*. New York: Knopf.
Graves, Theodore D. 1972. "The Personal Adjustment of Navajo Indian Migrants to Denver, Colorado." In *Native Americans Today: Sociological Perspectives*, edited by Howard M. Bahr, Bruce A. Chadwick, and Robert C. Day, pp. 440-66. New York: Harper and Row.
Kunitz, Stephen J. and Jerrold E. Levy. 1970. "Navajo Voting Patterns." *Plateau* 43 (1):1-8.
Lineberry, Robert L. 1977. *Equality and Urban Policy*. Beverly Hills: Sage.
McCool, Daniel. 1982. "Voting Patterns of American Indians in Arizona." *Social Science Journal* 19 (July): 104-11.
National Indian Youth Council. 1983. *American Indian Political Attitudes and Behavior Survey*. Albuquerque. Unpublished Data Report.
Price, John A. 1972. "The Migration and Adaptation of American Indians to Los Angeles." In *The Emergent Native Americans*, edited by Deward Walker, pp. 729-38. Boston: Little, Brown.

Ritt, Leonard G. 1979. "Views of American Indians." *Ethnicity* 6 (March): 46-68.
Taylor, Theodore. 1983. *American Indian Policy.* Mt. Airy: Lomond.
U.S. Department of Commerce. Bureau of the Census. 1983. *1980 Census of the Population General Population Characteristics, Part I United States Summary.* Washington, D.C.: Government Printing Office.

6

NEW PARTICIPANTS, OLD ISSUES: MEXICAN-AMERICAN URBAN POLICY PRIORITIES

Rodolfo O. de la Garza and Janet Weaver

The role that Mexican Americans have historically played in local politics is both predictable and surprising. It is predictable because they have had little effective voice in local decision making (as has been true in state and national level politics). Except for Mexican-origin residents of northern New Mexico, Mexican Americans have been unrepresented or underrepresented in local decision-making bodies across the southwest (Garcia and de la Garza 1977). The role of Mexican Americans is surprising because this lack of representation exists even though Mexican Americans comprise a significant percentage and sometimes constitute the majority of the local population. Yet when they have been able to mobilize their resources, it is at the local level that they have scored some of their most important and unexpected political victories. The mayoral triumph of Raymond Telles in El Paso in 1958 (D'Antonio and Form 1965), the Chicano takeover during the early 1970s of city council and county offices in Crystal City (Schockley 1974), and the city council takeover in Parlier, California (Riddell and Aguallo 1978) are particularly notable.

VOTING RIGHTS

The historical reasons for this lack of representation at the local level are, in several ways, similar to those that explain low representation at other levels of government. The depressed registration and voting rates of Mexican Americans are rooted in their lower socioeconomic status and in the higher incidence of political alienation found among Mexican Americans in this strata. Racial gerrymandering, at-large districting, and other procedural machinations too have had the effect of reducing both the extent and impact of Mexican-American electoral participation generally. However, Mexican Americans in the past often faced even greater barriers in the local political arena. The major political parties, particularly the Democrats, commonly used their resources to mobilize the Mexican-American vote in statewide and national elections. Those resources were rarely available in typically nonpartisan local elections. Here Mexican Americans had a much greater potential for directly challenging Anglo incumbents. In Texas, for example, the Democratic party traditionally contributed to voter-registration and "get out the vote" campaigns among Mexican Americans during presidential and gubernatorial elections. But the same Democratic leaders who organized those campaigns strongly opposed autonomous efforts by Mexican Americans to create an independent voting bloc (Allsup 1982). Furthermore, the viability of political machines in Texas and elsewhere depended on their ability to control the Mexican-American vote; when they lost that, they died (Anders 1982; Booth 1982).

The 1975 and 1982 Voting Rights Acts (VRA) eliminated many of the barriers to effective political participation that Mexican Americans had long faced. The 1965 VRA was intended to protect the voting rights of blacks in the South. The 1975 and 1982 VRAs were expanded to include jurisdictions across the Southwest, including every political jurisdiction in Texas.

The passage of the 1975 VRA was important to Mexican Americans for two major reasons. It required southwestern election officials to "submit or preclear all proposed electoral changes to the Attorney General or to the District Court for the District of Columbia . . . " (Lawyers' Committee 1982, p. 33). This prevented local and state officials from manipulating the electoral rules to the disadvantage of Mexican Americans. The 1975 Act also provided for bilingual election materials, which gave many Mexican Americans access to the polls for the first time.

While the 1975 Act enhanced Mexican-American political clout in statewide and national elections, it had little effect on improving the political fortunes of Mexican-American candidates at the local level because it left intact the system of at-large elections. At-large election systems are perhaps the principal obstacle that Mexican Americans and other minorities must overcome in their efforts to win local elections (Engstrom and McDonald 1981; Davidson and Korbel 1981).

The 1982 VRA established the conditions for challenging the legality of at-large systems in all types of jurisdictions. The language of the 1975 act was such that the Supreme Court had rejected numerous challenges to at-large elections, holding that only if there is proof of discriminatory purpose can there be a violation of Section 2 of the Voting Rights Act and the Fourteenth and Fifteenth Amendments. The 1982 version of the VRA altered Section 2 of the 1975 Act to prohibit any electoral practice "imposed or applied by any state or political subdivision in a manner which results in a denial or abridgement of the right of any citizen of the United States to vote on account of race or color" or minority language status (Lawyers' Committee 1982, p. 2). Thus, intent was no longer an issue; now only results mattered. Local Mexican-American leaders, armed with the new legislation and with the assistance of the Mexican American Legal

Defense and Education Fund, the Southwest Voter Registration Education Project, and legal corporations such as Texas Rural Legal Aid, have successfully moved to create single-member district systems in jurisdictions across the Southwest.

These changes mean that Mexican Americans are now in a position to be effective participants in local elections. The consequences of their participation are unknown. However, given the decades of exclusion they have experienced, it is reasonable to expect that they will come to local politics seeking relief from the problems that local governments have ignored for so long.

The objective here is to determine if this is indeed the case. Specifically, we will describe and compare how Mexican Americans in three major southwestern communities evaluate their ability to influence the political process. We will then examine from two perspectives the issues that Mexican Americans consider to be most important to their respective communities. First we will compare how Mexican Americans and Anglos in one city view local issues. Then we will compare the concerns of Mexican Americans in three different communities. In combination, the results of these comparisons will suggest how increased Mexican-American participation in local politics will affect local political processes. If Mexican Americans are most concerned about ethnic issues and feel that local officials do not represent them, then Mexican-American mobilization could lead to intense ethnic-based political struggles. On the other hand, if these are not the types of issues that concern them, Mexican-American mobilization is unlikely to disrupt the extant political process. Instead, these processes may simply expand to include Mexican-American concerns.

METHODOLOGY

The data analyzed here are taken from four surveys conducted under the supervision of the Southwest Voter Registration and Education Project in San Antonio, Unincorporated East Los Angeles (ELA), and Phoenix. The data are based on interviews with 361 Mexican-origin citizens in San Antonio, 265 in ELA, 402 in Phoenix, and 263 Anglo interviews in San Antonio. The Phoenix survey was conducted by telephone; the others were personal interviews.[1]

Table 6.1 presents some of the major socioeconomic characteristics of the Mexican-American respondents. It is important to emphasize that the Phoenix sample was limited to registered voters, while the other two samples were not. This probably accounts for the higher educational, income, and occupational characteristics of the Phoenix sample compared to the ELA and San Antonio samples. The great majority of Mexican-American respondents were bilingual. Most of the Mexican-American respondents had 12 years or less of formal education, although the Phoenix respondents had more education than Mexican Americans in San Antonio and ELA. Anglos had the highest education levels.

TABLE 6.1. Socioeconomic Characteristics of Respondents, by City and Ethnicity

Language Ability

	Mexican Americans San Antonio		Mexican Americans E.L.A		Phoenix		Anglos San Antonio	
	(N)	%	(N)	%	(N)	%	(N)	%
Spanish	41	11.4	26	9.8	0	0	0	0
English	17	4.7	19	7.2	19	4.7	213	81.0
Both	303	83.9	220	83.0	383	95.3	50	19.0

Education

	Mexican Americans San Antonio		Mexican Americans E.L.A		Phoenix		Anglos San Antonio	
Years Attended	(N)	%	(N)	%	(N)	%	(N)	%
0 – 8	184	50.9	152	57.3	144	27.3	36	13.6
9 – 12	88	24.4	60	22.6	109	26.0	73	27.5
13 +	89	24.7	52	19.7	177	42.2	155	58.5
No response	0	0	1	.4	19	4.5	1	.4

Income

	Mexican Americans San Antonio		Mexican Americans E.L.A		Phoenix		Anglos San Antonio	
	(N)	%	(N)	%	(N)	%	(N)	%
below $10,000	142	39.3	79	29.8	28	6.7	57	21.5
$10,000–19,999	105	29.1	72	27.2	75	17.9	65	24.6
$20,000–29,999	50	13.8	26	9.8	86	20.5	58	21.9
$30,000 +	38	10.6	22	8.2	103	24.5	55	20.6
No response	26	7.2	66	24.5	127	30.3	30	11.3

Occupation

	Mexican Americans				Phoenix		Anglos San Antonio	
	San Antonio		E.L.A					
	(N)	%	(N)	%	(N)	%	(N)	%
Professional & Technical	36	10.0	17	6.4	70	16.7	40	15.1
Managerial and Administrative	21	5.8	12	4.5	23	5.5	18	6.8
Sales	9	2.5	3	1.1	12	2.9	22	8.3
Clerical	32	8.9	19	7.2	48	11.5	16	6.0
Craftsmen	25	6.9	18	6.8	21	5.0	10	3.8
Operative	18	5.0	18	6.8	36	8.6	1	.4
Laborer	12	3.3	8	3.0	29	6.9	4	1.5
Service	28	7.8	21	7.9	25	6.0	13	4.9
Unemployed	30	8.3	34	12.8	27	6.4	19	7.2
Housewife	79	21.9	58	21.9	53	12.6	41	15.5
Student	16	4.4	14	5.3	17	4.1	9	3.4
Retired	46	12.7	37	14.0	30	7.2	72	27.2
No response	9	2.6	6	2.2	28	6.7	0	0
Mean Age		43		44		41		49

Source: Southwest Voter Registration and Education Project surveys: San Antonio and East Los Angeles, December 1981 - March 1982; Phoenix, October 1983.

Mexican Americans in San Antonio and ELA tended to be employed in nonprofessional and nonmanagerial positions or to be housewives. Phoenix residents were closer to Anglo respondents in occupational status, except that a fairly high proportion of Anglo respondents were retired. ELA had the highest percentage of unemployed respondents, but the percentages among the samples did not greatly differ. The average ages were 43 in San Antonio, 44 in ELA, 41 in Phoenix, and 49 for Anglos. The higher proportion of retired Anglos is probably related to the higher average age of the Anglo sample.

These urban areas represent three variants of the Mexican-American urban experience. Unincorporated East Los Angeles (ELA) is a city within a city. Composed almost entirely of Mexican-origin residents, it is located within East Los Angeles, the "Mexican" side of town. It is among the poorest Mexican-American sections in greater Los Angeles, and its situation is made to seem worse by the relative affluence of the neighborhoods on its northeastern border. Politically, the community is under the jurisdiction of the Los Angeles County Board of Supervisors. Despite the size of the Mexican-American electorate in Los Angeles County and the fact that supervisors are elected from single-member districts, no Mexican American has ever been elected to the board. Residents of ELA have been so dissatisfied with their situation that on several occasions they have tried to incorporate as a separate jurisdiction. The efforts failed, and the historic situation of the community continues (Macias et al. 1972).

Of San Antonio's 785,880 residents in 1980, 54 percent were of Mexican-origin. Although Mexican-origin citizens have played a major role in the history of that city, they were effectively excluded from having any real voice in local affairs until the mid-1970s (Booth 1982). The change occurred in 1978 when the city abandoned its at-large electoral system in favor of a single-member system with a mayor elected at-large. Since then, Mexican Americans have played a major role in all aspects of local decision making. In 1984, the mayor and four of the ten council members were Mexican American.

The Mexican-origin population comprised only 15 percent of Phoenix's 789,704 residents in 1980. This is one of the reasons why under an at-large system no Mexican American had ever served on the city council. In addition to their relatively small numbers, Mexican Americans in Phoenix, as in the rest of Arizona, have long confronted racial hostility. Those seeking office have suffered from maneuvers designed to limit the effects of voter registration drives and from the unwillingness of party leaders to support their candidacy (Garcia and de la Garza 1977). With the shift to single-member districts in 1984, the first Mexican-American council member was elected.

This study, then, compares the attitudes of Mexican Americans who reside in communities that are in some ways similar and in some ways dissimilar. The Mexican-American respondents are all members of ethnic communities that have been denied equal access to local decision-making centers. The absolute size of those communities varies greatly, however, as does the size of the Mexican-origin population relative to the rest of the city. They also are governed by different types of local electoral systems. At the time of the surveys, San Antonio had already instituted a single-member system, and Phoenix was in the process of doing so. ELA remained under the jurisdiction of the Los Angeles Board of Supervisors and had no prospects of becoming an independent political entity. Are Mexican Americans in those communities primarily concerned about discrimination and lack of services and representation that may be attributed to ethnic divisions? These are the questions we will now examine.

PATTERNS OF POLITICAL EFFICACY

Individuals who believe they can influence the political process are much more likely to be politically interested and involved than those who think their efforts will be futile (Almond and Verba 1963; Verba and Nie 1972). In view of the obstacles they have confronted historically, it is not surprising that Mexican Americans have long exhibited a low sense of efficacy (Grebler, Moore, and Guzman 1970). When those obstacles are removed, however, Mexican Americans have manifested high levels of efficacy, interest, and participation (Hirsch 1973).

As Table 6.2 shows, Mexican Americans differ among themselves in their articulated levels of political efficacy. What is most significant about this finding is that these differences are associated with differences in types of local political systems rather than with differences in the socioeconomic status (SES) of our respondents. Given that efficacy is usually positively correlated with SES, we would expect Mexican Americans in Phoenix to feel the most efficacious. Instead, San Antonio respondents report the highest efficacy levels, while Phoenix and ELA residents report comparably lower levels. This pattern reflects the differences in the political systems of the respective communities. Respondents in San Antonio, where single-member districts are well established, have a significantly higher sense of efficacy than do respondents in ELA and Phoenix, which were governed by at-large systems at the time of the survey.

Mexican Americans in all three cities feel less efficacious than do San Antonio Anglos. This pattern reflects both the historical pattern of Anglo hegemony as well as the higher SES of Anglo respondents.

Together, these findings indicate that Mexican Americans differ among themselves in how they relate to their local political systems. These differences may influence Mexican-American local policy concerns. For example, San Antonio respondents may feel efficacious because they have in fact been able to influence local decision making, while respondents in the other cities feel inefficacious because their concerns have been ignored by local officials. Anglo and Mexican-American respondents in San Antonio may be expected to voice distinct

TABLE 6.2. Political Efficacy of Respondents, by City and Ethnicity

| | | Mexican Americans ||| Anglos |
		San Antonio %	E.L.A. %	Phoenix %	San Antonio %
"People like me don't have any say"[1]	Agree	28	37	31	25
	Disagree	72	63	66	75
	(N)	(343)	(254)	(406)	(261)
"Public officials don't care what people like me think"[2]	Agree	43	51	53	35
	Disagree	57	49	47	65
	(N)	(337)	(245)	(406)	(253)
"Politics is too complicated"[3]	Agree	70	71	65	64
	Disagree	30	29	35	36
	(N)	(349)	(254)	(402)	(261)

[1] "People like me don't have any say about what the government does."
[2] "I don't think public officials care what people like me think."
[3] "Sometimes politics and government seem so complicated that a person like me can't really understand what is going on."
Source: Southwest Voter Registration and Education Project surveys: San Antonio and East Los Angeles, December 1981 – March 1982; Phoenix, October 1983.

concerns for similar reasons. The following section of this chapter examines the extent to which these patterns exist.

PUBLIC POLICY CONCERNS

Mexican Americans and Anglos in San Antonio

To appreciate fully the potential significance of Mexican-American local policy concerns, it is necessary to compare those views with the views of the other political actors with whom Mexican Americans interact and compete. In San Antonio, the principal group with which Mexican Americans compete for political influence is the Anglo. If there are major differences in the policy concerns of these groups, then the political contests in which they engage may become ethnically charged. Under these conditions, increased Mexican-American mobilization could destabilize existing political processes. On the other hand, if there are no major differences in the concerns of these groups, then increased Mexican-American participation will be easily accommodated by the extant system.

The history of San Antonio suggests that Anglos and Mexican Americans would have distinct and mutually exclusive policy concerns. Mexican Americans there have a long history of social discrimination and political exclusion. For a brief period following Texas independence, Mexican Americans were among the city's political elite; indeed, in 1836 all of San Antonio's council members were of Mexican origin (Booth 1982, p.113). Within a decade, however, non-Mexican immigrants had won control of the city's social, economic, and political arenas, and from then until the mid-1970s, Mexican Americans in San Antonio were effectively prevented from having any autonomous voice in public decision making.

Although they were unable to function as independent political actors, Mexican Americans were important to the political process because of their numbers. By the late nineteenth century, political machines were becoming a major feature of San Antonio and South Texas politics, and these machines used the Mexican-American "vote" to develop and maintain themselves (Anders 1982). In San Antonio, Mexican Americans traded their votes for construction jobs with the city. "In order to work for a local government, a Mexican American had to register to vote and to turn his or her poll tax receipt (as well as those of as many family members as possible) to his supervisor." When Mexican Americans attempted to organize independently, law enforcement officials used "violent repression" to prevent them from doing so (Booth 1982, pp.117-18).

This situation remained relatively unchanged until after World War II. For almost a century, Mexican Americans were taught explicitly and implicitly that they should stay out of politics. While there are no systematic data to document their views of the political process, it is reasonable to conclude that these experiences produced high levels of alienation toward political institutions and participation among the great majority of Mexican Americans in San Antonio. Their level of alienation is suggested by the response a Mexican-American worker gave when asked if he planned to pay his poll tax. "No, I don't have to because I have a job at Kelly Field now" (quoted in Booth 1982, p.119–20). In other words, now that he didn't depend on the machine for a job, there was no reason to vote.

These political machines ruled San Antonio until the 1950s when the Good Government League (GGL) took control of local politics. A coalition of Anglo business elites, the GGL did not need Mexican-American votes to maintain itself. Where the bosses had manipulated Chicano voters, the GGL simply ignored them. When the GGL could no longer ignore Mexican-American voters because of their size and new levels of political activism, it attempted to court them by nominating carefully selected Mexican-American candidates. Chicano voters rejected this tactic and would not vote for these candidates. By 1973 the GGL's rule had ended (Booth 1982, p.120).

Changes in the national political structure also affected developments in San Antonio. In 1971, federal courts ruled against the State of Texas and in support of Mexican-American and black defendants in San Antonio and Bexar county generally in declaring multimember state legislative districts a violation of the one-person one-vote principle of representation. This ruling led to immediate increases in Mexican-American political activity, which resulted in a dramatic increase in the number of Chicanos seeking and winning state legislative office (Booth 1982, pp.129–30). Even more significant was the passage of the 1975 Voting Rights Act (VRA), which now was extended to include the entire state of Texas and selected jurisdictions within the remaining southwestern states. The 1975 version of the VRA signaled the development of a new era in the politics of the Mexican-American community across the Southwest (Garcia and de la Garza 1977; de la Garza and Vaughan 1984).

In San Antonio, the effect of the VRA was dramatic and immediate. It facilitated an increase in Mexican-American electoral participation. More important, the passage of the act was a major factor in influencing the city council's decision to change from an at-large to a single-member election system. The council took this action rather than risk defeat in what surely would be a lengthy, expensive, and image-damaging lawsuit. This shift was followed by an immediate increase in the number of Mexican Americans seeking and winning local office. Beatrice Gallegos, the head of Communities Organized for Public Services (COPS), a Chicano grass-roots organization, concluded that the VRA

> made a complete change...Before, city council representatives knew nothing about us (Mexican Americans) and our issues. There was no understanding and no communication...We were constantly confronted with many problems, issues that weren't recognized by others...(in Booth 1982, p.162).

With the demise of the GGL, the stage was set for the radical restructuring of the San Antonio political system, and with that, Mexican Americans began to play a major role in local decision making.

Local and national factors combined to effect this restructuring. Within San Antonio, dissension within the GGL contributed to its downfall. During the period of the GGL's reign, furthermore, Mexican Americans had begun to organize and develop their own political organizations. By the early 1970s, San Antonio activists were among the leaders of the Chicano movement, and organizations such as the Mexican American Youth Organization, the Mexican American Legal Defense and Education Fund, El Partido Raza Unida and the Southwest Voter Registration and Education Project articulated Chicano concerns in the streets, in courtrooms, at city hall, and wherever else decisions might be influenced. Then, in 1973, COPS was established. All of these organizations explicitly and continuously attacked the GGL's practice of exclusion and, directly or indirectly, worked to develop the Mexican-American voters into a cohesive voting bloc to insure that Chicano interests would be heard. Ironically, then, the GGL's policy of exclusion contributed directly to the development of an ethnic voting bloc among Mexican Americans.

The new electoral structures provided Mexican-American voters with their first opportunity in over a century to elect their own candidates. They made good use of this opportunity. They increased their registration rate from 36 percent of the total registered voters in 1971–74 to 41 percent in 1976–81. In 1981 this increased level of participation combined with the new electoral structures to enable Chicanos, in coalition with blacks, to elect five of the city's ten council members and Henry Cisneros as Mayor. Significantly, in that election it was the non-Anglo vote that provided Cisneros his margin of victory. In 1983, Cisneros won reelection with 92 percent of all votes cast, and he carried each of the city's ten districts with at least a 90 percent majority.

While Cisneros' resounding triumph suggests that the social distance between Mexican Americans and Anglos has diminished over the past century, there is also evidence that the legacy of a century of ethnic divisions and tensions still divides these two populations. For example, Chicano-Anglo housing segregation is higher in San Antonio than in most other southwestern cities (Lopez 1981; Hwang and Murdock 1982), and the segregation index did not change substantially, 1970–80 (Valdez 1983). As of 1980, average family income in the census tracts with high Anglo concentrations ranged from $22,669 to $15,484, while in Mexican-American tracts the range was from $13,352 to $12,940. Housing values in these same tracts ranged from $55,700 to $25,722 in Anglo neighborhoods but from $22,020 to $20,150 in Chicano areas (Valdez forthcoming).

Politically, these differences were manifested in the results of the 1983 council election in district 6, the only district with a substantial Mexican American-Anglo mix. In that election, the Anglo candidate received 83 percent of the vote in the precincts that were over 80 percent Anglo. The Mexican-American candidate received 79 percent of the vote in precincts that were over 94 percent Mexican American. The Anglo precincts had a turnout rate of 25 percent, compared to 20 percent among Mexican-American precincts, and the Anglo candidate won with 60 percent of the vote (Brischetto and Avina 1983).

Thus, despite the mayor's impressive 1983 victory it is reasonable to expect that as is true in other southwestern cities (Lovrich 1974; MacManus and Cassel 1982), Chicanos and Anglos in San Antonio have distinct local policy concerns that reflect the historical division between the two groups.

To determine the local policy concerns of our respondents, we asked Mexican Americans, "What is the most serious problem facing Mexican Americans in your community?" Anglos were asked, "What is the most serious problem facing persons in your community?" The responses to the open-ended questions were coded into seven categories. While the same proportion of Mexican Americans and Anglos viewed unemployment as the most important problem, the two groups differed in the importance of the remaining problems. As Table 6.3 shows, many more Anglos were concerned with crime and the lack of services, while Mexican Americans were more evenly distributed over the remaining issues.

These results indicate that there are both important differences and similarities in the local issues that most concern Mexican Americans and Anglos. They also suggest that neither group sees ethnic issues as the city's key problem, though it is important to note that many more Mexican Americans than Anglos are concerned with discrimination.

TABLE 6.3. Most Important Problem Facing Mexican Americans and Anglos in San Antonio

	Mexican Americans %	Anglos %
Unemployment	21	22
Crime	9	24
Discrimination	11	2
Lack of municipal services	12	22
Social service cuts	8	2
Education	10	2
Other	39	28
(N)	(334)	(244)

Notes: Mexican Americans were asked, "What is the most serious problem facing Mexican Americans in this community?" Anglos were asked, "What is the most serious problem facing persons in this community?"

Source: Southwest Voter Registration and Education Project surveys: San Antonio and East Los Angeles, December 1982 - March 1982; Phoenix, October 1983.

Mexican Americans in Three Cities

A comparison of the issue concerns of Mexican Americans in the three cities (see Table 6.4) also reveals some striking similarities and differences. First, it is noteworthy that in none of the cities is discrimination considered to be the principal issue affecting Mexican Americans. Second, the single most important concern our respondents identify in common is unemployment. Third, there is considerable variety in the issues that concern our respondents. Fourth, only in Phoenix do respondents express a concern about the lack of political representation and about local leaders in general. Fifth, San Antonians are more concerned about the lack of social services than are residents of ELA, and yet they have more control over local decision making than do the latter.

The variation among respondents in different cities may be viewed as reflective of specific local conditions as well as of the characteristics of the respective samples. In Phoenix, for example, the respondents are all registered voters and have high SES compared to respondents in ELA and San Antonio. It is not surprising, then, that they are more concerned about social service issues than are respondents in ELA or San Antonio.

San Antonio respondents, on the other hand, are more concerned about social service issues than are residents of Phoenix and ELA. Since their SES characteristics are only somewhat higher than those of ELA respondents, the saliency of this issue for San Antonio residents may be primarily a function of local structural characteristics rather than of either the real level of need of the respondents or of the differences in need levels between ELA and San Antonio residents. These concerns, for example, may reflect differences in current levels of service delivery by local government. ELA residents may simply have access to more services than do residents of San Antonio. Also, COPS has generated among Mexican Americans in San Antonio an attitude that they have a right to expect local governmental agencies to respond to their needs. It may be that San Antonio respondents are more concerned about this type of issue because they expect more from government agencies than do ELA residents.

CONCLUSION

From one perspective the findings here strongly suggest that increased Mexican-American political participation will not significantly alter local political processes or polarize local political systems. Mexican Americans do not define their policy concerns in ethnic terms, and they do not seem to perceive local politics as being polarized along ethnic lines. Instead, they are most concerned about the kinds of issues that concern "typical" Americans—unemployment and education. The respondents are also relatively unconcerned about a lack of political representation. Only in Phoenix do respondents identify this as

TABLE 6.4. Most Important Problem Facing Mexican Americans, by City

	San Antonio %	East Los Angeles %		Phoenix %
Unemployment	21	18	Unemployment	24
Education	10	11	Education	19
Discrimination	11	10	Prejudice/Discrimination	11
Lack of municipal services	12	3	Lack of political representation	9
Social service cuts	8	1	Attitudes toward political participation	8
Crime	9	35	Poverty and crime	6
Other	29	22	Local leaders	5
			Low wages/Cost of living	3
			Other	15

Note: The differences in the problems listed by Phoenix respondents and those in the other communities may reflect the fact that the Phoenix data were not coded by the same individuals who coded the East Los Angeles and San Antonio data.

Source: Southwest Voter Registration and Education Project surveys: San Antonio and East Los Angeles, December 1981 – March 1982; Phoenix, October 1983.

an issue, and there only nine percent raise it as an important problem. This, combined with the high percentages of respondents who reject the proposition that people like them have no say in government, may indicate that Mexican Americans in these three communities feel that incumbent officials represent their interests, despite the fact that only in San Antonio do the incumbents include Mexican Americans.

Also supportive of this perspective is the fact that in San Antonio neither Anglos nor Mexican Americans perceive ethnic issues as central to local politics. This may be why the increase in Mexican-American participation and representation there has not resulted in continuous bitter ethnic conflicts. In view of the long history of ethnic antagonisms in San Antonio, the relatively low salience of explicitly ethnic issues in local politics is indeed surprising.

From another perspective, however, ethnic divisions may be seen as underlying the principal political concerns of Mexican Americans in these three cities. Mexican-American unemployment, for example, differs from Anglo unemployment in that it is at least in part a function of the historical patterns of discrimination that Mexican Americans have experienced in the labor market (Barrera 1977). The legacy of those patterns helps explain why Mexican-American unemployment is so much higher than Anglo unemployment (National Council de la Raza 1984). The concern that Mexican Americans voice regarding education, the lack of social services, and cuts in social services may also be seen as reflective of the discriminatory experiences of the Mexican-American community. Throughout most of this century Mexican Americans have struggled to improve their educational opportunities (Allsup 1982; Carter 1970); it is therefore not surprising that educational issues are among the most salient problems concerning Mexican Americans. Because of their experiences in the labor market and in school, many Mexican Americans are in need of social services in order to survive. Cuts in government programs thus have a disproportionately negative effect on Mexican Americans (Freeman 1984).

The validity of viewing these issues as reflective of ethnic divisions is suggested by some of the differences between Anglo and Mexican-American perceptions of key local problems. Anglos have not been denied educational and social services and thus are relatively unconcerned about educational issues and social service cuts. They are, however, quite concerned about the lack of municipal services. While it is beyond the scope of this paper to determine if Anglos in San Antonio are in fact being denied their "fair share" of services, there is little reason to think that that is the case. Instead, it may be that Anglos are reacting negatively to the undeniable success that COPS has enjoyed in redirecting local spending toward Mexican-American neighborhoods in recent years. That success may lead Anglos to perceive that the rise of Mexican-American political actors has resulted in Mexican Americans receiving more than their due from local government.

The contemporary policy concerns of Mexican Americans may thus be viewed as reflective of long-standing ethnic divisions. This, however, is not meant to suggest that increased Mexican-American political mobilization will necessarily result in overtly ethnically polarized political competition. To the contrary, the fact that neither Mexican Americans nor Anglos perceived discrimination to be a major problem indicates that local political processes may be free of overt ethnic appeals. Nonetheless, it also seems reasonable to conclude that Mexican Americans will use the political process to address the problems that have long plagued them. That effort may generate Anglo resentment and perceptions that Mexican Americans are being too well treated. As the San Antonio example illustrates, that may lead to intense Anglo–Mexican-American competition without necessarily producing overt ethnic political conflict.

If the patterns described here are typical of patterns in other southwestern cities, increased Mexican-American political participation will not disrupt established political practices. Instead, it most likely will lead to more intensely contested local elections which, if Mexican Americans win, will result in important shifts in spending practices of local governments.

NOTES

1. The San Antonio Mexican-American survey and the East Los Angeles survey were conducted from November 1981 to January 1982. These interviews were conducted in person by bilingual interviewers. In San Antonio, a systematic random sample of households was drawn from the 1980 San Antonio criss-cross Polk directory. Only households with Spanish-surnamed occupants were selected, and a total of 415 interviews were completed. In ELA, a multistaged sampling of three adjacent households was drawn. First, the census blocks were selected by using an appropriate skip interval from the 1970 census block list of housing units. Then clusters of three adjacent households were randomly selected. A total of 488 interviews were completed in ELA. In Phoenix, a telephone survey of 419 Spanish-surnamed registered voters was conducted by the Public Opinion Research Center at Arizona State University between October 15 and October 30, 1983. The sample was stratified to ensure that age, sex, and residential groups were adequately represented. The survey of San Antonio Anglos, conducted in March 1982, used the same procedures as the San Antonio Mexican-American survey.

REFERENCES

Allsup, Carl. 1982. *The American G.I. Forum: Origins and Evolution*. Austin: Center for Mexican American Studies, University of Texas.
Almond, Gabriel A. and Sidney Verba. 1963. *The Civic Culture*. Princeton: Princeton University Press.
Anders, Evan. 1982. *Boss Rule in South Texas*. Austin: University of Texas Press.
Barrera, Mario. 1979. *Race and Class in the Southwest*. Notre Dame: University of Notre Dame Press.
Booth, John. 1982. "The Impact of the Voting Rights Act in San Antonio, Texas." In *Bilingual Elections at Work in the Southwest: A Mexican American Legal Defense and Education Fund Report*, edited by Robert Brischetto, pp. 111–78. San Antonio: MALDEF.

Brischetto, Robert and Annette Avina. 1983. "Registration and Voting in 1983 City Election in San Antonio, Texas." San Antonio: Southwest Voter Registration Project. Unpublished Report.
Carter, Thomas. 1970. *Mexican Americans in School: A History of Educational Neglect.* Princeton: College Entrance Examination Board.
D'Antonio, William U. and William H. Form. 1965. *Influentials in Two Border Cities: A Study in Community Decision-Making.* Notre Dame: University of Notre Dame Press.
Davidson, Chandler and George Korbel. 1981. "At-large Elections and Minority Group Representation: A Re-examination of Historical and Contemporary Evidence." *Journal of Politics* 43 (November): 982-1005.
de la Garza, Rodolfo O. and David Vaughan. 1984. "The Political Socialization of Chicano Elites: A Generational Approach." *Social Science Quarterly* 65 (June): 290-307.
Engstrom, Richard L. and Michael D. McDonald. 1981. "Election of Blacks to City Councils: Clarifying the Impact of Electoral Arrangements on the Seats/ Population Relationship." *American Political Science Review* 75 (June): 344-54.
Freeman, Gary. 1984. *The Working Poor Under the Reagan Administration: The Case of Texas Mexican Americans.* Occasional Paper No.6. The Mexican American Electorate Series. San Antonio: Southwest Voter Registration Education Project and Austin: Center for Mexican American Studies, University of Texas.
Garcia, Chris F. and Rodolfo O. de la Garza. 1977. *The Chicano Political Experience: Three Perspectives.* North Scituate, Mass.: Duxbury Press.
Grebler, Leo, Joan Moore, and Ralph C. Guzman. 1970. *The Mexican American People: The Nation's Second Largest Minority.* New York: Free Press.
Hirsch, Herbert. 1973. "Political Scientists and Other Camaradas: Academic Myth Making and Other Stereotypes." In *Chicanos and Native Americans: The Territorial Minorities*, edited by Rodolfo O. de la Garza, Z. Anthony Kruszewski, and Thomas Arciniega, pp. 10-22. Englewood Cliffs: Prentice-Hall.
Hwang, Sean Shong and Steve H. Murdock. 1982. "Residential Segregation in Texas in 1980." *Social Science Quarterly* 63 (December): 737-48.
Lawyers' Committee for Civil Rights Under Law. 1982. *Section 2 Litigation Manual.* Washington, D.C.: Voting Rights Project.
Lopez, Manuel M. 1981. "Patterns of Interethnic Residential Segregation in the Urban Southwest, 1960 and 1970." *Social Science Quarterly* 62 (March): 50-63.
Lovrich, Nicholas P., Jr. 1974. "Differing Priorities in an Urban Electorate: Service Preferences among Anglo, Black and Mexican American Voters." *Social Science Quarterly* 55 (December): 704-17.
Macias, Reynaldo et. al. 1972. *A Study of Unincorporated East Los Angeles.* Los Angeles: Chicano Studies Research Center, University of California at Los Angeles.
MacManus, Susan A. and Carol Cassel. 1982. "Mexican Americans in City Politics: Participation, Representation, and Policy Preferences." *Urban Interest* 4 (Spring): 57-69.
National Council de la Raza. 1984. *Socioeconomic Demographic Highlights of Hispanics in the 1980 Census.* Washington, D.C.: unpublished report.
Riddell, Adaljiza Sosa and Robert Aguallo, Jr. 1978. "A Case of Chicano Politics: Parlier, California." *Aztlan* 9 (Spring, Summer, Fall): 1-22.
Shockley, John. 1974. *Chicano Revolt in a Texas Town.* Notre Dame: University of Notre Dame Press.

Valdez, Avelardo. 1983. "Recent Increases in Intermarriage Among Mexican-American Males: Bexar County, Texas from 1972-1980." *Social Science Quarterly* 64 (March): 136-44.

———. Forthcoming. "Changes in Residential Segregation of Chicanos and Undocumented Mexicans in San Antonio (Bexar County), Texas: Consequences on Minority Status." In *Mexican American Community: An Evolving Relationship*, edited by Harley Browning and Rodolfo O. de la Garza. Austin: Center for Mexican American Studies, University of Texas.

Verba, Sidney and Norman H. Nie. 1972. *Participation in America*. New York: Harper and Row.

7

SEEKING EQUALITY: THE ROLE OF ACTIVIST WOMEN IN CITIES

*Joyce Gelb
and Marilyn Gittell*

Urban politics occupies a special place in the U.S. policy process. The particular character of federalism has established a tradition of the three-tiered government in which cities are not only the major direct deliverers of services but are also the source of new programs and laboratories for demonstrating the effectiveness of social programs. The underlying concept of federalism, that local governments provide an important balance to centralized power and a mechanism for responding to particular community needs, has been a sustaining factor in the continued reliance on strong local governments. Cities, in particular, have been the source of ideas and experience in the development and initiation of programs which address the needs of a changing society. This history of cities and urban service systems is synonymous with the expansion of the public sector in U.S. politics. Underlying the demand for government to provide direct services and address social needs was the assumption that only the government could fulfill egalitarian goals. Although largely ignored in the history of cities, the women's movement, in some form, has been instrumental in influencing the formulation of this ideology as well as in political struggles to shape new services and delivery systems.

It is in movement politics that women have made their contributions to shaping the character of urban society. The earliest form the movement took was in voluntary organizations, whose membership was and is largely comprised of women activists. It is not surprising that the first full-scale study of these groups and the role of women in them was a product of feminist scholarship. Berg (1978) in her research on early nineteenth century voluntary associations demonstrates the vital role of the women in those organizations and their particular contribution in characterizing urban problems as social needs resolvable only through new city services. This early tradition of female activism at the community and city level—its emphasis on the social causation of inequality and reliance on government to redress these problems—is an ideological thread of the women's movement which can be traced throughout the history of the U.S. city.

This study has as its focus several aspects of women's role in the urban arena: their role in the structure of power and control in the city; the quest for social equality in relation to the distribution of prestige and social status; juridical equality—before the law and in the opportunity structure; and, finally, distributive equality, involving the allocation of economic goods and resources and urban services. Our emphasis, while it includes all of these, will be on juridical and especially distributive equality in order to demonstrate how urban resources, service delivery, and policy outcomes have been affected by the feminist movement.

While women do not constitute a distinct economic or consumer group, they have always related in groups to local government service delivery, employment, and political representation (Goss 1984). More than any other level of government, local government intervenes in women's lives (Gelb and Klein 1983), and they, in turn, have sought to shape its character.

The structure of the contemporary women's liberation movement—grass roots, antihierarchical, and decentralized—inevitably took root at the local level of politics. Consciousness-raising groups, which served to create a recognition of the collective nature of sexism, discrimination, and oppression experienced by women, also helped to heighten awareness of the need for new and different approaches to urban services for women in areas such as health, safety, and poverty. It became evident that opportunities for equality were limited by the absence of choices for women regarding work, leisure, and political participation. Bureaucratic services that failed to meet the needs of women in general or those of specific groups of women were challenged by the creation of alternative modes of service. Our particular emphasis will be on three aspects of women's efforts to achieve more equitable and just allocation of services and economic resources: the role of women in restructuring traditional urban services, such as welfare and education; the role of contemporary feminism in creating alternative urban services; and the role of women as policymakers aiding in the redefinition of urban priorities.

The women's movement, as we have defined it, includes local voluntary organizations. Women were the most active participants in those organizations that in the nineteenth and twentieth centuries were in the forefront of major efforts to expand the role of government in the social services. Although these are now viewed as traditional urban services, the role of the women's movement in securing their adoption and expansion, first at the local level and ultimately at the national level, was vital. These activist women recognized the importance of public action in addressing social problems. Using their voluntary and charitable organizations, they established the community as the center for service delivery. It was responsive to local needs and more readily accountable to their pressures. In later years they recognized that equity was more likely to be achieved through national programs and expansion of the welfare state. They continued to be strong suppporters of decentralization, however, and maintained their activist tradition at the local level through community organization. The role of these activist women in the community is recorded in the history of voluntary organizations throughout the nineteenth century, of the settlement house movement, and in recent and more complete studies of community organizations.

TRADITIONAL URBAN SERVICES

How can we effectively measure the impact of the women's movement on the delivery of traditional urban services? Unlike the specific services clearly identified with the campaigns of contemporary feminist groups, the origin and early history of these more traditional service areas is selectively recorded. The major development in the character of urban services over the last several decades has been their expansion. For specific programs, we can trace the influence of organized groups in securing the approval of new and expanded services as well as increased funding.

For example, the recently written history of the tenants' movement has demonstrated the primary role of women's organizations in promoting public construction and regulation of housing and in expanding awareness of the need for greater equity in the distribution of adequate housing (Lawson 1980). Women's groups also played a key role in the struggle to establish public education in Illinois in the mid-nineteenth century (Tax 1980) and in every educational reform movement since that time. Many of the traditional human services as well were first provided in cities by voluntary associations and only later, as a result of long campaigns by activist local organizations, were administered or funded by government. And as Ware (1981) demonstrates in her history of the New Deal, many of the activist women who promoted social welfare programs at the national level in the 1930s had earlier experience in state and local government where they created and ran those programs.

Although they did not often hold leadership positions, women constituted an overwhelming proportion of those active in movements to reform urban social services. Feminists at the turn of the century were active in the populist and progressive movements which promoted government reorganization and centralization of the political system (Lemons 1973). The Fainsteins' (1974) extensive history of urban social reform movements concludes that women were the major participants in these struggles and that a primary concern was to establish equity in the delivery of urban services. Later reformers organized in community organizations were seeking more responsive local delivery of services. Studies of grass roots community organizations in the 1960s agree that a majority of members were women (Perlman 1976; Gittell 1980).

The welfare rights organization was an example of a women's group which succeeded in making important policy changes in the 1960s. Comprised primarily of black, poor women, the National Welfare Rights Movement (NWRM) organized locally throughout the United States in the 1960s. Like other domestic programs, the welfare system is funded by the federal and state governments. However, the programs are developed and administered at the local level—hence, discretionary policies and specific variations in service delivery are locally determined. During the 1960s, welfare rights groups confronted welfare authorities and jammed local welfare departments in order to demand special grants for clothing, furniture, and other necessities, as well as higher benefit levels. This was clearly a local level women's movement, fighting for more equitable treatment, more funds, and equality in the job market through better jobs and day care (West 1981).

As a result of the movement's activities, millions of dollars were transferred to the poor—the number of women receiving AFDC tripled from 1966 to 1979 (West 1981). Local and state laws were successfully challenged to increase eligibility and to loosen restrictive requirements. As a result of legal and protest activity, public consciousness was aroused (Hertz 1981) and welfare women became participants in the policy-making process itself (Hertz 1981; West 1981). They gained increased representation on local and county welfare boards, and bargained for funding and advocacy space with welfare department administrators (West 1981). Finally, many "welfare" departments adopted the more humane term, "human services." The debate on equity for poor women was reopened and a legacy of political activism remained (West 1981).

CHANGES IN STRUCTURED DELIVERY OF SERVICES

Other institutional changes in city government were achieved in the 1960s and 1970s as a result of women's activism in community organizations. These changes included affirmative action programs to include greater representation of women and minorities within city bureaucracies; a return to ward elections, which reestablished the neighborhood as a center for electoral politics; party reorganization, which broadened representation of women and minority groups; decentralization and expansion of city services; and the creation of alternative forms of service delivery, which made human services more responsive to the needs of marginal populations.

Women's activist efforts also produced fundamental changes in interest group politics in U.S. cities in the 1960s and 1970s. The traditional upper- and middle-class bias of interest group politics was broadened in many cities. The character, role, and structure of traditional voluntary associations were changed. Lower-income groups no longer viewed these associations as intermediaries for them in the polictical system. Once again, women used community organizations to press for public policies to meet the special needs of women and their families. They again utilized these groups for service delivery but shifted their focus from traditional voluntary associations to more broadly based, advocacy-oriented grass roots organizations.

The expansion of neighborhood and community services in urban areas in the 1960s was a dramatic change in the thrust of urban service delivery. This was in sharp contrast to the centralization of city services and the development of professional bureaucracies that began at the turn of the century and was followed by six decades of growth. In the 1960s, health care clinics, day care centers, after-school programs, multipurpose centers, and senior citizens programs—all based in the neighborhood and controlled by client-participants—became the new mode of urban service. The major characteristics of this new mode were neighborhood orientation, direct participation of residents in the policy process, and emphasis on equitable, responsive, and representative service. In public housing it required direct participation of residents in the administration of their buildings; in schools it resulted in decentralization of large city school systems or the creation of community controlled and alternative schools. The aim was to redistribute power, personalize government programs, and reduce bureaucratic control. At the same time increased federal involvement provided compensatory funding and regulations to reduce inequities. The women's movement had a direct and instrumental role in the city reforms of this era. In Los Angeles, the women activists who organized the alternative school movement succeeded in getting the school system to create a separate structure for alternate schools. They were also major supporters of school desegregation. That group of women activists later organized as "Women For," which became an influential political organization in the electoral politics of the city. In Chicago, community activist organizations joined with the national civil rights movement but were less successful in their efforts to desegregate and gain a voice in the operation of housing projects.

Combined with the concept of providing better service was the goal of equitable and compensatory funding. Many of the civil rights and community advocacy organizations of the 1960s became the service deliverers of the 1970s. The neighborhood school districts in New York City, created in 1967 to test the concept of community control, were run largely by the activists who had fought to integrate the schools in the early 1960s. Organizations like TWO in Chicago and the Oakland Community Services Organization became multiservice centers funded by federal, state, and local governments. Each provided services to neighborhoods long denied those services by city and state bureaucracies. Low-income and minority women comprised a majority of the membership of these organizations (Gittell and Shtob 1980; Perlman 1976) and were central to the reform of city government which spread across the country. Middle-income women continued to be active in more traditional voluntary organizations, which were also enlisted in the new reform efforts.

In addition to the expansion of human service, health, and educational programs, the influence of the women's movement can be identified in such major changes as in the institution and development of paraprofessional training in each of these service areas so as to include more women and minorities as service deliverers, and in the removal of discriminatory hiring, promotion, and recruitment policies. Affirmative action programs became an integral part of the service delivery reform policies. Legislative reform in the 1960s and 1970s embodied broad principles that characterized differentiation in the quality of service delivery according to sex, class, or race as unacceptable. Women's groups utilized monitoring of Title IX to promote nondiscriminatory practices in local education agencies. Other changes in policies were sought to include the excluded and develop more equitable allocation of resources in every service area. Compensatory funding was to become more common as cities adopted a more redistributive role.

Alliances and coalitions at all levels of government between women's organizations and activist community organizations were instrumental in achieving city reforms. Joint action was most often evident in efforts to expand neighborhood and community facilities, especially for battered families, health care, day care, and senior care. At the local level the women's movement is most cohesive when it is addressing the issues of service delivery. Conflict, when it occurs (and it has), generally has involved efforts by women's groups to gain state ERA legislation or establish women's commissions. Community activists have supported these efforts but have not given them top priority. In selected instances differences of opinion on abortion rights, particularly in Hispanic communities, have created some conflict between community groups and women's groups.

As the backlash policies of the 1980s began to undermine the reforms of the 1970s, the ties between women in community organizations and women's organizations were strengthened. Although Chicago women's groups supported Jane Byrne's candidacy in the 1983 primary, women's groups and activist women in community organizations joined forces to help elect Harold Washington in the general election. The combined groups are now a major force in the Washington administration and are consulted on policy in all areas of city government. Interviews with women activists in community and women's groups in Chicago before and after the elections suggested that the mayoralty campaign was a pivotal event for joint action (Gittell and Naples 1984).

Although this review of the role of women in local reform movements suggests uniform support for equity in urban communities, we should also note that some women were active in groups that opposed these efforts. Women were the most important participants in the neighborhood preservation movement that opposed school integration and public housing in the 1970s. The right to life movement, too, has strong support from activist women, and the movement for abolition of the income tax has been led by women.

The overwhelming thrust of women's activism in community and women's organizations, however, has been to expand government services and the social welfare state, to decentralize service delivery and achieve equality. The recognition that women's needs in urban communities relate specifically to the life-styles and circumstances of those communities has influenced the agendas and priorities of women's groups, and they increasingly have joined in coalitions with other organizations to maintain service levels. This was particularly true in reponse to the Reagan budget cuts, which most directly affected women in cities. State coalitions organized to preserve urban education and health programs under the new block grants included activist women in all kinds of organizations—women's groups, community organizations, and professional associations. On the national level, the major women's organizations campaigned actively for preservation of social and human service programs.

FEMINISM AND THE CREATION OF ALTERNATIVE PUBLIC SERVICES IN THE CITY

While women have played an important role in reforming traditional urban functions, their most notable contribution is in the creation of new and alternative services. Present-day feminists have initiated a variety of new public services directed at the changing needs of contemporary urban women. These new services have taken on a nontraditional form, stressing participatory democracy, self-help, and absence of hierarchical leadership and structures. In these efforts, the movement has added a new dimension to the concept of equality and the goals of an equitable society. Feminists have provided a new voice in the political arena, pressing for an end to the physical separation of households from the public sphere and the economic separation of the domestic economy from the rest of the political system (Hayden 1984).

An important development in urban politics and policymaking has been a redefinition of needed public services and a reexamination of the line dividing the public and private spheres. Particularly in the areas of health, the role of displaced homemakers, and treatment and aid for female victims of male violence, feminists have succeeded, at least in part, in raising new issues, placing them on the public agenda, and thus contributing to the restructuring of policy concerns.

Feminists have tried to respond to the unmet needs of women as well. New institutions were begun and networks created between grass roots feminists, legal and professional organizations, and, sometimes, city officials. Public consciousness was often altered and existing separations between the public and private spheres ceased to be rigidly maintained.

Health Care

One area of such activity was in the redefinition of modes of health care. The desire for equal access to information and self-help in a group setting led to the creation of over 1,200 groups connected with women's health (Gottlieb 1980). Often, these groups grew out of workshops and discussions of women's bodies and women's health during the late 1960s (Gelb and Klein 1983). Concern among members of the Boston Women's Health Collective regarding the inaccessibility of medical information to women resulted in the publication of *Our Bodies, Ourselves*, a now widely used feminist manual on medical aid for women. In Los Angeles in 1973, the Women's Health Center grew out of a consciousness-raising group which emphasized self-help. The Los Angeles center provides abortion services, pregnancy screening, and treatment of venereal and vaginal diseases. Other groups, such as the Women's Center in Seattle, train health care specialists to be more responsive to the needs of women. The Gynecorps project in Seattle also provides enhanced services to high-risk and underserved women (Gottlieb 1980).

Specialized services have been created in several cities for women with special problems. Among these are the Boston-based Women, Inc., which provides drug treatment for addicts and their children. The emphasis on this group of women again reflects concern for a population not served by traditional therapeutic services. Minority women from Dorchester, Roxbury, and the South End, largely older women, are the primary participants in the collective, supportive service structure (Schwingl et al. 1980).

Another effort that reflects particular concern for the unmet needs of specialized groups of women is the Alcoholism Center for Women, Inc., founded in Los Angeles in 1974. Here the particular emphasis is on lesbian alcoholics. CASPAR (Cambridge and Somerville Program for Alcoholism Rehabilitation) is a similar East Coast organization which, in addition to reaching more and different women, targets community agencies and groups such as hospitals and welfare agencies. It provides sensitivity training for their personnel and information about problems specifically related to women (Schwingl et al. 1980).

Violence Against Women

As in the health arena, consciouness-raising (C.R.) groups created public awareness of the pervasiveness of violence against women. The National Organization for Women (NOW) helped to arouse additional interest in and awareness of the issue through the creation of 300 state and local task forces (Schechter 1982). One of the first shelters to be created in St. Paul (in 1971) was a direct outgrowth of a C.R. group. The creation of rape crisis centers and shelters for battered women concerned with addressing acts of violence against women represents dramatic institutional innovations in the creation of alternative urban services.

Around 1970, health services for rape victims were developed and rape crisis centers formed in order to influence the helping professions and institutions unresponsive to the victim's plight. By 1972, a half-dozen rape crisis centers providing an alternative service structure existed; today there are hundreds that provide victim assistance through counseling support, legal advocacy, medical care, and data gathering functions (Stevens 1980). Their innovative approach has influenced community institutions, which began to rethink their own procedures and develop specialized training programs to deal with victims' needs. Today, police departments, hospitals, district attorneys' offices, and mental health agencies, as well as other municipal institutions, have coordinated efforts and adopted many of the techniques of the rape crisis movement.

The movement to aid rape victims has a multifaceted approach. Peer counseling, support networks, information about police and legal procedures, as well as health service and 24-hour hotlines are all provided by the movement (Burgess and Holmstrom 1979). In Cleveland the great demand for services led to the creation of a NOW Task Force on Rape. In mid-1973, women's groups at a local university, Case-Western Reserve, requested and received funds from the Gund and Cleveland foundations. Although like many other similar groups, the center relied on a large number of volunteers, this funding helped to establish a 24-hour hotline and to hire full- and part-time staff to provide advocacy at hospitals, police stations, and courts. A speaker's bureau kept the issue before the public, and foundation-funded instructors conducted self-defense classes. A major goal of the center was to reform the structure of enforcement, especially the police and the courts. The reeducation of city bureaucracies in traditional service areas is an important component of the special approach of feminist reform.

The Women's Center in Houston and Women In Action developed ways to connect local community organizations to their special hot-line services. Direct contacts with local governments were necessary in order to increase funding and improve legal procedures. These have included emphasis on better treatment for rape victims and emphasis on prevention. In Danbury, Connecticut, a coalition of police, state attorneys, the local hospital, and the rape crisis center combined to educate the community about assault and how to deal with it and to compile information related to rape (Burgess and Holmstrom 1979).

A program developed in Los Angeles in the mid-1970s provided support for female victims at all stages of crisis. In New York City a "model" approach to the apprehension of rapists was developed; it included a program of attitudinal and skill training for police officers (Stevens 1980). The rape crisis movement has resulted in greater community concern with problems created by rape—both in terms of services to aid the victim and public education—while implementation varies within specific communities. New interest may turn to broader issues related to patterns of violence. There is no doubt that at present attitudes and behavior in hospitals, police, and the courts have been altered by the movement (Schechter 1982). Numerous procedures related to police treatment of rape victims, requirements for corroborative evidence and evidence related to "prior sexual contact" have been changed and judicial proceedings expedited (Taylor 1981).

As the rape victim's plight became more a matter for public concern, feminists and grass roots women were successful in raising issues related to other forms of violence against women, particularly spouse abuse. Emphasis was placed on creating services for victims of domestic violence, changing laws, and arousing public consciousness (Schechter 1982). Multipurpose task forces, often affiliated with local NOW chapters, were among the first to recognize wife abuse as a widespread phenomenon, and the shelter movement in many cities was also an outgrowth of rape hot lines (Hutchins and Baxter 1980). Drawing on their experience in the creation of rape crisis centers, feminists and activists organized at the local level to seek state and local funding as well as foundation aid for these new services. Activists had to relate to traditional social service agencies including welfare, health, and legal departments as well as to fire and zoning departments in order to obtain, for example, emergency housing space. By 1982, there were between 300 and 700 "safe houses" and shelters in the United States (Schechter 1982).

Women used a variety of techniques to force police to make arrests and intervene in family violence in compliance with the law. Changed practices included larger numbers of arrests and reforms in police training and procedures. Courts, which formerly had been hostile to the dissolution of intact families and thus were reluctant to force males to leave their families (a practice which often resulted in delays and further injury and abuse), modified their practices. This was due in part to stepped-up court monitoring and attitudinal changes in judicial personnel as a result of new training. (The district attorney's offices were similarly affected.) Divorce, support, and child custody laws were amended to increase compliance. Increased criminal penalties and better data collection were adopted in many cities. Options for victims were increased and ignored groups (for example unmarried women) were particularly targeted. Federal funding, especially during the 1970s, helped to support many movement activities under such legislation as the Law Enforcement Assistance Act, Title XX of the Social Security Act, and Title I of the Elementary and Secondary School Act.

The need for funding sometimes transformed feminist-organized and -run rape crisis centers and shelters into municipally operated social services. As a result, the feminist self-help participatory approach to service structures has been modified (Ahrens 1980). Often gaps have occurred between grass roots innovation and service delivery (Kahn and Kamerman 1982). In cities like New York, where battered women's programs developed from the top down in the absence of a feminist-sponsored coalition, the original conceptual framework and approach were essentially destroyed as institutional welfare requirements limited the scope and aims of the programs (Schechter 1982).

Community Education

There are also some highly effective women's community education programs in several large cities. Their efforts range from the granting of

GEDs (high school diplomas) to college degree programs. The Community Women's Education Project in Philadelphia, a spinoff of a women's education program at the Lutheran Settlement House, is a college-degree-granting program affiliated with Philadelphia Community College. Its curriculum stresses math and technology. The college is housed in an old school building, which The Women's Education Project refurbished and maintains. The program provides day care and strong counseling services. Peer group support and career counseling are also emphasized.

One of the earliest community-based women's college programs was developed by the Congress of Neighborhood Women in the early 1970s in a lower income area in Brooklyn. Credit is granted through the state and city universities. The curriculum is directed at training women as community leaders through the analysis of community issues and needs. The Carroll Gardens Women's College program is a spinoff of the Congress effort and provides a more traditional college offering.

Women, Inc., which established the first residence where addicted mothers could live with their children, has since developed a GED program and a college basic skills preparatory program for neighborhood women. The programs include peer group support and day care facilities as well.

Nontraditional job training is another thrust of the women's educational programs. The Women's Technical Institute in Boston trains women for careers in electronics and drafting. It places over 90 percent of its graduates in jobs at an average salary of $9,000. A similar program is run by Wider Opportunities for Women (WOW) in Washington, D.C. It annually trains 400 local women in its technical education programs.

Approaches to urban women's equality have tended to reflect a single-issue orientation, although the concept of multiservice centers enjoys considerable support among feminists and their political allies. There is no current parallel in the United States to the effort to provide a coherent urban level approach to women's issues as in the case of the United Kingdom. There women's committees have been organized in municipalities to provide funding and support for a broad range of women's services and needs. In the United Kingdom there has been an emphasis on mass participation across issue lines. Outreach efforts such as the Women's Bus in the Borough of Camden in London, which travels around the community to focus attention on women's issues and concerns, have not developed in U.S. cities (Goss 1984).

WOMEN IN CITY GOVERNMENT

Historically women have been underrepresented in the formal appointive and elective offices in cities, as they have been in other aspects of public life. As a result of the influence of the feminist movement, women's roles in the political sphere have increased, although they continue to lack adequate representation at the upper levels and are the first to suffer from retrenchment policies.

The gains made by women from 1975 to 1981 in the urban sphere are evident; for example, the number of women serving as mayors and governing officials of local municipal governments and townships rose from 4 percent to 10 percent in the six-year period. In 1981, women were 7 percent of urban mayors (compared with 1 percent in 1971) (Mueller 1983). By 1983, women comprised 8.7 percent of American mayors, including those in Houston, Chicago, San Francisco, and San Jose. During the period 1971–83, the number of female county officials doubled and female municipal officials tripled (Flammang 1984).

Women have moved into key roles in shaping urban public policy in related professions as well. As of 1980, they comprised 10–15 percent of professional planners—a number that almost tripled in a decade (Leavitt 1980). The significance of women as municipal office holders and managers goes beyond mere statistics. In these positions, women have helped to foster affirmative action, protest the existence of discrimination, encourage the hiring of other women, and serve as role models (Burns 1979).

Numerous studies have demonstrated that women as city officials hold different opinions about policy issues than their male colleagues. Among these are support for ERA ratification, day care, affirmative action, legalization of prostitution, and eradication of sexism in education (Mezey 1978). Women are also likely to be more supportive of homemaker social security and opposed to an abortion amendment to the Constitution. In general, studies have found that women are more likely to be "humanistic" in approaching such policy issues as criminal penalties, busing, and the like (Antolini 1984). Hence, the increased election of women to local offices should have important policy repercussions in terms of service and policy priorities.

In addition to the growing policy significance of women officeholders in a variety of municipal roles, women in office also create access to power for other women (Antolini 1984). Women officeholders favor upgrading the status of women and are more supportive than their male colleagues of the women's movement and efforts to secure women's rights. Several studies support the view that women politicians think they have a responsibility to represent women's interests and take a lead role in advocacy of women's issues (Mezey 1982; Stewart 1980). A large majority of women officeholders say that they have helped to involve women in appointive commission roles in urban politics, while a smaller group (40 percent) say they have helped to employ women in bureaucratic positions (Burns 1979). Similar findings have been reported for women school-board members (Johnson and Stanwick 1979).

Women officeholders have also had positive effects on public attitudes toward women in politics. A Houston study demonstrated that Mayor Kathy Whitmire's strong performance as city controller resulted in far greater support among voters for female participation in local political offices (McManus 1981).

Women in decision-making roles also perceive themselves as role models for other women (Mezey 1982).

Another aspect of women's participation in local politics has been the creation of commissions on the status of women. These institutional efforts to provide for women's advocacy were supported initially by such groups as the League of Women Voters and the National Women's Political Caucus (Flammang 1984). The commissions serve a number of key functions including public education, administrative or budgetary oversight, and sometimes investigations of sex discrimination complaints (Rosenberg 1982). As part of the educational function, commissions raise consciousness about feminist concerns by holding conferences, hearings, and workshops, publishing newsletters, and distributing materials on key public issues. This function has been aptly called the "convenor/catalyst" function, the generation of support for programmatic action (Stewart 1980). Some commissions lobby, initiate proposals, and seek direct influence in policymaking. Many commissions are particularly important in seeking more appointments of women and keep talent or data banks in order to expand feminist influence. Finally, they assess particular needs, keep track of hiring/promotion policies and contract awards, and monitor law enforcement (Rosenberg 1982; Stewart 1980). At their most effective, commissions provide a key link between feminist interest groups and the formal political process and a vehicle for publicity about women's concerns. It should be noted, however, that many commissions are hampered in their effectiveness by limited power and funding (Rosenberg 1982).

Another important role for professional and political women in the urban arena is that of providing networks consisting of ad hoc or more formal coalitions or caucuses. Networks typically include elected and/or appointed women officials, members of the media, feminist activists, and community and/or specialized issue groups. Such coalitions may be activated around a key policy issue, the campaign of a prospective feminist officeholder, or efforts to get more women into local bureaucracies. They have helped to reshape both the gender composition and policy priorities of local politics. Although this analysis suggests effective change in the status of women, it should not obscure the inequities in representation, rank, and salary that continue to exist.

THE CHALLENGE OF THE 1980s

Starting with the fiscal crisis in New York City in 1975, many of the urban reforms of the 1960s and 1970s experienced a sharp transformation. Governments became more concerned with balancing budgets; the economy, it was claimed, could no longer support the expansion of the social welfare state. The election of Ronald Reagan and his policies reinforced an antigovernment mood at the same time that the needs of women were expanding.

The increased participation of women in the work force has produced additional needs. Supports provided by the family in earlier generations no longer exist, and the only substitute is government support; yet the leadership at the federal level is moving toward further reduction in services. Urban services have certainly not kept up with growing needs. Given the limited tax base of local communities, their ability to support service cutbacks is exceedingly limited.

Obstacles to full equality for women persist in the urban environment. As the traditional family has declined, there have been only a few successful efforts by feminists and others to rethink structures of opportunity for women, particularly as they relate to the everyday needs of particular groups of women. Women activists have had little or no impact in redesigning the urban environment so that it better reflects the needs of working women for more efficient transportation networks, child care, and home care services. Limitations in low cost public transportation that could aid working women, placement of worksites in often inaccessible locations, inflexible schedules which are insensitive to the needs of parents of small children, and the lack of publicly funded, high quality day care—all place limits on the options of women who continue to be underemployed and overburdened (Wekerle, Peterson, and Morley 1980). By 1978 almost 60 percent of all women were in the paid labor force, while close to a majority of women with children under six worked, two-thirds of them full time. With the discovery of the feminization of poverty—a concept that emphasizes the disproportionate number of female-headed families that are disadvantaged economically, and a large number of whom are urban dwellers—the inhospitality of the work force and the (man-made) urban environment loom even more significantly. The urban system needs to take into account the changing economic role of women and the needs of single female heads of households who are poor and/or on fixed incomes (Wekerle, Peterson, and Morley 1980). By 1990 only 25 percent of women will be full-time housewives. Only 35 percent of children under six with working mothers are currently in federally funded day care (Zeigler and Gordon 1982). Only 19 percent of those who seek child care can currently find places (Clarke-Stewart 1982). The absence of child care alternatives is a barrier to equity in the job market and other aspects of the public sphere. Issues of ideology, cost, and professionalization have prevented meaningful change in this policy area.

The achievement of greater equality of opportunity for women involves changes in traditional housing patterns with particular attention to the needs of single mothers and poor women. Selected experiences suggest the direction future planning must take. In 1978 in Providence, Rhode Island, several women sought to work with low-income urban women in order to develop an economic and spatial program to meet their needs. Connections were made with church, community, city and other government agencies. By 1980 the community of Elwood, where the median income fell below the poverty line, saw the establishment of the Women's Development Corporation with 225 participants, mostly single parents in their twenties. They sought to rehabilitate residential housing, develop an economic base, and establish day care, using self-help approaches. By 1983 they had completed considerable construction and revitalization, emphasizing the creation of rental housing (Hayden 1984).

In some cities, the need for urban safety related to women has been addressed. The greenlight program in Jamaica Plains (Massachusetts) and Safehouse in San Francisco seek to provide refuge for frightened women, as well as emergency counseling and other assistance. In Madison, Wisconsin, and Whitehorse, Alaska, specialized women's transportation services provide flexible, personalized transportation. In Madison, the city, county, and university share funding costs. While these beginning efforts to reach out to underserved and neglected groups of urban women are noteworthy, policies related to inadequate transportation, which limits access to jobs and other aspects of public participation, have often been overlooked.

New efforts must seek to end women's isolation in the home and increase access to a nonsexist city. More thought must be given to policies that will provide for alternative home care for children's play, sick children, meal distribution, assistance with repairs, service for victimized women, and socialization of homemaking tasks (Hayden 1984).

CONCLUSION

There is a historical tradition of women's role in city reform which can barely be gleaned from the literature. In each era, women pushed for fundamental social reform through the expansion of urban services. Their sociopolitical analysis of the problems of society provided a rationale for new public sector efforts. The era of the 1960s and early 1970s follows this tradition and is distinguished by expanded participation, particularly the engagement of lower-income working-class and minority women in political activism through community organization. Their activism set new goals, including a sensitivity to the needs and enhancement of the role of marginal populations in the political system through expanded concepts of representation, citizen participation, and alternate approaches to service delivery. While earlier reform efforts of women activists concentrated on service and programs, the 1960s and 1970s reforms established new and continuing roles for women in the political system through institutional change. The next era will require that the women who have secured positions of power join with community activists to secure more equitable distribution of urban services to meet the growing needs of women in cities.

REFERENCES

Ahrens, Lois. 1980. "Battered Women's Refuges and Feminist Cooperation v. Social Services Institutions." *Radical America* 14 (May-June): 41-48.
Antolini, Denise. 1984. "Women in Local Government: An Overview." In *Political Women: Current Roles in State and Local Government*, edited by Janet A. Flammang, pp. 23-40. Beverly Hills: Sage.
Berg, Barbara J. 1978. *The Remembered Gate: Origins of American Feminism: The Woman and the City.* New York: Oxford University Press.
Burgess, Ann and Lynda Holmstrom. 1979. *Rape: Crisis and Recovery.* Bowie, MD: Robert J. Brady.
Burns, Ruth Ann. 1979. *Women in Municipal Management: Choice, Challenge and Change.* New Brunswick: Center for the American Woman and Politics, Rutgers University.
Clarke-Stewart, Alison. 1982. *Day Care.* Cambridge, Mass.: Harvard University Press.
Fainstein, Norman I. and Susan S. Fainstein. 1974. *Urban Political Movements: The Search for Power by Minority Groups in American Cities.* Englewood Cliffs: Prentice-Hall.
Flammang, Janet A. 1984. "Filling the Party Vacuum: Women at the Grass-roots Level in Local Politics." In *Political Women: Current Roles in State and Local Government*, edited by Janet A. Flammang, pp. 87-114. Beverly Hills: Sage.
Gelb, Joyce and Ethel Klein. 1983. "Women's Movements: Organizing for Change in the 1980s." Washington, D.C.: American Political Science Association.
Gittell, Marilyn. 1980. *Limits to Citizen Participation: The Decline of Community Organizations.* Beverly Hills: Sage.
_____ and Nancy Naples. 1984. "The Gender Gap and Coalescing for Power." In *Beyond Reagan*, edited by Alan Gartner, Colin Greer, and Frank Riessman, pp. 243-55. New York: Harper and Row.
_____ and Theresa Shtob. 1980. "Changing Women's Roles in Political Volunteerism and Reform of the City." *Signs* 5 (Spring): S67-78.
Goss, Sue. 1984. "Women's Initiatives in Local Government." In *Local Socialism*, edited by Martin Boddy and Colin Fudge, pp. 109-23. London: Macmillan.
Gottlieb, Naomi, ed. 1980. *Alternative Social Services for Women.* New York: Columbia University Press.
Hayden, Dolores. 1984. *Redesigning the American Dream.* New York: W.W. Norton.
Hertz, Susan Hendley. 1981. *The Welfare Mother's Movement.* Washington, D.C.: University Press of America.
Hutchins, Trova and Vee Baxter. 1980. "Battered Women." In *Alternative Social Services for Women*, edited by Naomi Gottlieb, pp. 179-211. New York: Columbia University Press.
Johnson, Marilyn and Kathy Stanwick. 1979. "Local Office Holding and the Community: The Case of Local School Boards." In *Women Organizing*, edited by Bernice Cummings and Victoria Schuck, pp. 61-81. Metuchen, N.J.: Scarecrow Press.
Kahn, Alfred and Shelia Kamerman. 1982. *Helping America's Families.* Philadelphia: Temple University Press.
Lawson, Ronald. 1980. "Tenant Mobilization in New York." *Social Policy* 10 (March/April): 30-40.

Leavitt, Jacqueline. 1980. "The History, Status and Concern of Women Planners." *Signs* 5 (Spring): S226-30.
Lemons, J. Stanley. 1973. *The Woman Citizen: Social Feminism in the 1920's*. Urbana: University of Illinois Press.
McManus, Susan A. 1981. "A City's First Female Officeholder: 'Coattails' for Future Female Officeholders." *Western Political Quarterly* 34 (March): 88-99.
Mezey, Susan Gluck. 1982. "Perceptions of Women's Rights on Local Councils in Connecticut." In *Women in Local Politics*, edited by Debra Stewart, pp. 177-97. Metuchen, N.J.: Scarecrow Press.
_____. 1978. "Support for Women's Rights Policy: An Analysis of Local Politicians." *American Politics Quarterly* 6 (October): 485-97.
Mueller, Carol. 1983. "Social Movement Success and the Success of Social Movements." Working Paper 710. Wellesley: Center for Research on Women, Wellesley College.
Perlman, Janice. 1976. "Grassrooting the System." *Social Policy* 7 (September/October): 4-20.
Rosenberg, Rina. 1982. "Representing Women at the State and Local Levels: Commissions on the Status of Women." In *Women, Power and Policy*, edited by Ellen Boneparth, pp. 38-46. New York: Pergamon.
Schechter, Susan. 1982. *Women and Male Violence*. Boston: South End Press.
Schwingl, Pamela J. et al. 1980. "The First Two Years: A Profile of Women Entering Women, Inc." In *Alternative Social Services for Women*, edited by Naomi Gottlieb, pp. 131-57. New York: Columbia University Press.
Stevens, Doris A. 1980. "Rape Victims." In *Alternative Social Services for Women*, edited by Naomi Gottlieb, pp. 235-54. New York: Columbia University Press.
Stewart, Debra. 1980. *The Women's Movement in Community Politics in the U.S.: The Role of Local Commissions on the Status of Women*. New York: Pergamon.
Tax, Meredith. 1980. *The Rising of the Women*. New York: Monthly Review Press.
Taylor, Stuart Jr. 1981. "Rape Crisis Centers Reduced." *New York Times*, August 31, p. B4.
Ware, Susan. 1981. *Beyond Suffrage in the New Deal*. Cambridge, Mass.: Harvard University Press.
Wekerle, Gerda, Rebecca Peterson, and David Morley, eds. 1980. *New Space for Women*. Boulder: Westview Press.
West, Guida. 1981. *The NWRO: The Social Protest of Poor Women*. New York: Praeger.
Zeigler, Edward and Edmund W. Gordon, eds. 1982. *Day Care: Scientific and Social Policy Issues*. Boston: Auburn House.

8

AN EXCHANGE APPROACH TO COMMUNITY POLITICS: A CASE STUDY OF WHITE ETHNIC ACTIVISM IN STATEN ISLAND, NEW YORK

Irene J. Dabrowski, Anthony L. Haynor, and Robert F. Cuervo

Those studying community politics have approached the topic from a variety of perspectives. Four of these are particularly important. One involves the analysis of power relationships within the city. Elitist (Hunter 1953), pluralist (Dahl 1963), neo-elitist (Bachrach and Baratz 1962; Crenson 1971; Hayes 1972), bureaucratic (Lowi 1964), and triangular (Lineberry and Sharkansky 1978, pp. 179-88) models have been presented. Others have addressed the question of service distribution by examining the shares allocated to various groups and classes within the city and the basis on which allocations are made (Lineberry 1977; Jones 1980). A second important area of concern is the decision-making process in urban politics. Rationalistic, incrementalist, and street-fighting pluralist approaches, for example, have been advanced (see Jones 1980; Yates 1976). The goal is to understand the process through which authoritative decisions are made by urban government. A third important area of concern involves the relationship between community organizations and their environment. Analysts here often employ a systems perspective (see Sharp 1981). Finally, a considerable literature has developed around the issue of collective action (see Hechter, Friedman, and Appelbaum 1982; Rich 1980; O'Brien 1975). Attention here is on the conditions under which individuals will participate in various urban interest groups, given rational choice assumptions, and the structure of incentives which can and do motivate people to participate in collective efforts aimed at achieving particular goals.

A MODEL OF COMMUNITY POLITICS

The purpose of this chapter is to present a conceptual model which is capable of integrating these four strands of the community politics literature and guiding research on community politics in a systematic and rigorous fashion. We argue that an exchange approach to community politics is best given its comprehensiveness, parsimony, and clarity. An exchange approach to community politics (see Bredemeier 1978; Haynor 1983; Curry and Wade 1968; Bredemeier and Stephenson 1962; Ilchman and Uphoff 1969; Salisbury 1970) begins with the identification of principal categories of actors. It then examines the goals or interests of these actors; the relationships between and among these goals and interests; the decisions made; the resources, strategies, and tactics employed; and the outcomes or products of interaction among actors.

Principal Categories of Actors in Urban Politics

Four types of actors can be identified: (1) elected and appointed government officials, who can be classified even more precisely on the basis of functional jurisdiction; (2) fiduciaries, who are interest group leaders in whom members have vested decision-making authority; (3) beneficiaries, who are interest group members benefiting from the activities of fiduciaries; and (4) spectators, who are neutral observers of an issue and who may or may not be affected by the outcome or resolution of the issue.[1]

Goals or Interests of Actors

Government officials occupy the status of leaders, by which is meant that they hold and exercise political authority. Thus, they legitimately make binding decisions for a collectivity. Interest group members have the status of followers, which means that they attempt to influence the decisions of political leaders (see Bredemeier and Stephenson 1962, p. 381). Politics in general, and community politics in particular, involves the struggle over authority. As Charles Lindblom (1977, p. 119) puts it, "In an untidy process called politics, people who want authority struggle to get it while others try to control those who hold it." In the urban political context, leaders make decisions regarding the allocation, distribution, and delivery of services such as police, transportation, sanitation, fire, energy, and housing (see Yates 1976, p. 241). It is the goal of leaders to process various interest group claims and make allocative decisions within the appropriate jurisdictional domain and in accordance with some decisional rule (based on demand, need, equality, efficiency, or some combination of these) that will receive sufficient public support (see Jones 1980, pp. 88-89; Lineberry and Sharkansky 1978, pp. 270-73). Followers, on the other hand, seek "distributive justice" (see Homans 1974, chapter 11), by which is meant a service allocation level which conforms to their expectations, not their wants, desires, or preferences. Expectations are based on hard-headed, realistic assessments as to the allocation level that is possible, given such constraints as scarce resources and the recognized need to contribute to system-wide goals. Support is withdrawn from those decisions which diverge from expectations. In short, leaders seek claims and support from followers; followers expect authoritative decisions and responsiveness from leaders. It is in this sense that leaders and followers attempt to successfully adapt to each other in what is an exchange relationship.

Relationships Among Goals and Interests

The urban political system is made up of a multiplicity of government officials and interest groups, each of whom seek particular goals. It is possible for actors to have (1) the same goals; (2) different yet potentially compatible goals; (3) divergent goals; or (4) unrelated goals (in which case each is a spectator vis-a-vis the other). In the first three cases, interests are interdependent; in the last case they are not (see Haynor 1983, pp. 66-70).

Decisions, Strategies, Tactics, and Resources

Dissatisfaction among leaders or followers with the exchange relationship does not necessarily result in organized action aimed at amelioration. A decision to act is based not only on perceived need but also on a belief that (1) the investments of time, energy, and resources are outweighed by the benefits that would result if the desired allocation level were to be achieved and (2) the action is strongly related to goal attainment (see Bredemeier 1978, pp. 428-29). Decisions can be made on a highly rationalistic basis whereby all options are carefully identified, consequences scrupulously delineated, and probabilities assigned. Alternatively, decision making may be highly reactive. Here there is little planning, calculation, or systematic thought in the decision process, given both the pressures of time and a perception that the environment is untrustworthy, chaotic, and unstructured (see Yates 1976, pp. 244-52). It is also possible to vest decision-making authority in someone else on the basis of expertise or in order to simplify the decision-making process.

Successful adaptation to the environment (meaning getting the environment to respond in a desired way) depends on available resources and their utilization in strategically effective ways. Actors can appeal to the sympathy or obligation of other actors; dangle "carrots" (especially electoral support, patronage) in front of others; or threaten others with various "sticks" (especially lawsuits, protests, withholding government funds) (see Etzioni 1975, pp. 3-100; Bredemeier 1978, pp. 438-42). Successful adaptation may also entail establishing alliances with others or seeking advocates or publicists for one's cause from among the ranks of spectators (especially the mass media) (see Curry and Wade 1968, pp. 41-47; Cobb and Elder 1972). Power, from an exchange perspective, is a function of having resources that others find valuable, that are in limited supply, and that are thus capable of eliciting desired responses from others. Power is not to be confused with bargaining power, which refers to getting something from another on good terms by adopting a stance of "least interest" (see Kuhn 1975, pp. 107-8; Bredemeier 1978, p. 423; Homans 1974, pp. 73-74).

Outcomes and Feedback Processes

If a given strategy elicits a desired response from another actor such that the goal is completely achieved, no further action is necessary. Failure, however, can trigger a number of responses: (1) a change in strategies for dealing with the frustrating environment; (2) a lowering of expectations; or (3) abandoning the relationship with the frustrating environment and seeking alternative relationships (see Bredemeier and Bredemeier 1978, pp. 214-22).

The urban polity, in summary, is best analyzed in terms of the transactions which take place between and within four categories of goal-directed, adaptation-seeking role-players: public officials, fiduciaries, beneficiaries, and spectators. An exchange model incorporates within it four important approaches to community politics found in the literature. "Power" is defined by the resources controlled by various actors and their consequent success in eliciting desired responses from others. "Decision making" is approached in terms of the strategies actors choose to achieve their goals and the mode of that choice (rationalistic or reactive). Both exchange and systems models have as an analytic concern the relationship between organizations and their environment and thus are in many respects compatible and parallel perspectives. Finally, the question of "collective action" can easily be incorporated within an exchange perspective. In exchange terms, the issues are (1) how fiduciaries (meaning leaders within civic organizations) attempt to adapt successfully to beneficiaries by procuring a desired level of support and resources; (2) how beneficiaries (meaning followers within civic organizations) attempt to adapt successfully to fiduciaries by procuring a desired level of responsiveness and results; and (3) how beneficiaries attempt to adapt successfully to other beneficiaries.

In the next section, the exchange model of community politics will be applied to white ethnic community activism. In the process, we hope to demonstrate the utility of the model as a coherent interpretative framework for empirical data.

EXCHANGE PROCESSES IN SELECTED WHITE ETHNIC COMMUNITIES

In the summer of 1984, ten prominent white ethnic community leaders living in the largely working-class New York City borough of Staten Island were interviewed at length about their political activities.[2] They were asked to discuss: (1) salient issues in their communities in recent years, particularly those in which civic associations played a major role; (2) the power of civic associations in the policy process and those tactics and strategies which were most effective; and (3) the role of leadership within civic associations. The interviewees (with the exception of one who has a borough-wide focus) live or work in the older, established, white ethnic neighborhoods of Staten Island and have established strong roots in their neighborhoods. Five of the leaders were past or present presidents of their civic associations; four were past or present community board members (including a district manager); one was the head of a prominent environmental protection group; one was actively involved in a transit workers' union; and one was an officer in a local development corporation.

Identification of Actors

The primary focus was on fiduciaries within white ethnic block and neighborhood associations, community planning boards, and local development corporations. Of central importance were the goals and interests of these leaders and their exchange or adaptive relationships with (1) government officials, both elective and appointive; (2) beneficiaries (meaning organization members or followers); (3) other fiduciaries (meaning other civic leaders, community planning board members, private sector representatives); and (4) spectators (meaning government officials, other fiduciaries, or potential beneficiaries who are at any given point indifferent to a particular issue).

Specification of Goals and Interests

A prominent exchange theorist has defined "adaptation" as follows:

> Adapting to an environment involves four processes: obtaining things from it, disposing of things to it, avoiding things that are in it, and retaining things inside the actor that might "escape." (Bredemeier 1978, p. 423).

Applied to the present context, community members (fiduciaries, beneficiaries, or both) can have obtaining, avoiding, retaining, or disposing goals or interests in relationship to their environment (consisting of other community members, other communities, government officials, or private sector elites).

In the first case, community members seek to receive or consume those valued things which environments can produce or are producing. In our study, examples included the 13-year effort of a civic association to obtain a new school; the effort of a local development corporation to obtain funds for economic development and home improvement; the successful attempt of a civic association to get funding for community beautification; the activities of a civic association in support of townhouse construction in a transitional area; and the efforts of various community groups and leaders to obtain for their neighborhoods increased police and sanitation services, as well as items like bus shelters and traffic lights.

In the second case involving avoidance, community members seek to prevent the imposition on their neighborhoods of things in the environment defined as "bads." The grass-roots activities which generate the most passion are those which respond to avoidance concerns.[3] A broad range of avoidance issues was mentioned by our respondents. First, the city approved a proposal by a private concern to place a coal export facility on Staten Island. Fearing adverse environmental impact, a number of civic associations (both inside white ethnic neighborhoods and outside) joined forces to eventually defeat the proposal. Second, a proposal put forward by the Power Authority of the State of New York (PASNY) to construct a power plant in a given community triggered strident local oppostion. Area residents feared further environmental deterioration in an already polluted locale. After an arduous six-year fight, the plan was defeated. A third issue was a city proposal to convert a shipping terminal to a bus garage. Residents vehemently opposed this project on the grounds that it would produce traffic bottlenecks and increase pollution. A fourth avoidance concern involved the siting of low-income housing in two communities. In one, a proposal to build a subsidized housing complex in a neighborhood in which a high-rise low-income project was already present, was withdrawn after a vigorous two-year community effort. In the other, a federally subsidized project was built despite a vehement four-year effort to prevent it. In each case, the arguments against building the project were that (1) high-rise housing was incompatible with the existing neighborhood housing stock; (2) the density of the project would place an undue burden on existing services; and (3) the project might attract an undesirable element. A fifth example was the effort of local residents, in partnership with a prominent local environmental organization, to demand stricter adherence to sewerage treatment regulations on the part of condominium developers. This same environmental group also had taken steps to prevent the Army Corps of Engineers from burying sludge too close to the shore line and the city from dumping raw sewerage into the harbor. Finally, one community group had attempted to alter plans for a senior citizen housing development in order to avoid what were believed to be negative features.

In pursuit of the third type of goal, involving retention, community members seek to hold on to valued things which are in their possession, and prevent their being taken away. Issues which involved the efforts of community members to "retain" something of value against external threats include the following: the mobilization of community members to prevent the closing of a local elementary school; the activities of a community in preventing the cancellation or modification of bus routes; and the activities of the environmental organization to preserve natural resources (for example acting to prevent large fishing boats from depleting the supply of certain kinds of fish in local waters, a practice which the group contends had adverse ecological consequences for the entire harbor, and seeking to preserve the wetlands as well as a large area of undeveloped forest land).

In the fourth case, involving disposal, community members seek to rid their neighborhoods of things defined as "bads" or transfer things to the environment. For example, the problem of noise pollution (caused by trucks, airplanes, and factories) was identified as a priority issue by one leader and mentioned by another. A second type of disposal issue was traffic congestion, brought about by the community's proximity to commercial establishments, a major highway, and a bridge connecting two boroughs, as well as overutilization of local streets by commercial vehicles. A third was the effort of a community group to address the negative spillover effects associated with the placement of court assigned youths in community-based group homes. The civic assocation sought to have input into site selection and monitoring. It also felt that the community was bearing a disproportionate burden in dealing with the problem; whereas this community contained four such homes, other communities had none. A fourth issue was the efforts of one community to dispose of an odor emanating from a city landfill. The community was able to get the city to place a ceiling on the quantity of garbage that will be buried in this landfill in the future. A fifth example involved the efforts of two civic leaders to effect changes in zoning ordinances so as to restrict and curtail the presence of certain kinds of commercial buildings in order to reduce congestion and improve the visual and aesthetic qualities of the largely residential neighborhood. During the past two-and-a-half years, community leaders have worked closely with the city planning commission and other government officials to help bring this about, and some progress has been made.

The Relationship Between Goals or Interests

Community members can have preferences or interests which are either identical to, complementary with, or divergent from those of government agencies or other community groups or members (but see Sharp 1981; Yates 1976, pp. 240-43). A community member has an identical interest to that of the environment to the extent that both seek either to obtain the same thing, dispose of the same thing, retain the same thing, or avoid the same thing. This condition can lead either to a competitive, systemic, or cooperative relationship. A competitive relationship is one which is perceived in zero-sum terms—that is, in terms of a struggle over the allocation of "goods" and "bads." A systemic relationship is characterized by the subordination of different interests to a utilitarian allocative standard of some kind. A cooperative relationship is one of direct partnership and alliance.

Community members or groups are in "potential" competition with each other over: (1) the placement of group homes, landfills, and low-income projects; and (2) allocations of various services (for example bus routes), capital budgets, and local development funds. We say "potential" because the competitive dimension tends to be downplayed by community leaders and members. For the most part, the community leaders we interviewed refused to cast their relationships with other community groups in "we-they" terms. Instead, they insisted that elementary utilitarian standards of fairness be applied and that services should be allocated on the basis of need. Some leaders believed that their neighborhoods were not being fairly treated. For example, the leader of the civic association involved in the group-home controversy argued that his neighborhood was absorbing a disproportionate share of the costs associated with group homes. A few leaders complained that their communities were not receiving an adequate level of sanitation and police services, particularly as compared to wealthier communities. On the other hand, other leaders were quite satisfied with their neighborhood's share of the pie. There were specific instances of cooperation as well. For example, the coalport and power plant issues involved considerable coalition-building efforts among a number of community groups.

A complementarity of interests occurs in the following circumstances: (1) when what a community group seeks to obtain, its environment seeks to dispose of; (2) when what a community group wants to avoid, its environment seeks to retain; (3) when what a community group seeks to dispose of, its environment seeks to obtain; and (4) when what a community group seeks to retain, its environment seeks to avoid. These situations reflect a relative absence of conflict—that is, an alignment of interests between community groups and their environments. One example from our data involved the efforts of a community group to limit the amount of garbage to be buried in a local landfill (an avoidance issue). The city in this case came to accept this general goal. The key question became: "At what level?" A bargaining process between the two parties ensued and it resulted in a workable agreement. In short, complementary relationships can involve either nonissues or negotiations, the resolution of which depends on the bargaining power of the respective participants.

Divergence or conflict occurs when what a community member or group desires and what its environment desires are clearly at cross-purposes. The following circumstances are conflictive: (1) when what a community group wants to retain, its environment seeks to obtain; (2) when what a community group seeks to dispose of, its environment seeks to avoid; (3) when what a community group seeks to avoid, its environment seeks to dispose of; and (4) when what a community group seeks to obtain, its environment seeks to retain. An example of the first kind of conflict is that between a community group which seeks to retain an elementary school or bus route and a city agency which seeks to take these services away; or that between a community group which seeks to retain natural resources and real estate developers who wish to use them for their own purposes. An example of the second type is that of a community group which attempts to dispose of noise, congestion, group homes, and landfill pollution to communities which seek to avoid those "things." Examples of the third type of conflict include relationships between a community group which seeks to avoid a coalport, a power plant, or low-income housing and an environment (a corporation, PASNY, and a developer, respectively) which desires to produce (or "dispose" of) those "things." An example of the fourth type of conflictive relationship is that between a community group which desires to obtain something (for example, a new school) and a government which for 13 years sought to withhold funds for that purpose. Rivals in conflictive relationships can see each other as enemies or as partners in a joint enterprise, who happen to have a serious difference of opinion.

There are two other situations which can lead to either a complementary or conflictive relationship, depending on the circumstances. First, there is the situation in which a community group wishes to avoid some thing and its environment (namely another community group) wishes to obtain that thing (or vice versa). This situation leads to conflict if the environment in question is another community group in the same neighborhood or immediate area but results in complementarity if the two groups are located in different neighborhoods. The same applies to another situation in which a community group seeks to retain a thing which another group seeks to dispose of (or vice versa). An example of intracommunity conflict was the issue of whether a Navy facility should be based in a Staten Island community. Some residents wanted to "avoid" it; others wanted to "obtain" it. The result was a conflictive relationship between these two camps. An example of complementarity did not present itself, although such an occurrence is empirically possible. One reason for this appears to be the existence of a consensus on Staten Island regarding what is desirable or undesirable. Therefore, what one community seeks to avoid, another does not desire to obtain; what one seeks to dispose of, another would not seek to obtain.

What the preceding discussion illustrates is the ineluctable interdependence of community groups with other actors in their environmental field (see Bredemeier and Bredemeier 1978, chapter 2). However, there are occasions when interdependence does not occur. The desires of one community group may be those to which other community groups are indifferent (for example, efforts to save the wetlands). What is sometimes described as selfishness, localism, and parochialism may in reality be a function of a lack of interdependence. The range of interdependence tends to vary directly with the scope (both spatial and functional) of the community group. Thus, the environmental organization whose interests extend even beyond the borough level is involved in a larger web of interdependence regarding environmental issues than a neighborhood civic association.

Decisions, Strategies, Resources, and Power

Another component of the exchange model is the strategies and tactics that community groups utilize to maximize their neighborhoods' stock of valued things and minimize their stock of costly things. Community groups have at their disposal resources that they can use to elicit desired responses from environments with whom they are interdependent or from spectators who present potential allies. Effective strategies reflect accurate perceptions of the environment's attitude toward the community group (see Parsons and Shils 1951, pp. 105-7). That is, if government agencies encourage community input, then persuasion might be appropriate and effective; if, on the other hand, government agencies insulate themselves from community groups, then more militant strategies might be appropriate.

For the most part, community groups try to influence government officials and agencies who are authorized to make binding decisions for the collectivity. Either the government is the direct protagonist, having embarked upon a policy defined as contrary to the community group's expectations (for example, the PASNY plant), or community groups "retreat to government" (Thurow 1980, pp. 15-16), requesting the latter to intercede on their behalf in disputes with other community groups or private sector entities (for example, real estate developers). Involved is the process of "agenda-building," through which a community interest becomes a genuine issue and is placed on the public docket as a priority concern (Cobb and Elder 1972). In addition, community groups might attempt to elicit desired responses directly from community groups with whom they are in conflict, or enlist the latter's assistance and support in demanding certain things from government agencies or officials. Finally, community groups might seek the support of selected government officials or entities in their disputes with other government officials or entities.

In their efforts to achieve "distributive justice," community groups can utilize three basic types of strategies. The first is to try to convince the frustrating environment that the policy decided upon was not sound, did not make sense, and should be altered. This strategy entails a reliance on expertise, persuasion, and knowledge. A few leaders believed that some government officials were capable of and willing to engage, at least occasionally, in a rational dialogue over issues. The second strategy is to bargain with other entities by offering them something that they value in exchange for their support for your claims. Several community leaders, for example, enlisted the support of government officials in their disputes with government agencies by offering the officials electoral support. Third, community groups can attempt to elicit desired responses from entities by imposing or threatening to impose costs on them (for example negative publicity, disruption of operations, public embarrassment). These costs can be imposed through protests at public hearings and town meetings or law suits. These strategies are considered by community leaders to be a critical part of the arsenal of community groups in their disputes with government agencies.

All of the civic leaders with whom we spoke believed that their associations had made a difference in preserving or upgrading the quality of life in their neighborhoods. However, they also recognized the considerable obstacles that they have to confront in their dealings with government agencies and officials. These include the limited accountability and inertia of many agencies (referred to by different leaders as "dictatorships," "corporations," and as entities which often make decisions before affected communities have had a chance to express their point of view) and the apathy and negligence of many government officials. Such obstacles make it more difficult for community groups to achieve their goals because considerable energy must be devoted to getting the attention of government officials.

The civic leaders believed that it is possible to overcome these obstacles if certain measures are taken to increase a community group's power vis-a-vis government agencies. First, there was overwhelming consensus as to the need for "numbers" and "bodies," particularly at an initial stage. This need was well expressed by one leader:

> To get the city's or any bureaucracy's attention, you must be perceived as worth giving attention to; and in the political sphere, most of the time what they will respond to are numbers, numbers of voters. I can say I speak for Travis and there are 500 families and 2000 people... It doesn't matter if they vote or not. The fact that you are communicating with those people on a regular basis means, "Hey, maybe we better listen to this guy." That's your foot in the door. If you come down to see a politician as Joe Blow private citizen, you will be treated cordially and dismissed.

Issues involving group homes, the coalport, the power plant, and low-income projects generated widespread community response. Issues such as these might be called beneficiary-initiated or beneficiary-based. They often trigger the formation of civic associations, the leaders of which come to serve in a fiduciary capacity. Beneficiary-initiated action not only increases the power of residents in relation to the triggering issue, but also increases their power on other issues as well. To the extent that fiduciaries are perceived to be representing the interests of a considerable number of residents (whether they are or not is irrelevant), the power of fiduciaries increases (see Lindblom 1977, pp. 24–25).

Several other issues (for example industrial zoning, dredging permits, wetlands preservation) can best be called fiduciary-initiated or fiduciary-based. Here there is a noticeable lack of mass interest, and fiduciaries assume primary responsibility. As one civic leader states:

> As a civic leader, I'm always questioning myself. Who am I speaking for? Is this what the people want? Or is it for Tony?

An instructive typology is generated when the adaptation dimension is cross-classified with the initiation dimension. Avoidance, retention, obtaining, and disposal issues can be subdivided in terms of the mode of initiation involved.[4] (See Table 8.1.)

We found that organizations that emerged from issues that were beneficiary-based tended to become, over time, fiduciary based.[5] The main reason is that residents who were originally active eventually either (1) lose interest in the organization when the issue that triggered their involvement is resolved or partially addressed[6]; (2) become impatient and disenchanted when results are not immediately forthcoming; or (3) act as "free riders," believing

TABLE 8.1. A Typology of Grass-Roots Activities

Type of Adaptation	Mode of Initiation	
	Beneficiary	*Fiduciary*
Disposing	Noise pollution Traffic congestion Group homes Landfill pollution	Industry (Zoning)
Avoiding	Coalport Power plant Pouch terminal Low-income projects Condominium sewerage Senior housing	Sludge dumping Raw sewerage dumping Dumping of toxic materials
Retaining	Elementary school Bus routes	Wetlands Greenbelt
Obtaining	New school	Economic development Jobs Home improvement Beautification Townhouses

Source: Compiled by the authors.

it to be rational not to contribute time and energy to an activity that, if successful, will benefit them regardless of their participation and to whose success their contribution is felt to be negligible (see Olson 1971; Rich 1980; Hechter, Friedman and Appelbaum 1982).

What is needed, according to the leaders interviewed, is enough popular or mass participation so that government officials perceive community activists both as fiduciaries and as a small band of dedicated people who are willing to put a considerable amount of time and energy into securing the association's goals. This leadership nucleus must exhibit various qualities. First, leaders must be prepared for the long haul. A successful community movement requires great patience, perseverance, and pacing in order to avoid premature burn-out. Second, the civic leaders stressed that in order to establish credibility, which is critical to success, it is necessary to be very well informed, to be prepared to give logical and rational reasons for the group's goals, and to be ready with acceptable alternatives. One civic leader put it this way:

> What we didn't want to do is put any facts or statements together that were ours. We wanted to use theirs or what somebody else said. This established credibility. We did a lot of research. Many hours we put into this; and we found that they (politicians) were not educated on the issues. It became very easy for us to paint them into a corner.

Third, fiduciaries must be persistent in their challenge; they must keep on the "backs," so to speak, of government officials by immediately challenging what are thought to be fallacious statements. Fourth, political neutrality was considered to be important. Several leaders charged that many organizations lost effectiveness when community leaders became part of the formal political apparatus and thus were coopted. Fifth, leaders must be able to build bridges to other residents and other communities. It is important to communicate with residents on their own terms, including, if necessary, on very simplistic terms. Explanations should be accessible, nontechnical, and graphic in nature and general enough to make the issue relevant to the lives of various segments of the community and to other communities (see Cobb and Elder 1972, chapter 7). In addition, community support can be gained by the force of the leader's personality. One leader spoke of the need to balance the "intellectual" and "expressive" dimensions of leadership:

> I like to think I'm a rational person, a little more intellectual than a lot of my neighbors. On the other side of the spectrum, if you have strictly a person who is an egghead or intellectual who will do nothing but cite chapter and verse, he will be very ineffective. Any kind of leader must have some kind of charisma to be able to relate to people.

Outcomes and Feedback Processes

Reactions to maladaptation can range from moving out of the neighborhood, changing strategies toward the frustrating entity, or taking one's case to another entity. The leaders with whom we spoke were strongly committed to their neighborhoods and had no intention of ever leaving; exit was not an option (see Hirschman 1970; Lineberry and Sharkansky 1978, pp. 99-101). The comments of one leader are representative:

> The reason I remain (involved in community politics) is greed, not in a pecuniary sense. I have made a decision that Travis is going to be my home. I was born there and I intend to stay there. It's certainly not a fancy neighborhood... All is not roses in Travis. It is roots....

The other two reactions (changing strategies, taking one's case elsewhere) were much in evidence.

CONCLUSION

In this chapter an exchange model of community politics was presented and then applied to the activities of selected white ethnic community groups. Several dimensions appropriate for analyzing politics in any community context were identified: (1) the roster of actors involved; (2) the kinds of goals and interests that the actors pursue; (3) the relationships between the goals and interests of various actors; (4) the decisions, strategies, resources, and power of different actors; and (5) reactions to maladaptation. In this section, several conclusions drawn from our interviews of white ethnic community leaders are linked wherever possible to existing theories and studies in the field. Because of the selection process used here and the limited number of interviews conducted, these conclusions should be viewed as hypotheses requiring much more systematic testing.

It is clear, however, that white ethnic neighborhoods are not monolithic; different neighborhoods have different adaptive problems. There are, at a minimum, two distinct types of white ethnic communities: (1) neighborhoods which have experienced a decline in recent years in the quality of life; and (2) neighborhoods which have enjoyed considerable stability (see Perlman 1979, pp. 46-47, 50-51). The former constitute fertile ground for revitalization movements in which both block associations and local development corporations are significant participants (see Wilson 1984; Schoenberg and Rosenbaum 1980; Dabrowski 1983). Such neighborhoods attempt primarily to obtain additional services, while seeking to retain what they already have, dispose of present "bads," and avoid additional "bads." The latter type of neighborhood seeks to preserve a quality of life with which it is essentially satisfied. The priority of such neighborhoods is to avoid threats to that quality of life, while seeking to dispose of present "bads," to obtain additional "goods," and retain present "goods." One could locate each type of neighborhood in a Maslowian hierarchy of needs. Declining neighborhoods are primarily concerned with lower-order needs (for example fire, sanitation, and police services, and economic prosperity); stable neighborhoods shift attention to such higher-order needs as clean air and visual aesthetics (see Thurow 1980, p. 105). This might explain the potency of environmental issues, particularly in stable neighborhoods. As declining neighborhoods are revitalized, one might expect a greater sensitivity to environmental issues.

In addition, neighborhoods in decline appear more likely than stable neighborhoods to have community groups involved in "coproduction," that is, the assumption of responsibility for service delivery (see Sharp 1981, p. 416; Gittell 1980; Rosenbloom 1979; Yates 1973, chapter 4; Perlman 1979, pp. 49-50). In our study, this took the form of local development corporations, which bid on government contracts and are responsible for dispensing funds for economic development, home improvement, and summer jobs for youths. "Coproduction" does not appear to be a major item on the agenda of community residents in stable white ethnic neighborhoods. Community groups in such neighborhoods are more interested in honest government and are content to leave responsibility for service delivery in government hands.

Finally, in both stable and declining white ethnic neighborhoods, three features were particularly conspicuous. The first was the reactive nature of community activism. For example, community groups in both types of neighborhoods played only a nominal role in the budgetary and policy formulation process. Community groups, for the most part, responded to policy decisions after they had been made by governmental officials.[7] This is probably due to personnel or time restraints, an overly passive orientation to the policy process, and the ability of government officials to keep items off the agenda until they are a *fait accompli.*

Second, within the context of this limited role and limited resources, we found white ethnic community groups to be quite effective.[8] This is primarily attributed to the effectiveness and zeal of community fiduciaries. Mass participation is, at best, highly sporadic because of the lack of private incentives and the free rider problem. We found a leadership core with considerable political savvy. It consisted of remarkable individuals intensely committed to their neighborhood's welfare. Each will always prefer "voice" to "exit."[9]

Third, fiduciaries did not define their activities in relation to a "white ethnic" cause (but see Horowitz 1972; Bell 1975; Ryan 1973; Weed 1973; Wenk, Tomasi, and Baroni 1977). In general, the leaders view the issues with which they are concerned as primarily "neighborhood" and not narrowly "ethnic" problems (see Rosenbloom 1979, pp. 106-8). Ethnicity is a powerful source of pride and identity for many community leaders and residents in these white ethnic neighborhoods. It is on some level associated with a way of life (for example family-centeredness, close-knit relationships between neighbors, stability, a small-town atmosphere) that they wish preserved or regained. However "ethnic purity" (understandable in terms of the goal of "avoiding" certain ethnic groups) does not appear to be an overriding goal of civic action.

In conclusion, we believe that an exchange perspective generates the right questions to be examined. It is hoped that its potential usefulness in analyzing community politics has been demonstrated here. Even so, much further research is needed to explain observed differences in terms of the five dimensions, both within white ethnic communities and between white ethnic and other kinds of neighborhoods.

NOTES

1. This typology of actors is based on the classification presented in Curry and Wade (Robert L. Curry and L.L. Wade, *A Theory of Political Exchange* [Englewood Cliffs: Prentice-Hall, 1968], pp. 39-49. We prefer the category, "government officials," to Curry and Wade's category, "politician," because we think it is important to distinguish between political officials who are elected (politicians) and those who are civil service bureaucrats.

2. A list of white ethnic community leaders was furnished by the news editor of a local paper that specializes in covering grass-roots activism on Staten Island.

3. Our interview data suggested that avoidance issues dominate community politics. This was substantiated in a content analysis of the 1983 and 1984 "Year in Review" editions of a local newspaper. Of those local issues attracting active community involvement, 45 percent reflected avoidance concerns. The remainder were divided fairly equally among the other three categories.

4. One other type of initiation has been omitted: those activities undertaken by individual citizens. Our concern here is restricted to the activities of white ethnic community groups.

5. The opposite situation can also occur. An issue that was formerly fiduciary-initiated can begin to generate increasing mass concern. For example, the leader of the environmental group observed a heightened level of interest and awareness in recent years with respect to environmental issues.

6. An excellent example of this was recounted by a community leader actively involved in mass transit on Staten Island. According to his account, four or five years ago both mass and individual protest were directed against inadequate bus service to Manhattan. The public transit authority withheld such service, opening the way for private bus companies to provide this service. This leader argued that the transit authority's decision to withhold a profitable service was the result of a political deal. Furthermore, it should be fought because it was costing the taxpayers a considerable amount of money. But public opposition lessened considerably and responsibility for this cause fell squarely on the civic leader and other fiduciaries.

7. This reactive quality of community activism is consistent with the notion of "street-fighting pluralism" advanced by Yates (Douglas Yates, "Urban Government as a Policy-Making System," in *The New Urban Politics,* eds. Louis Masotti and Robert Lineberry [Cambridge, Mass.: Ballinger, 1976], pp. 235-64). Block associations become active during crisis situations and lie dormant during other periods. This implies a cyclical model rather than the growth-decay models advanced earlier by Yates (Douglas Yates, *Neighborhood Democracy.* [Lexington: D.C. Heath, 1973], pp. 35-39).

8. Both Gittell and Yates argue that groups without formal decision-making authority may be more effective than groups with such authority, owing to the former's independence and spontaneity (Marilyn Gittell, *Limits to Citizen Participation: The Decline of Community Organizations* [Beverly Hills: Sage, 1980]; Douglas Yates, *Neighborhood Democracy*). Lineberry and Sharkansky, as well as Perlman, note that effectiveness is enhanced when community groups organize around specific and perceptible threats (Robert L. Lineberry and Ira Sharkansky, *Urban Politics and Public Policy* [New York: Harper and Row, 1978], p. 111; Janice Perlman, "Neighborhood Research: A Proposed Methodology," *South Atlantic Urban Studies* 4[1979]: 49).

9. Rosenbloom, as well as Lineberry and Sharkansky, argue that blue-collar, lower middle-class neighborhood groups are more active and effective than the poor (who are difficult to mobilize) or the affluent (who can "exit"); Dabrowski, in addition, has analyzed the emerging role of women in the leadership core of working-class community groups (Richard Rosenbloom, "The Politics of the Neighborhood Movement," *South Atlantic Urban Studies* 4[1979]: 104; Lineberry and Sharkansky, *Urban Politics*, p. 111; Irene Dabrowski, "Working Class Women and Civic Action: A Case Study of an Innovative Community Role," *Policy Studies Journal* 11[March 1983]: 427-35).

REFERENCES

Bachrach, Peter C. and Morton S. Baratz. 1962. "The Two Faces of Power" *American Political Science Review* 56 (December): 947-52.

Bell, Daniel. 1975. "Ethnicity and Social Change." In *Ethnicity*, edited by Nathan Glazer and Daniel P. Moynihan, pp. 141-74. Cambridge, Mass.: Harvard University Press.

Bredemeier, Harry C. 1978. "Exchange Theory." In *A History of Sociological Analysis*, edited by Tom Bottomore and Robert Nisbet, pp. 418-56. New York: Basic.

———— and Richard M. Stephenson. 1962. *The Analysis of Social Systems*. New York: Holt, Rinehart and Winston.

Bredemeier, Mary E. and Harry C. Bredemeier. 1978. *Social Forces in Education*. Sherman Oaks, Cal.: Alfred Publishing.

Cobb, Rober W. and Charles D. Elder. 1972. *Participation in American Politics: The Dynamics of Agenda-Building*. Boston: Allyn and Bacon.

Crenson, Matthew. 1971. *The Unpolitics of Air Pollution: A Study of Non-Decision Making in the Cities*. Baltimore: Johns Hopkins University Press.

Curry, Robert L. and L.L. Wade. 1968. *A Theory of Political Exchange*. Englewood Cliffs: Prentice-Hall.

Dabrowski, Irene. 1983. "Working Class Women and Civic Action: A Case Study of an Innovative Community Role." *Policy Studies Journal* 11 (March): 427-35.

Dahl, Robert. 1963. *Who Governs? Democracy and Power in an American City*. New Haven: Yale University Press.

Etzioni, Amitai. 1975. *A Comparative Analysis of Complex Organizations*. New York: Free Press.

Gittell, Marilyn. 1980. *Limits to Citizen Participation: The Decline of Community Organizations*. Beverly Hills: Sage.

Hayes, Edward C. 1972. *Power Structure and Urban Policy: Who Rules in Oakland?* New York: McGraw-Hill.
Haynor, Anthony L. 1983. "A Systems Approach to Personality and Social Structures with an Application to Selected Writings on Modernity." Ph.D. dissertation, Rutgers University.
Hechter, Michael, Debra Friedman, and Malka Appelbaum. 1982. "Theory of Ethnic Collective Action." *International Migration Review* 16 (Summer): 412-34.
Hirschman, Albert. 1970. *Exit, Voice, and Loyalty.* Cambridge, Mass.: Harvard University Press.
Homans, George. 1974. *Social Behavior: Its Elementary Forms.* New York: Harcourt, Brace, Jovanovich.
Horowitz, Irving. 1972. "Race, Class, and Ethnicity." In *Foundations of Political Sociology,* edited by Irving Horowitz, pp. 535-38. New York: Harper and Row.
Hunter, Floyd. 1953. *Community Power Structure.* Chapel Hill: University of North Carolina Press.
Ilchman, Warren F. and Norman T. Uphoff. 1969. *The Political Economy of Change.* Berkeley: University of California Press.
Jones, Bryan D. 1980. *Service Delivery in the City.* New York: Longman.
Kuhn, Alfred. 1975. *Unified Social Science.* Homewood: Dorsey.
Lindblom, Charles. 1977. *Politics and Markets.* New York: Basic.
Lineberry, Robert L. 1977. *Equality and Urban Policy.* Beverly Hills: Sage.
_____ and Ira Sharkansky. 1978. *Urban Politics and Public Policy.* 2nd ed. New York: Harper and Row.
Lowi, Theodore. 1964. *At the Pleasure of the Mayor.* New York: Free Press.
O'Brien, David. 1975. *Neighborhood Organizations and Interest Group Processes.* Princeton: Princeton University Press.
Olson, Mancur. 1971. *The Logic of Collective Action.* Cambridge, Mass.: Harvard University Press.
Parsons, Talcott and Edward Shils. 1951. *Toward a General Theory of Action.* Cambridge, Mass.: Harvard University Press.
Perlman, Janice. 1979. "Neighborhood Research: A Proposed Methodology." *South Atlantic Urban Studies* 4:43-63.
Rich, Robert C. 1980. "Political Economy Approach to the Study of Neighborhood Organization." *American Journal of Political Science* 24 (November): 559-92.
Rosenbloom, Richard. 1979. "The Politics of the Neighborhood Movement." *South Atlantic Urban Studies* 4:103-20.
Ryan, Joseph. 1973. *White Ethnics.* Englewood Cliffs: Prentice-Hall.
Salisbury, Robert H. 1970. "An Exchange Theory of Interest Groups." In *Interest Group Politics in America,* edited by Robert H. Salisbury, pp. 32-67. New York: Harper and Row.
Schoenberg, Sandra Perlman and Patricia Rosenbaum. 1980. *Neighborhoods That Work.* New Brunswick: Rutgers University Press.
Sharp, Elaine B. 1981. "Organizations, Their Environments, and Goal Definition: An Approach to the Study of Neighborhood Associations in Urban Politics." *Urban Life* 9 (January): 415-40.
Thurow, Lester. 1980. *The Zero Sum Society.* New York: Basic.

Weed, Perry. 1973. *The White Ethnic Movement and Ethnic Politics.* New York: Praeger.

Wenk, Michael, S.M. Tomasi, and Gino Baroni, eds. 1977. *Pieces of a Dream.* New York:
Center for Migration Studies.

Wilson, Cicero. 1984. *Neighborhood Revitalization Project: Summary of Findings.* Washington, D.C.: American Enterprise Institute.

Yates, Douglas. 1976. "Urban Government as a Policy-Making System." In *The New Urban Politics,* edited by Louis Masotti and Robert Lineberry, pp. 235–64. Cambridge, Mass.: Ballinger.

——. 1973. *Neighborhood Democracy.* Lexington: D.C. Heath.

PART IV
EQUALITY OF ACCESS

9

HOUSING ASSISTANCE PROGRAMS FOR AMERICA'S URBAN POOR: AN ANALYSIS OF POLITICAL CHOICES VERSUS SOCIAL REALITY

Byran O. Jackson

The report of the National Advisory Commission on Civil Disorders concluded that the United States was moving toward two societies, "one Black, one White—separate and unequal" (U.S. National Advisory Commission on Civil Disorders 1968, p.1). Today, after the launching of a number of antipoverty programs for the poor and the adoption of civil rights legislation, great social inequities remain in U.S. society. The "underhoused" as well as the homeless in U.S. cities painfully illustrate this reality. Housing stands at the center of social inequality in this country. As Anton and Williams point out, housing is the core mediator of access to a wide variety of social values available in urban areas.

> Depending on where it is located, a house or an apartment may carry with it more or fewer public services, better or worse schools, more or less access to commercial activities, more or less interaction with people who are prized or people who are shunned (Anton and Williams 1971, p. 1).

Unfortunately, the plight of the poor in terms of their access to a decent, safe, and sanitary living environment has not changed over the years despite government intervention. This chapter explores the federal government's role in providing housing assistance for the poor. Three major questions are addressed: What has been the rationale for federal intervention in housing? How has the government intervened on behalf of the poor? And, what difference has government intervention made?

FEDERALLY ASSISTED HOUSING FOR THE URBAN POOR

Housing assistance was among the first areas addressed by federal social welfare policy. Beginning with the low-income public housing program established by the Housing Act of 1937, an assortment of housing and urban development programs have been enacted to provide decent housing for low and moderate income families. The Housing Act of 1949, passed during the administration of Harry Truman, set as a national goal "a decent home and suitable living environment for every American family." This goal was reaffirmed in the Housing Act of 1968 when the federal government committed itself to the construction or rehabilitation of 26 million housing units within a ten-year period.

Although there are now a variety of federal housing programs for low- and moderate-income families, prior to the administration of Lyndon Johnson, low rent public housing was the only major program. Public housing is constructed and operated by local Public Housing Authorities (PHAs). These are governmental authorities that are usually independent of city government. The federal government is responsible for the construction costs of public housing units and shares the operating cost of public housing with the local PHA (see Struyk 1980, pp.3-20).

Johnson's Housing Assistance Policy Initiatives

The substantive provisions found in the Housing Act of 1968 grew out of two major studies: the President's Committee on Urban Housing (the Kaiser Committee) and the National Commission on Urban Problems (the Douglas Commission). The estimates of housing need and the level of government assistance to accommodate those needs were taken directly from the Kaiser Committee Report. The Kaiser Committee set out to answer several major questions: How many American families are too poor to afford the market rate price for adequate housing? How many existing homes are unfit for occupancy given the nation's standard of living? How many homes must be built to meet the growing needs of the total population? (U.S. President's Committee on Urban Housing 1968, p.39).

The committee showed concern for the general condition of the nation's housing stock. Housing needs in terms of quality, affordability, and the changing rate of household formation were the principal areas of concern. At the time the committee began its work, massive population shifts had taken place. By 1960, 73 percent of the nation's black population resided in urban areas, compared to 20 percent in 1910. The location of the white population had also undergone change. The white urban growth rate showed a slight decline between 1950 and 1960, from a 7 percent increase to a 6 percent increase. By 1970 this had slowed to only 2 percent.

The committee concluded that "our nation must build 26 million houses and apartments in the next decade to provide for all the new households forming, to allow enough vacancies for our increasingly mobile population, to replace houses destroyed or demolished, and to eliminate all substandard housing"

(U.S. President's Committee on Urban Housing 1968, p.42). The committee also concluded that massive government assistance was essential not only to enable these families to afford adequate quarters, but also to make feasible the production target of 26 million units. They estimated that 6 to 8 million families would need housing assistance by 1978.

To accommodate these needs, the Housing Act of 1937 was amended to include two major subsidy programs: section 235, which provided assistance to low- and moderate-income families for homeownership, and section 236, which provided assistance to low-income families for rental assistance. Taken together, the low rent public housing program (1937), the rent supplement program (1965), the 235 program (1968) and the 236 program (1968) formed the core of the Great Society's approach to providing housing assistance to low-income families.

Review and Critique of the Johnson Policy Initiatives

A number of important political questions and policy issues surface in reference to Johnson's policy initiatives. For example, how accurate were the estimates of housing need? Were resources adequate to meet the public goals? How stable was the political support that placed low-income housing on the national policy agenda?

Estimating the quality of the U.S. housing stock has proven to be problematic. Estimates of substandard housing based on 1960 Census indicators (for example "dilapidated" or "lacking adequate plumbing facilities") yielded 9 million substandard units as of 1960. A special housing study commissioned by the Kaiser Committee concluded that 6.7 million substandard units, as well as 2 million deteriorated units, were still in the housing stock in 1967.

Even though some critics argue that the use of "lack of plumbing" as an indicator of substandard housing is too conservative in that the installation of plumbing is only one aspect of improved housing quality, researchers using both the Census Bureau's "lack of adequate plumbing" plus other indicators (for example leaky roofs, holes in walls and floors, adequate heat) have found a continuous improvement in the quality of the housing stock. Similarly, these observers have noted a steady increase in the proportion of income that low-income families devote to shelter. Thus, housing quality may not be the major problem confronting the average low-income urban dweller. The problem may be affordability.

Another criticism regarding the emphasis on housing quality relates to the absence of concurrent improvements in "residential services." Aaron has argued:

> Even if the goals were achieved, they would not directly affect the quality of residential services consumed with housing. The hope held out by the housing goal that both the "too little" and the "bad" housing problem can be

solved is certain to be frustrated because the improvement of residential services depends on other programs that have not been undertaken (Aaron 1972, p.42).

Another issue surrounding Johnson's policy initiatives is resource commitment. The Housing Act of 1968 called for 5 million newly constructed units and 1 million rehabilitated units over a ten-year period, an average of 600,000 subsidized units per year. The cost of such a program was estimated at $800-1000 per unit or 6 billion dollars annually (Schultze 1972, p.241). Yet, even without attempting to add 600,000 assisted housing units a year, federal housing assistance costs were 8 billion dollars in fiscal year 1984.

A final issue is the changing political climate. The Housing Act of 1968 was passed at a time when public concern about "poverty" was quite high. The program also had the enthusiastic support of not only the president but also organized labor, the home building industry, and social welfare groups. By 1973 public concern about poverty had declined tremendously. Richard Nixon was president and the political climate was quite different. The weaknesses in Johnson's housing policy initiatives set the stage for Nixon's housing policy reforms.

The Nixon-Ford Era

Housing assistance programs were included in President Nixon's 1973 spending moratorium. At the same time, the president commissioned an elaborate study of the Johnson administration's housing assistance programs (U.S. Department of Housing and Urban Development 1973). Earlier, Congress had enacted the Housing and Urban Development Act of 1970, which authorized a multimillion dollar project to test the feasibility of housing allowances as a policy alternative to the Johnson programs.

Three major topics were covered in the 1973 housing study: (1) the current involvement of the federal government in housing and housing finance; (2) the appropriate role of the government in housing and housing finance; and (3) the changes in policy and programs necessary to achieve the latter (U.S. Department of Housing and Urban Development 1973, p.3). The study based its evaluation of current housing assistance programs on three criteria: equity, impact, and efficiency. The study concluded that the subsidized programs enacted in 1968 were inequitable in the following ways: comparable subsidy benefits were not being provided for all those with comparable problems; many moderate-income families benefited while most lower-income families did not; and millions of people with incomes only slightly above those of program beneficiaries lived in units older and in poorer condition than those subsidized with their tax dollars (U.S. Department of Housing and Urban Development 1973, pp.86-138).

The Nixon suspension of housing assistance was not taken lightly in Congress, as demonstrated in a congressional report that critically evaluated his claims. According to Senator John Sparkman (D.-Ala.), the chairman of the Subcommittee on Housing and Urban Affairs at the time:

> On the basis of a 215 page Congressional Research analysis, I must report that the "mounting evidence" of program failure alleged by HUD officials, turns out to be more theory than fact. Its conclusions rest, like a house of cards, on an unsteady foundation. The document which we have received is not an adequate evaluation of federal housing programs. Nor can it be considered an adequate base for formulating national housing policy. It does not contain justification for the past year's suspension of homeownership and rental housing programs to assist low- and moderate-income families, elderly families, rural families, or families dependent on low-rent public housing for decent shelter (U.S. Senate 1974, pp.v–xi).

Despite this congressional concern, the low-income housing assistance programs were overhauled with the passage of the Community Development Block Grant Act of 1974 during the Gerald Ford administration. Section 8 amended the Housing Act of 1937 to provide housing assistance to low-income families in three forms: use of the existing stock (section 8 existing), new construction (section 8 new construction) and substantial rehabilitation (section 8 substantial rehabilitation).

Section 8 Existing. This program subsidizes rents in housing chosen by participating households selected by local public housing authorities. Under the program's income standards, all households with incomes up to approximately 80 percent of median family income in the local area (with adjustments for family size) are eligible for assistance.

Section 8 New Construction/Substantial Rehabilitation. This program subsidizes the rents in apartments built or renovated by developers. The developers may be private or public and the projects may be privately financed or publicly financed through state or local housing agencies. The apartments are leased to households chosen by the landlord. Under the program's income standards, all households with incomes up to approximately 80 percent of median family income in the local areas are eligible. In each apartment project, HUD requires the landlord to choose at least 30 percent of the initial tenants from households with "very low incomes," defined as incomes below 50 percent of median income in the area.

In addition, to the three subsidy programs provided under section 8, the 1974 Community Development Block Grant (CDBG) program also called for local communities to develop housing assistance plans.

Review and Critique of the Nixon-Ford Policy Initiatives

The Nixon-Ford reforms of Johnson's housing programs came at a time when public criticisms of the War on Poverty were high. Congressional hearings were held on landlord and homeowner defaults and abandonments in the Section 236 and Section 235 programs. In addition, the Nixon administration had also begun a set of housing allowance experiments in 1970. In theory at least, housing allowances addressed most of the shortcomings of the Johnson policies and thus received enthusiastic support from some housing policy analysts (for example de Leeuw 1971). Housing allowances were particularly attractive in that: (1) they rely heavily on existing stock; (2) they allow certificate holders freedom of choice in terms of neighborhood; and (3) they cost less than programs utilizing newly constructed units.

The attractiveness of the program, public concern about welfare reform, and President Nixon's own agenda on welfare reform made housing allowances a "politically acceptable" policy alternative in 1974. However, little empirical evidence had been gathered on the effectiveness of housing vouchers at the time the program was adopted. Results from the Experimental Housing Allowance program had only just begun to trickle in at the time the Section 8 program was adopted. Many questions were still unanswered. Among these were: (1) Would the housing allowance generate low-income residential mobility to better neighborhoods? (2) Would housing allowances create price inflation in the housing market? (3) Would housing allowances bring about improvements in housing quality?

Carter's Urban Reform Package

Both the political and economic climates had again changed by the time Jimmy Carter was inaugurated. High inflation and unemployment were the major issues that dominated the political agenda. There was also a general decline in trust of government, as well as a decline in the public's perception of government's ability to solve social problems.

The Carter administration's approach to urban reform was much more comprehensive than those of his predecessors. Attention was focused on developing a broad urban policy. Furthermore, emphasis was placed on targeting aid to distressed urban centers, as opposed to the use of the "entitlement concept" begun under the Nixon administration. The Urban Development Action Grant program, enacted in 1977, and the 1974 Community Development Block Grant program were used extensively. Twice as many Section 8 new and rehabilitated units were subsidized under the Carter administration as during the administrations of either Gerald Ford or Ronald Reagan.

The costs associated with these units as well as the inequities (defined here in terms of the number of eligible people actually served) resurfaced as political issues. Implicit in the Carter approach was the use of housing assistance through new construction as a means of providing aid to the general economies of distressed urban areas.

The Reagan Administration's Commission on Housing

The report of the President's Commission on Housing, appointed by the Reagan administration, viewed affordability as the number one housing problem facing low-income families. The commission approached its task with the belief that

> the genius of the market economy, freed of the distortions forced by government housing policies and regulations that swing erratically from loving to hostile, can provide for housing far better than federal programs. (U.S. President's Commission on Housing 1982, p.xvii).

The commission, as in the case of the Kaiser Committee, devoted considerable attention to the problem of low-income housing. After reviewing data on the housing conditions of the poor in terms of housing quality, affordability, and crowding, the commission concluded:

> The nature of housing problems in the 1980s suggests that a fundamental redirection of subsidized housing is in order. The Commission proposes a consumer-oriented Housing Payments Program as the preferred alternative to production programs. Such a program directly addresses the housing affordability problems of lower-income persons by providing a subsidy to help pay monthly housing costs. With their housing payment, lower-income households are free to occupy any unit that meets the minimum standards for housing set by the program (U.S. President's Commission on Housing 1982, p.17).

In addition, the commission also recommended restructuring the Community Development Block Grant program to assist local areas still suffering from a supply problem. Proposed changes included the addition of new construction as an eligible activity under CDBG and the addition of a housing component to the CDBG program as a replacement for previous categorical programs. The commission believed that with these changes, state and local programs could be more flexible and responsive "than Federal housing production programs" (U.S. President's Commission on Housing 1982, p.28).

In reviewing the recommendations by the commission, it is clear from the outset that its work was guided by a clear philosophy: direct government intervention in the housing market through tools such as production-oriented subsidies, rent control, and zoning were inefficient and should be avoided. Another theme that emerged was that local governments are better at addressing local housing needs than the national government and thus should be accorded this responsibility. These guiding principles aid in understanding those problems the commission chose to emphasize as well as those they deemphasized. The commission viewed affordability as the major low-income housing problem, rather than crowding or housing quality. Neighborhood quality was not discussed at all. Instead, a critique of Great Society production-oriented subsidies, results from the Experimental Housing Allowance program, and data from the Annual Housing Survey were used to justify the commission's position and recommendations.

There are a number of substantive criticisms that can be raised against the commission's recommendations. First, there is insufficient evidence that the low-income housing problem is mainly one of affordability and that emphasis on housing assistance payments will solve this problem. Second, the commission mentioned two major factors restricting the supply of low-cost rental housing: residential zoning and building codes. Many communities are able to prevent the construction of rental units through zoning ordinances. Building codes raise the cost of housing production. But in both cases, the commission failed to make substantive recommendations for change. Another weakness found in the commission's recommendations involves equity. The commission failed to view the housing assistance program as an entitlement program comparable to the tax deduction on interest payments afforded homeowners. As in the case of housing studies conducted during the Johnson and Nixon administrations, the commission was constrained by a political environment that made some ideas and choices more "politically marketable" than others.

MEASURING CHANGES IN HOUSING ASSISTANCE PROGRAMS

So far, this analysis has focused on the programmatic choices made by each administration since Johnson in the area of housing assistance and the rationale for those choices. In this section, I examine two sets of policy outputs stemming from the adoption of the various programs under review. First is a measure of the volume of federal housing assistance offered to the poor in a given year. This is operationalized by summing the total number of unit reservations made for each assistance program by year. Unit reservations are the number of newly constructed units or existing units that are recommended for addition to the total assisted housing stock in a given fiscal year. They represent the level of commitment in a given fiscal year to housing assistance for the poor. Another measure of output includes unit starts and completions. Unit starts show construction activity in a given fiscal year for assisted units that were previously reserved. Unit completions show the number of reserved units actually completed in a given fiscal year. Therefore, the number of unit reservations represents magnitude of outputs; starts reflect the implementation of program choices; and completions represent outcomes.

Unit reservations will be used here to measure the level of assistance allocated each fiscal year by presidential administrations beginning with Johnson. By summing the unit reservations for each low-income housing

HOUSING ASSISTANCE PROGRAMS / 139

assistance program for each fiscal year since 1965, it is possible to trace the growth of total assisted unit reservations under each administration.

As shown in Figure 9.1, in 1965, 100,000 assisted units were reserved under the Johnson administration. The Low Rent Public Housing program and the Rent Supplement programs were the major programs in effect between 1965 and 1968. The rapid acceleration in unit reservations between 1968 and 1973 reflects the Johnson administration's commitment to add 6 million assisted housing units to the housing stock in a ten-year period. President Nixon maintained this commitment during this first three years in office.

A rapid decline in unit reservations followed President Nixon's 1973 moratorium on assisted housing programs. At the time of the moratorium, the following assisted housing programs were in effect: Low Rent Public Housing, Rent Supplements, Section 235, and Section 236.

The rise in assisted unit reservations came with the adoption of the 1974 Community Development Block Grant program. The section 8 program under this act accounted for 56 percent of the assisted unit reservations in 1976. In 1977, President Carter increased the total number of unit reservations by almost four times the 1965 level; however, due to the 1979 recession and other problems that led President Carter to adopt a more fiscally conservative posture during the latter portion of his administration, total assisted unit reservations declined sharply.

Figure 9.2 classifies unit reservations by type: newly constructed units, existing stock, and the combined total of both approaches. As shown, Presidents

FIGURE 9.1. Total Units Reserved, by Presidential Administration

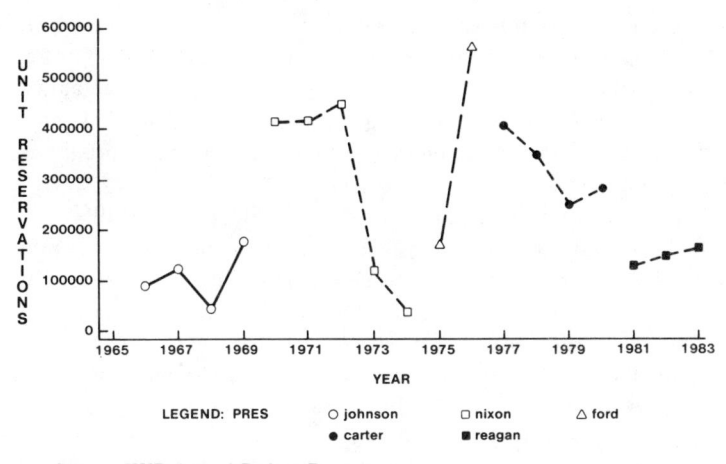

Source: HUD Annual Budget Reports

FIGURE 9.2. Units Reserved: 1965-1983

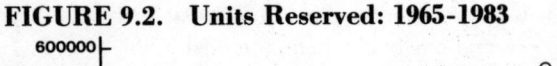

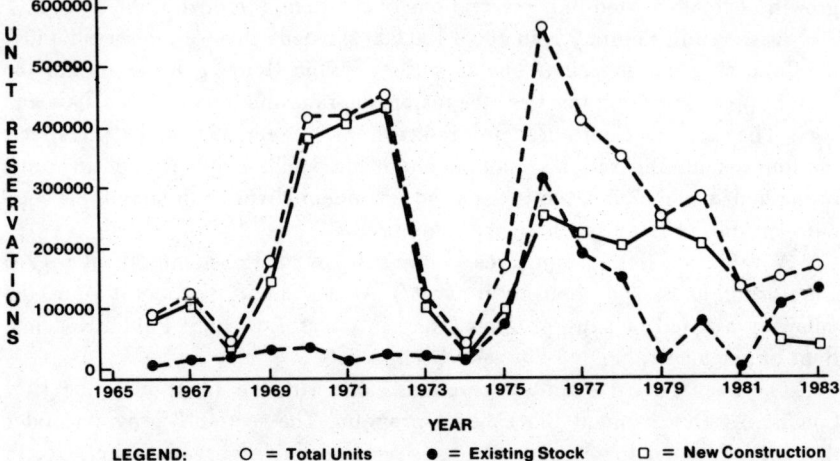

LEGEND: O = Total Units   ● = Existing Stock   □ = New Construction

Source: HUD Annual Budget Reports

Ford and Reagan utilized the existing stock more than did Presidents Johnson and Carter. According to Nixon, the Johnson administration's housing assistance programs were too costly and reached too few people. Also note the dramatic cuts by the Reagan administration in the number of assisted unit reservations. These cuts reduced program activity here to the 1965 level. As the data show, the nation has fallen far short of the 1968 goal of adding 6 to 8 million "additional assisted" units to the housing stock.

A second measure of policy output used here is yearly expenditures for low-income housing assistance programs. Expenditures provide a measure of the growth in federal spending in this area, as well as comparisons between expenditures on housing assistance and other government programs. Budget outlay data on housing assistance are used, since these figures represent the actual expenditures incurred by the government in a given fiscal year. Figure 9.3 shows the growth in 1972 dollars of federal outlays for housing assistance programs, 1957-83.

Expenditures in this area remained stable 1957-68. Beginning in 1968, continuous growth in the total cost of housing assistance is evident. The variation in growth rates, 1975-83, may be attributed to two factors. One is simply the difference in the number of unit reservations made in the Ford and Carter administrations. And second, the Carter administration emphasized new construction to a greater extent. The rapid acceleration during the late 1970s and early 1980s supports this. (Outlays reflect the costs of unit reservations made in previous years.) Although the growth of housing assistance expenditures expressed in dollars is substantial, these outlays in 1983 represented only 1.25 percent

FIGURE 9.3. Federal Low Income Housing Assistance Annual Budget Outlays: 1957-1983

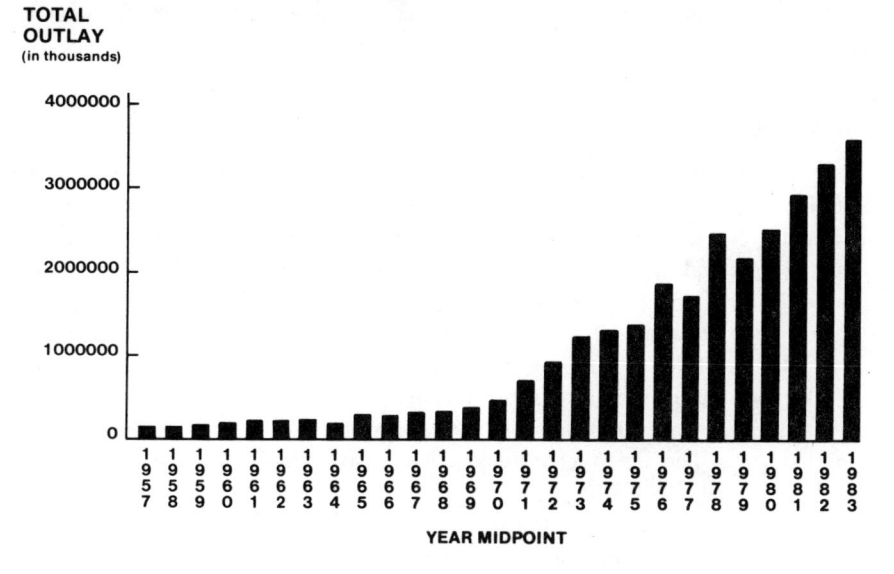

TOTAL OUTLAY (in thousands)

YEAR MIDPOINT

(In 1972 Dollars)

Source: HUD Annual Budget Reports

of nondefense federal expenditures and less that 1 percent of total federal expenditures.

CHANGES IN THE RENTAL HOUSING MARKET, 1973-83

This chapter has thus far examined two major components of the domestic policy-making process, decision making and policy outputs. The purpose of this section is to discuss the impact of these policies. The question addressed here is how have the housing needs of the poor changed over the last ten years in the light of fluctuations in the level of government housing assistance, changes in the domestic economy (high inflation and unemployment), and changes in the condition of the housing market. Since approximately 70 percent of poor families are renters and federal housing assistance activity has been primarily directed at the rental housing market, most of this analysis will address changes in the rental housing market.

Three measures of the need—housing quality, housing affordability, and neighborhood quality—are used. The first two were given major attention in the Housing Acts of 1949 and 1968. The third, neighborhood quality, is recognized as an important component of an assessment of housing but has received little attention from scholars in the field. Yet, improving and maintaining the quality of U.S. neighborhoods are necessary conditions for solving the low-income housing problem in this country.

Housing Quality

The measure of housing quality is based on data from the U.S. Department of Housing and Urban Development's *Annual Housing Survey*.[1] The standard evaluates housing units based on eight factors: plumbing, kitchen, sewage, heating, general maintenance (for example leaky roof, cracks, floor condition), building exterior, toilet access, and electricity (Yezer 1979). Four years were selected for the analysis: 1973, 1976, 1979, and 1981. A longitudinal approach was taken in order to measure the nature and level of changes in the housing stock over time. The three-year intervals between 1973 and 1979 were selected to assess the cumulative effects of policies during the Nixon, Ford, and Carter administrations. The most recent housing survey available at the time the analysis was performed was 1981.

Table 9.1 shows the incidence of substandard rental housing by geographic, socioeconomic, and demographic characteristics. It gives both the percentage of substandard housing found within each category and the total number of households constituting each group.

In 1981, 16.8 percent of the nation's renters occupied substandard housing, compared to 8.47 percent of homeowners. The decline in the rental housing market within central cities is especially pronounced, particularly in the Northeast. As suburban areas age, they also show decline, although far less than central cities. The analysis also reflects population shifts to areas outside Standard Metropolitan Statistical Areas (SMSAs). Earlier studies have shown that there has been an increase in housing construction in these areas (see Jackson 1983). As more affluent families migrate to these areas, improvements occur. However, a vast number of poor renters continue to reside in rural areas in substandard housing.

Even though there has been a slight decline since 1973, almost 30 percent of the nation's renters who are poor continue to live in substandard housing. Over 25 percent of black households who rent live in substandard housing. A special analysis (not shown in Table 9.1) showed that among those of Spanish origin, approximately 25 percent of the renters lived in substandard housing. The problem was particularly acute for Puerto Ricans (30 percent) and less so for Cubans (7 percent).

No gender gap appeared in terms of the incidence of substandard housing between male and female renters. However, beginning in 1976, the elderly appeared to be better housed than the nonelderly.

TABLE 9.1. Substandard Rental Housing Stock, 1973-81

	1973 N	1973 Percent	1976 N	1976 Percent	1979 N	1979 Percent	1981 N	1981 Percent
Region								
Northeast Metro								
City	661,565	18.73	630,014	21.37	712,795	22.77	684,318	21.86
Suburb	198,731	10.71	194,284	11.99	229,818	12.84	215,560	12.43
Outside SMSA	156,538	19.90	254,043	16.08	298,528	17.31	281,388	15.65
Midwest City	301,147	12.33	340,793	16.56	366,169	17.34	363,495	17.16
Suburb	124,353	8.28	141,881	10.57	161,284	11.00	156,517	9.74
Outside SMSA	256,939	18.24	335,916	16.00	343,344	15.34	377,322	15.79
South City	390,088	14.07	324,134	16.61	426,594	20.12	374,524	16.25
Suburb	193,824	11.36	146,284	9.80	198,201	12.03	219,616	12.29
Outside SMSA	720,463	29.16	876,048	22.74	918,989	22.40	917,221	20.44
West City	350,326	17.92	287,433	16.91	337,222	16.94	352,423	16.85
Suburb	210,463	10.93	242,107	12.74	315,513	13.80	387,549	15.35
Outside SMSA	163,288	21.12	251,395	17.88	278,061	17.65	330,131	18.68
Income								
Nonpoverty	2,514,849	13.16	2,684,164	13.88	2,969,266	14.57	2,712,903	13.26
Poverty	1,212,789	30.15	1,340,168	29.07	1,617,352	27.90	1,947,161	26.17
Race								
White	2,493,634	13.20	2,784,763	14.41	3,163,194	15.13	3,101,140	14.25
Black	1,100,780	29.35	1,089,658	27.24	1,240,733	27.46	1,347,421	26.82
Other	133,224	27.34	149,911	24.03	182,691	23.93	211,503	22.34
Sex								
Male	2,411,586	15.51	2,607,373	17.01	2,664,558	17.38	2,745,521	16.91
Female	1,316,052	17.35	1,416,959	16.43	1,922,060	17.85	1,914,543	16.65
Age								
Nonelderly	3,106,505	16.00	3,664,791	17.26	4,122,514	18.30	4,228,849	17.52
Elderly	621,133	16.71	359,541	13.26	464,104	12.72	431,215	11.99
National	3,727,638	16.12	4,024,332	16.80	4,586,618	17.52	4,660,064	16.80

Source: HUD Annual Housing Survey National Files: 1973, 1976, 1979, and 1981.

Affordability

Affordability is also a dimension of the low-income housing problem that federal programs are designed to address. Measures of affordability are based on the proportion of income a family devotes to shelter. For a long period, families paying more than 25 percent of their income for shelter were considered to have "a shelter burden." However, under legislation recommended by the Reagan administration and adopted by Congress in 1981, 30 percent of income will be phased in as the criterion. This means that for assisted households, the government will pay the difference between 30 percent of an eligible family's income and the cost for shelter. In this analysis, families paying 30 percent or more of their income for shelter were considered to have "a shelter burden." Only renters were included in this analysis.

As shown in Table 9.2, the national trend has been a consistent rise in the proportion of a family's income being devoted to shelter. In 1973, 24.58 percent of the nation's renters paid more than 30 percent of their income for shelter; by 1981, this figure was 38.57 percent. This pattern is consistent across all groups but tends to affect some groups much more than others.

For example, in 1981, 71 percent of the renters living below the poverty line paid more than 30 percent of their income for shelter. Fifty-one percent of female heads of households had a rent burden, compared to 30 percent of male-headed households. This problem also affects the elderly. In 1981, 46.52 percent of the elderly households had a rent burden, compared to 37.38 percent of the nonelderly. Blacks too have been afflicted with above average rent burdens. Between 1973 and 1981, rent burdens for black households increased tremendously. In 1973, 28 percent of black renters had shelter burdens. In 1981, this figure had increased to 43 percent.

Neighborhood Quality

A final indicator of housing need is neighborhood quality, as measured by data on neighborhood physical characteristics and the quality of neighborhood services taken from the *Annual Housing Survey*. Measures of the physical environment were the presence of abandoned buildings in the neighborhood and the presence of crime. Respondents were asked if these conditions existed in their neighborhoods. The respondents were coded (1) if the condition was not present; (2) if the condition was present but respondent did not want to move; and (3) if present and the respondent wanted to move. In terms of services, respondents were asked if they found services adequate or inadequate. The respondents were coded (1) if satisfied with the service; (2) if dissatisfied but respondent did not want to move; and (3) if dissatisfied and the respondent wanted to move. Finally, the results were used to label each respondent as (1) satisfied, (2) dissatisfied, or (3) strongly dissatisfied.

TABLE 9.2. Renters Paying More Than 30 Percent of Income for Housing, 1973-81

		1973 N	1973 Percent	1976 N	1976 Percent	1979 N	1979 Percent	1981 N	1981 Percent
Region									
Northeast	**Metro**								
	City	1,009,819	28.58	1,081,365	36.68	1,297,387	41.44	1,322,299	42.25
	Suburb	462,260	24.91	489,628	30.22	643,835	35.97	649,210	37.43
	Outside SMSA	182,610	23.22	436,050	27.60	610,136	35.38	646,904	35.98
Midwest	City	722,093	29.57	694,703	33.75	816,107	38.66	878,270	41.47
	Suburb	318,426	21.21	340,570	25.37	500,904	34.17	572,598	35.64
	Outside SMSA	289,948	20.59	532,111	25.34	750,976	33.55	905,267	37.87
South	City	661,572	23.87	552,016	28.28	726,241	34.25	865,641	37.55
	Suburb	367,502	21.55	383,355	25.67	515,144	31.27	635,747	35.58
	Outside SMSA	396,977	16.07	947,898	24.61	1,215,837	29.64	1,567,610	34.94
West	City	621,011	31.76	547,118	32.20	761,714	38.27	933,649	44.64
	Suburb	485,868	25.24	631,688	32.30	930,480	40.71	1,071,897	42.47
	Outside SMSA	166,838	21.58	386,695	27.51	536,913	34.08	649,612	36.75
Income									
	Nonpoverty	3,439,361	18.00	4,112,605	21.26	5,266,024	25.83	5,417,510	26.69
	Poverty	2,245,563	55.83	2,892,592	62.75	4,039,650	69.69	5,281,194	70.99
Race									
	White	4,564,985	24.17	5,490,879	28.41	7,280,735	34.84	8,143,716	37.41
	Black	1,036,825	27.64	1,366,906	34.16	1,766,397	39.10	2,149,030	42.78
	Other	83,114	17.06	147,412	23.63	258,542	33.86	405,958	42.89
Sex									
	Male	2,585,599	16.63	3,067,174	20.01	3,806,105	24.69	4,826,149	29.72
	Female	3,099,325	40.87	3,938,023	45.66	5,499,569	51.08	5,872,555	51.07
Age									
	Nonelderly	3,996,313	20.59	5,779,231	27.21	7,523,208	33.39	9,025,932	37.38
	Elderly	1,688,611	45.43	1,225,966	45.21	1,782,466	48.83	1,672,772	46.52
National		5,684,924	24.58	7,005,197	29.25	9,305,674	35.54	10,698,704	38.57

Source: HUD Annual Housing Survey National Files: 1973, 1976, 1979, and 1981.

Physical Quality. As shown in Table 9.3, crime was frequently viewed as a serious problem. In 1981, 16 percent of the nation's households (both renters and homeowners) expressed dissatisfaction with the level of crime present in their neighborhoods. As expected, central cities were most affected, particularly in the Northeast. Dissatisfaction with abandoned buildings, conversely, was rarely expressed except by those living in northeastern and midwestern central cities. There was a dramatic decrease in blacks and those below the poverty line expressing dissatisfaction with abandoned buildings in their neighborhoods, 1979–81. This may reflect an increase in the demolition of abandoned buildings in the neighborhoods occupied by these residents; mobility on the part of dissatisfied low-income and black residents; or redevelopment and displacement. On the other hand, the number of females expressing dissatisfaction with abandoned buildings in their neighborhood sharply increased, 1976–81. This rise may be due to the growing number of female heads of households.

Service Quality. As shown in Table 9.4, residents expressed the greatest dissatisfaction with hospitals. And here dissatisfaction levels were greatest among suburbanites and rural residents. Residents also reported relatively high levels of dissatisfaction with the police. Central city residents and those outside SMSAs expressed greater dissatisfaction than did suburban dwellers. Blacks too were consistently more dissatisfied with police. A separate analysis on Hispanic respondents (coded as other in Table 9.4) showed a similar growth in dissatisfaction with police. In viewing the findings on resident dissatisfaction with public schools, it should be remembered that many households either do not have children or do not have children of school age. Therefore, the low percentage of residents expressing dissatisfaction may reflect some indifference on the part of these groups. Nevertheless, the pattern is as expected. Central city residents are most likely to express dissatisfaction with schools, particularly in the Northeast and the Midwest. And corresponding to differences in perceived "stake," the elderly were less likely to express dissatisfaction with schools than the nonelderly.

In sum, great inequalities exist among households in terms of access to decent and safe communities. Residents of central cities suffer the most from crime and abandonments. Residents in these areas are also more likely to be dissatisfied with their schools than residents in other areas. The same pattern holds true for police services. Blacks and other minorities too are more likely than whites to express dissatisfaction with their neighborhoods. There is also growing dissatisfaction with some services among females, which reflects the growth in the number of female-headed households during the past few years. Overall, these data support the contention that access to decent communities is still a dream for many Americans and thus should form the basis of federal housing assistance policy.

TABLE 9.3. Changes in Neighborhood Quality, 1976-81: Physical Attributes

		CRIME						ABANDONMENT					
		1976		1979		1981		1976		1979		1981	
		D %	SD %	D %	SD %	D %	SD %	D %	SD %	D %	SD %	D %	SD %
Region													
Northeast	Metro												
	City	16	13	18	14	21	13	5	5	7	6	6	6
	Suburb	10	3	10	4	14	4	1	1	2	1	2	1
	Outside SMSA	7	3	8	2	10	3	1	1	2	1	2	1
Midwest	City	12	9	14	8	17	9	3	2	4	4	5	3
	Suburb	0	0	9	3	8	3	1	0	1	1	1	0
	Outside SMSA	5	1	6	2	8	2	1	2	2	0	2	0
South	City	9	6	12	6	16	8	2	1	2	1	3	2
	Suburb	9	3	10	3	12	4	1	0	3	1	2	1
	Outside SMSA	6	2	6	2	9	2	2	1	2	1	2	1
West	City	14	7	15	9	20	8	2	1	2	1	2	1
	Suburb	12	5	12	5	14	5	2	1	1	1	1	1
	Outside SMSA	9	4	10	3	12	4	2	0	2	0	1	0
Income													
Nonpoverty		9	4	10	4	13	4	2	1	2	1	2	1
Poverty		7	6	8	6	10	7	2	2	7	5	3	2
Race													
White		9	3	9	3	12	4	1	1	2	1	2	1
Black		8	8	10	9	13	10	5	5	7	5	3	2
Other		7	3	7	5	14	6	1	1	2	1	2	1
Sex													
Male		9	4	9	4	12	4	2	1	2	1	1	1
Female		9	5	10	5	12	6	2	1	3	2	2	1
Age													
Nonelderly		9	4	10	4	13	5	2	1	2	1	2	1
Elderly		7	3	7	2	10	2	1	1	2	0	1	0
National		9	4	9	4	12	4	2	1	2	1	1	0

Note: D = Dissatisfied; SD = Strongly Dissatisfied.
Source: HUD Annual Housing Survey National Files: 1973, 1976, 1979, and 1981.

TABLE 9.4. Changes in Neighborhood Quality, 1976-81: Services

		Police						Hospitals						Schools		
		1976		1979		1981		1976		1979		1981		1976	1979	1981
		D%	SD%	D%	SD%	D%	SD%	D%	SD%	D%	SD%	D%	SD%	D%	D%	D%
Region	**Metro**															
Northeast	City	9	6	12	9	12	8	5	2	7	3	6	2	6	10	9
	Suburb	4	1	5	1	4	2	8	0	9	1	6	1	3	4	4
	Outside SMSA	7	1	8	2	7	1	13	1	13	1	8	0	4	5	5
Midwest	City	5	3	8	4	8	4	5	1	7	1	6	1	3	8	8
	Suburb	4	1	5	1	5	1	9	1	10	1	7	0	2	4	3
	Outside SMSA	7	1	7	1	7	1	13	1	16	1	11	1	2	3	4
South	City	6	2	7	2	8	3	7	1	11	1	5	1	3	5	6
	Suburb	7	2	8	1	7	2	14	1	14	2	11	1	4	5	4
	Outside SMSA	10	1	10	2	7	2	14	1	19	1	15	1	5	6	5
West	City	6	2	8	4	7	4	7	1	8	1	5	1	5	7	5
	Suburb	6	2	8	2	7	2	9	1	9	1	6	1	5	6	3
	Outside SMSA	9	2	10	2	10	2	15	2	19	1	13	1	5	4	4
Income																
Nonpoverty		7	2	8	2	7	2	11	1	13	1	9	1	4	5	5
Poverty		9	3	9	4	9	4	12	2	15	2	11	2	4	5	4
Race																
White		7	1	8	2	7	2	11	1	13	1	9	1	4	5	5
Black		9	4	10	7	9	6	9	2	14	4	10	3	5	7	5
Other		5	2	8	3	11	4	8	2	12	1	8	1	3	7	3
Sex																
Male		7	2	8	2	8	2	11	1	13	1	10	1	4	6	5
Female		6	2	8	3	7	3	10	1	13	2	9	1	3	4	4
Age																
Nonelderly		7	2	8	3	8	2	11	1	13	1	9	1	4	6	5
Elderly		7	1	7	1	7	1	11	1	14	1	10	0	2	2	2
National		7	2	8	2	8	2	11	1	13	1	9	1	4	5	5

Notes: D = Dissatisfied; SD = Strongly Dissatisfied.
Responses to the question on the education system were coded as either satisfied or dissatisfied.
Source: HUD Annual Housing Survey National Files: 1973, 1976, 1979, and 1981.

CONCLUSION

There are a number of factors which structure the housing policy agenda and policy choices. Political ideology plays a significant role in the selection of policy alternatives (for example production-oriented subsidies vs. demand-oriented subsidies). Democratic administrations have emphasized the construction of new subsidized housing over the use of existing stock. The opposite is true for Republican administrations. Ideology also influences the level of federal intervention. For example, the Johnson administration set out to "eliminate all substandard housing" and defined eligibility for housing assistance programs in very broad terms. On the other hand, the Reagan administration has redefined the affordability criterion, using 30 percent instead of 25 percent of income as the standard. In addition, only persons making less than 55 percent of the median income in their metropolitan area are now eligible to participate in the Section 8 housing assistance program. Previously, the ceiling was 80 percent of the median income.

Task forces are also influential in the housing decision-making process. Major changes in housing assistance policy were based on recommendations contained in housing commission reports issued during the Johnson, Nixon, and Reagan administrations. Norman Thomas and Harold Wolman (1969, p.125) compare the "old process" of developing presidential proposals with the increased use of presidential task forces. Prior to the Johnson administration, the president's proposals to Congress were normally developed by the departments and agencies and submitted to the president through the Bureau of the Budget. The Budget Bureau and the White House staff then analyzed these proposals and the legislative proposal emerged.

Beginning with Johnson, presidents have been able to control their policy agendas by using presidential task forces. Even though presidents are not compelled to accept task force recommendations, and in many cases do not, housing task forces have been influential. A major reason for the success of the housing commissions is that most of the appointees are selected from groups already predisposed to supporting the president's program (see Thomas and Wolman 1969, pp.142-43; Downs 1983, pp.182-91).

Shifts in party control also bring innovation. Presidents seek to differentiate their housing proposals from those of previous administrations, particularly those led by members of the other party. According to Schattschneider:

> Political conflict is not like an intercollegiate debate in which the opponents agree in advance on a definition of the issues. As a matter of fact, the definition of the alternatives is the supreme instrument of power; the antagonists can rarely agree on what the issues are because power is involved in the definition. He who determines what politics is about runs the country, because the definition of alternatives is the choice of conflicts, and the choice of conflicts allocates power (Schattschneider 1961, p.68).

Thus President Nixon's decision to emphasize vouchers as a policy alternative can be explained in part by his struggle to control the housing policy agenda. According to Nathan (1975), Nixon expressed frustration over the Johnson administration's housing policies during his first term in office but had not come up with an alternative. Recommending housing vouchers gave him an opportunity to redefine and control the housing policy agenda. The same holds true for the Reagan administration.

However, the current emphasis on housing vouchers has received support from scholars in the field (see Weicher 1980). There is a growing consensus that affordability is the major housing problem confronting low-income families, not substandard housing (Weicher 1980, pp.12-30). The data presented here do not support this argument. Although increasing percentages of the low-income population pay more than 30 percent of their income for shelter, this trend has been a national trend as well. High unemployment since the late 1960s, rising interest rates, inflation during the last decade—all have contributed to the affordability problem.

The large percentage of substandard housing found in the rental housing market, as well as public perceptions of housing and neighborhood conditions, suggest that the problem is more fundamental than affordability. The nation's central cities, particularly in the Northeast and Midwest, are deteriorating. In 1981, 22 percent of renters in the Northeast lived in substandard housing compared to 19 percent in 1973. If only 10 percent of the nation's housing stock was substandard in 1981, why did so many renters live in substandard housing? The trends suggest that housing quality is still a problem in the rental housing market.

Patterns of dissatisfaction with neighborhood services also follow the distribution of substandard housing. For example, concern about crime, abandonments, and city services is expressed most often in cities of the Northeast and Midwest. All of the trends reported here seem to suggest that the problem is one of access. That is, even though standard housing and good neighborhoods exist in the United States, they are unequally distributed.

Providing access to decent housing and neighborhoods should form the basis of federal housing policy. Housing vouchers, production-oriented subsidies, community development block grants, antidiscrimination laws such as the Fair Housing Act of 1968, and laws against unfair zoning ordinances that prevent the construction of low-income housing all have a role to play in providing social access to low-income families. At present, however, there is only a weak link between the selection of housing assistance policy alternatives and the problems facing the poor.

NOTES

1. The data and tabulations utilized here were made available, in part, by the Inter-university Consortium for Political and Social Research. The data for "*Annual Housing Surveys*, 1973, 1976,

1979 and 1981 (United States): National Files" were originally collected by the U.S. Department of Commerce, Bureau of the Census. Neither the collector of the original data nor the Consortium bear any responsibility for the analyses or interpretations presented here.

REFERENCES

Aaron, Henry J. 1972. *Shelter and Subsidies: Who Benefits from Federal Housing Policies?* Washington, D.C.: Brookings Institution.

Anton, Thomas and Oliver P. Williams. 1971. "On Comparing Urban Political Systems: Residential Allocations in London and Stockholm." Paper presented at the Annual Meeting of the American Political Science Association, September 7-11, Chicago.

de Leeuw, Frank. 1971. *The Design of a Housing Allowance.* Washington, D.C.: Urban Institute.

Downs, Anthony. 1983. "The President's Housing Commission and Two Tests of Realistic Recommendations." *Journal of the American Real Estate and Urban Economics Association* 11 (Summer): 182-91.

Jackson, Bryan O. 1983. "The Impact of Federal Housing Policy on Low and Moderate Income Black Americans: An Analysis of a Dream Deferred." Paper presented at the Annual Meeting of the National Conference of Black Political Scientists, April 27-30, Houston, Texas.

Nathan, Richard. 1975. *The Plot That Failed.* New York: John Wiley.

Schattschneider, E.E. 1961. *The Semi-Sovereign People.* New York: Holt, Rinehart and Winston.

Schultze, Charles. 1972. *Setting National Priorities: The 1972 Budget.* Washington, D.C.: Brookings Institution.

Struyk, Raymond. 1980. *A New System for Public Housing: Salvaging a National Resource.* Washington, D.C.: Urban Institute.

Thomas, Norman C. and Harold L. Wolman. 1969. "Policy Formulation in the Institutionalized Presidency: The Johnson Task Forces." In *The Presidential Advisory System*, edited by Thomas E. Cronin and Sanford D. Greenberg, pp. 124-43. New York: Harper and Row.

U.S. Department of Housing and Urban Development. 1973. *Housing in the Seventies.* Washington, D.C.: Government Printing Office.

U.S. National Advisory Commission on Civil Disorders. 1968. *Report.* Washington, D.C.: Government Printing Office.

U.S. President's Commission on Housing. 1982. *Report.* Washington, D.C.: Government Printing Office.

U.S. President's Committee on Urban Housing. 1968. *A Decent Home.* Washington, D.C.: Government Printing Office.

U.S. Senate. Committee on Banking, Housing and Urban Affairs. Subcommittee on Housing and Urban Affairs. 1974. *Critique of Housing in the Seventies.* Washington, D.C.: Government Printing Office.

Weicher, John C. 1980. *Housing: Federal Policies and Programs.* Washington, D.C.: American Enterprise Institute.

Yezer, Anthony. 1979. *How Well Are We Housed?* Washington, D.C.: Government Printing Office.

10

GENDER EQUITY AND THE URBAN ENVIRONMENT

Greta Salem

Policymakers and activists who seek to redistribute power and achieve a larger measure of equity in our society have learned slowly and often painfully that the removal of overtly discriminatory practices is a necessary but hardly sufficient condition to achieve that end. Obstacles to equal opportunity are embedded in and supported by a myriad of traditional values, orientations, perceptions, behaviors, and thought patterns that often militate against the equal opportunity authorized by the law.

Among the most frequently overlooked obstacles to gender equity, for example, is the design of the urban environment itself. Although generally perceived as a benign and neutral setting in which activity takes place, in regard to women, it is neither. All environments encourage some activities and inhibit others. Popenoe (1977, p.82) uses the concept "environmental fit" to characterize those situations in which the physical setting accommodates the needs, goals, and patterns of social behavior of the residents "without undue limitations and constraints, especially those which generate social and psychological stress." The urban environment currently provides this kind of support for households in which men go to work and women stay home. It does not, however, accommodate working women in this regard.

This lack of environmental fit must be taken into account by those seeking to understand as well as to remedy the failure of women to achieve economic equality. And this failure is critical, not only because a growing number of women bear primary responsibility for the economic well-being of their families, but also, and even more importantly, because economic power appears to be central to the achievement of equity in all areas.

Historical, anthropological, and sociological evidence indicates that gender equity is most likely to be achieved when women play an integral role in the productive economy (Boulding 1976; Moen et al. 1980). Such a role, however, is not derived from mere labor force participation alone. Women must have some control over the means of production and the distribution of available surplus. Furthermore, what they produce must be essential to the well-being of their society. This is more likely to occur, cross-cultural studies reveal, in societies in which the private and public spheres are more closely integrated (Rosaldo 1974). In the most egalitarian cultures men also value and participate in the life of the home. In such situations women have greater access to the resources that will facilitate the fullest development of their abilities.

An important and frequently overlooked resource for the achievement of economic power is physical mobility. A historical study of the geography of women notes that women's patterns of movement are different from those of men:

> They are less likely to have mobility associated with their regular work roles, and even where law and society permit them to move freely, they tend to move less than men and to move shorter distances (Hayford 1974, p. 5).

Yet mobility, and particularly movement beyond one's immediate environment, is an important instrument for the development of the capacity for growth and survival. As Coser notes:

> It is well known that organisms that reach outward have more survival value than organisms dependent on the immediate environment. Whether we compare shellfish with mammals, or the unborn with a baby that can walk, or the self-sufficient farm with the large farming enterprise, always it is the case that interdependence with other organisms creates increased opportunities for survival and growth (Coser 1975, p.476).

Coser argues that societies control the social status of their members by controlling their spatial movements. Thus restriction of horizontal movement leads also to restriction of upward mobility.

Support for this argument is provided in an analysis of two segments of the Kung tribe which found more gender equality among hunters and gatherers where both men and women spent equal time and went equal distances away from home. In the sedentary tribe, where men went off to hunt and women stayed home, the latter had access to fewer resources and did not develop as wide a range of abilities as the men (Slocum 1975). The importance of mobility is also underscored by Boulding (1976), who notes that studies of the nomadic life may provide some models for a more egalitarian society.

In summary, women are most likely to enjoy economic power and equity in general in societies in which the public and domestic spheres are closely integrated; in which domestic obligations are shared; and in which women have increased capacity to travel beyond their immediate environment. These conditions, as the following discussion will show, do not prevail in the contemporary urban environment.

WORKING WOMEN AND THE URBAN ENVIRONMENT

The design of contemporary urban communities reflects the values and assumptions characterizing industrialized urbanized societies. These include a commitment to a patriarchal family structure, which allocates domestic authority to the man and domestic responsibility to the woman. The man goes off to work and the woman stays home to tend to child care and home maintenance obligations. Domestic and public spheres are clearly separated. Thus Boulding (1976, p.191) speaks of urbanization as a process that by fostering the seclusion of women in the home, "encloses women and launches men."

The analysis below will deal with cities and suburbs separately only when experiences in these settings are compared. For the most part, the term urban region or environment will be used to describe an area that encompasses both suburbs and cities. This acknowledges the reality that most men and women, in the conduct of their daily affairs, move across a number of boundaries that may separate areas politically and symbolically, but function as a total environment in which the range of activities related to work, recreation, and domestic obligations take place.

The focus will be on the "built" or "man-made" characteristics of the environment. These include the spatial arrangements of residential and work sites, the placement of service institutions and recreational areas, and the transportation networks that make it possible to get from one place to another. And because the timetables in our communities affect the life we can live within them (Michaelson 1980), the time frame within which institutional services are available will also be considered.

Although the urban environment currently facilitates the activities of women who stay home and men who go to work, the U.S. mother who stays at home is increasingly rare. The most recently collected data indicate that six out of every ten mothers with children under 18 are in the labor force. These include approximately 50 percent of the mothers of infants and toddlers under three. A majority of these working mothers are employed full time. Furthermore, single heads of households constitute a growing segment of the population. Of the 12 million such families reported in 1984, 10 million were maintained by women (U.S. Department of Labor 1984).

All of these women find in their environment innumerable hurdles which must be overcome if they are to obtain work and accommodate both job and domestic responsibilities. These include: (1) dispersed and segregated dwelling, employment, and commercial sites; (2) limited public transportation, particularly in the suburbs; (3) transportation schedules that are designed primarily for the trip to and from work; (4) schedules in service institutions based on the assumption that consumers and clients will be available during the work day; and (5) limited availability of and access to child care facilities. Thus the spatial separation of home and workplace together with the minimal transportation options limit accessibility to jobs. And the paucity of environmental supports, which include the failure of service institutions to modify time schedules to accommodate working women, impose serious physical and psychological strains.

Michelson (1980) has defined as incongruent those situations in which the built environment makes certain activity either very difficult or impossible. The growing population of working women, who conduct their daily affairs in an environment designed for women who are supposed to stay at home, confront this incongruence regularly in the form of the increased opportunity costs they must pay. An examination of their perceptions about their environment and their experiences within it will indicate the nature of these costs.

Time is a frequently overlooked resource required for the attainment of other societal values. Individuals who must allocate more time than others to achieve the same ends are clearly disadvantaged. The dispersion of facilities, combined with the allocation of roles within the family unit, imposes burdensome demands on the time of working women. Although many of these women have full-time jobs, they retain their domestic obligations as well as their belief that their primary commitment must be to the home. Thus time studies show that a majority of the women who work simply add their job to their other tasks (Saegert 1982). Although working women do less housework than those who are not employed, little of that is shared. The big tradeoff is not so much in terms of work at home, but in terms of free time. One study showed that a woman's workload is increased by 13 hours per week when she enters the workforce (Kreps and Leaper 1976). And time studies in a number of nations reveal that the working mother sleeps less than any other segment of the population (Michelson 1973).

Additional time and energy costs are created by limited transportation options. Although only a small portion of the transportation literature focuses specifically on the travel patterns of women, the fragmentary evidence that does exist documents some real disadvantages. A number of studies show that women have less access to cars than men (Kannis and Robins 1974; Guiliano 1979; Hayden 1980). In a one-car family, the car is used by the male member for the journey to work 75 percent of the time (Kannis and Robins 1974). Not surprisingly, women are more dependent on public transportation.

In general people with less access to automobiles travel less frequently and make shorter trips, while at the same time they incur higher time costs when they do travel. The disproportionate public expenditures on highways is reflected in the increased differential between the mobility of automobile users and transit users. Guiliano (1979) reports that while automobile users are enjoying increased levels of mobility, bus travelers have suffered a loss.

Lack of access to the automobile would not be as much of a problem if public transportation took women where they needed to go. However, our systems were originally designed to take men from the suburbs to work in the cities. For the most part they do not provide adequate service between or within suburbs. Nor do they work well for those who use them at nonpeak hours. In such instances the time costs may be inordinately high.

A comparison of the travel patterns of women and men in Canada showed that women take many more short trips than men (Hayford 1974). This reflects in part the domestic obligations that require trips to a number of spatially dispersed facilities. Women who must combine trips to and from work with side trips to drop children off at schools, day care centers, lessons, recreation activities, and doctor's appointments, and who must fit in trips to the grocery store and other service institutions, confront serious problems even if they have access to a car. Dependence on public transportation exacerbates an already difficult situation.

Working women with children confront particularly serious problems in attending to their care. A value system that requires women to devote full time to home and child care is reflected in the paucity of child care arrangements available to working mothers. There has not been a systematic survey of day care needs since the mid-1970s. At that time day care centers accommodated one out of ten children of working mothers (Kreps and Leaper 1976). Since then increased use and need have been documented. Many mothers currently perform "desperate juggling acts" to create adequate care packages for their children (Kamerman 1983). When child care centers are available, they tend to be located at some distance from both the mother's home and work. Neither schools nor businesses consider schedules that might allow mothers to more easily meet their child care needs. One large city public school system, for example, starts the day at 9:30 a.m., creating serious problems for women who are confronted daily with a one-hour discrepancy between their work requirements and the school schedules of their children. Thus women who work pay with their time, energy, and increased levels of stress for a system that allocates to them primary responsibility for domestic affairs but offers minimal institutional support to help alleviate that burden and only limited access to transportation facilities that allow them to fulfill work and domestic obligations in an environment in which functions are segregated and dispersed.

AN EQUAL OPPORTUNITY ENVIRONMENT

Women who work require and desire high density communities with easy access to the central city (Rothblatt, Garr, and Sprague 1979; Saegert 1980). Yet such communities are not readily available. Those women who have locational options find themselves choosing between cities, which offer employment and social and cultural opportunities, and suburbs, which are perceived as better and safer environments for children. Married men prefer to live in the suburbs where they can take advantage of the best that both environments have to offer. The conflict between their domestic and work roles, however, forces women to choose which set of environmental disadvantages they will tolerate.

Because most locational choices tend to be made with the husband's needs in mind (Markusen 1980), working women most frequently find themselves living in environments that are less likely to accommodate their employment needs. Such environmental inequities, however, not only produce the frantic life-style documented above, they also constitute a serious obstacle to economic equity. The distances between activities outside the home, the lack of adequate transportation, and the conflicting schedules of work, household, and childcare obligations impose severe limitations on what women can do outside of the home. Thus they travel shorter distances and longer hours to work (Erickson 1977). These restrictions in employment options help to account for the fact that despite significant increases in educational preparation, women have failed to make significant inroads into the most valuable market occupations (Kreps and Leaper 1976).

The urban system has been described as a "geographical distribution of created resources of great economic, social, psychological and symbolic significance" (Harvey 1975, p. 69). Women are economically disadvantaged to an increasingly larger extent because the urban environment imposes on them greater accessibility costs. They are underemployed and unemployed because they lack the environmental support that would facilitate their ability to more readily and effectively accommodate their domestic obligations and their career and work aspirations.

Thus working women find themselves in the paradoxical position explicated by Hayden (1980). On the one hand, they cannot improve their position in the home without improving their economic status. And on the other, their economic position cannot be improved unless their domestic responsibilities are altered. The remedy for this dilemma ultimately will require changes in both behaviors and values. Public policies, however, are more likely to have an impact on behavior. And although eventually equity for women will depend on a value system that supports a more balanced distribution of obligations within the domestic sphere as well as equal opportunities in the work force, the changes in the former are more likely to take place in an environment that facilitates women's access to job opportunities.

Popenoe's (1977) comparison of a Swedish suburb and U.S. suburb gives us some idea about the contours such an environment might take. In contrast with the American suburb, which provided limited employment opportunities within reasonable commuting distances and where women were totally dependent on the automobile, the Swedish suburb provided a large job market readily accessible by public transportation. Whereas there were no child care facilities in the American suburb, Swedish women had access to excellent day care service in the immediate vicinity of the dwelling unit. Other services were also located close to the dwelling units so that shopping and other maintenance errands could easily be incorporated into the trip home from work. Furthermore, because most of the Swedish women were apartment dwellers, they had fewer home maintenance obligations.

An equal opportunity environment thus would have to start by eliminating the "friction of space" that imposes such heavy burdens on American women. Single-use zoning responsible for the segregation of functions would need to be replaced by mixed-use zoning to allow for the more proximate location of employment and residential sites and for more readily accessible commercial areas and service institutions. Child care facilities or arrangements will have to be available within the residential neighborhood. And public transportation networks that provide more regularly scheduled service both within and between suburbs will need to be designed.

These proposals for environmental modification, as well as the inequities previously described, indicate quite clearly that the physical structure of a community has a major impact on the activities that go on within it and that the power inherent in built environments must be understood within the context of the value system operative when they were designed.

POWER, VALUES, AND THE BUILT ENVIRONMENT

Many social theorists, according to Harvey, live in a spaceless world. But his examination of urban social justice indicates that "spatial design signifies much about the social processes that go on within it" (Harvey 1975, p. 28). According to Louis Wirth, the characteristics of the environment are at best conditioning factors "offering possibilities and setting limits for social and psychological existence and development" (quoted in Popenoe 1977, p. 81). However, these possibilities and limits are not randomly distributed. The built environment generally reflects the dominant values in a given society. Architect Susan Torre (1981) argues that building designs should be viewed as symbolic forms that embody specific ideologies about how people should live and what kinds of values and hierarchies should be fostered by them. This is also true of community designs.

Once these values have been embedded in physical structures and designs, they have more than a temporary impact. They tend to institutionalize, and "in some respects, to determine the future development of social process" (Harvey 1975, p. 27). Thus the built environment becomes an extension of the particular set of values operative at the time of its creation and continues to exert an independent influence on the activities that go on within it. It therefore functions as an instrument of social power and a force for the maintenance of the status quo.

Power is generally conceptualized in terms of a relationship in which one individual exerts influence over the activities of another (Dahl 1963). Community power studies focus specifically on how that influence is exerted in the decision-making processes that affect the allocation of values (Dahl 1961; Hunter 1953). For this reason, those who seek a redistribution of values have generally focused on strategies that will strengthen the influence of disadvantaged groups in this regard. However, if one looks at efforts to attain values rather than at strategies for influencing decisionmakers, one finds less visible manifestations of power, which nonetheless impose potent constraints on the powerless groups in society. One such power dimension is identified by Stone in his analysis of systemic power. This form of power is inherent in the socioeconomic stratification system and rests in the predispositions of public officials to favor the upper strata in their decision making. They do this, not in response to overt pressure, but because it is in their professional interest to do so (Stone 1980).

Three characteristics of systemic power are particularly relevant to the argument presented here. First, it is contextual. It is embedded in the social structure. Secondly, it is not intentional. It operates independently of the wishes of the power holders. And finally, because it is not overtly exercised, it is less visible than intentional efforts designed to influence decisionmakers. Indeed because it requires neither action nor intention to be in effect, systemic power is likely to be less visible to those who have it than to those who do not. Lower strata groups, for example, may fail in their efforts to achieve a goal because of the predispositions of public officials. In such instances, the beneficiaries of the power system may not even know that a contest has taken place and that they have won. However, the losers in such instances are well aware of the fact that power has been exercised to their disadvantage. They may not understand its source, but they know that there are barriers inherent in the system that make it difficult for them to elicit positive responses to their demands.

Because power is generally conceptualized from the perspective of those who exercise it, the focus has been on the intentional manipulation of others to secure desired outcomes and on overt conflict between individuals. Stone's notion of systemic power, however, suggests that power can be less visible, situational, and differentially perceived by those who have it and those who do not. If we focus on the experience of the disadvantaged, power assumes the form of barriers that either prevent the achievement of goals or raise the opportunity costs involved.

The power inherent in the social structure of society is also manifested in the spatial designs of communities. These exert an independent influence on the activities of those who live and work within them. And although those whose activities are facilitated may not be aware of the power inherent in the physical arrangements, it is clear to those whose options are limited by them.

Although such a manifestation of power is less visible, at least to the power holders, and not intentionally exercised, it has a potent impact on the allocation of values and works effectively as an instrument for the maintenance of the status quo. Thus those who seek to alter the distribution of values and power resources must take into consideration not only the power resources associated with the more visible exercise of influence, but also the less frequently considered manifestations of power that are visible primarily to the powerless as impediments to their quest for a more equitable distribution of societal values. In the case of women, the physical design of communities that sustains the economic disadvantages they confront must be taken into account and altered if equal employment conditions are to be achieved.

REFERENCES

Boulding, Elise. 1976. *The Underside of History*. Boulder:Westview Press.
Coser, Rose Laub. 1975. "Stay Home, Little Sheba: On Placement, Displacement and Social Change." *Social Problems* 22 (April):470-79.
Dahl, Robert. 1963. *Modern Political Analysis*. Englewood Cliffs: Prentice-Hall.
———. 1961. *Who Governs?* New Haven: Yale University Press.
Erickson, Julia A. 1977. "An Analysis of the Journey to Work." *Social Problems* 24 (April):428-35.
Guiliano, Genevive. 1979. "Public Transportation and the Travel Needs of Women." *Traffic Quarterly* 33 (October):607-15.
Harvey, David. 1975. *Social Justice In the City*. Baltimore:Johns Hopkins University Press.
Hayden, Dolores. 1980. "What Would a Non Sexist City Be Like? Speculations on Housing, Urban Design, and Human Work." *Signs* 5 (Spring):170-87.
Hayford, Alison M. 1974. "The Geography of Women: An Historical Introduction." *Antipode* 6 (2):1-19.
Hunter, Floyd. 1953. *Community Power Structure: A Study of Decision-Makers*. Chapel Hill:University of North Carolina Press.
Kamerman, Sheila. 1983. "The Child Care Debate: Working Mothers vs America." *Working Woman* 8 (November):131-35.
Kannis, Phyllis and Barbara Robins. 1974. "The Transportation Needs of Women." In *Women, Planning and Change*, edited by Karen Hapgood and Judith Getzels, pp. 63-70. Chicago:American Society of Planning Officials.
Kreps, Juanita M. and John R. Leaper. 1976. "Home Work, Market Work, and the Allocation of Time." In *Women and the American Economy*, edited by Juanita M. Kreps, pp.61-81. Englewood Cliffs:Prentice-Hall.
Markusen, Ann R. 1980. "City Spatial Structure, Women's Household Work, and National Urban Policy." *Signs* 5 (Spring):S23-S44.
Michelson, William. 1980. "Spatial and Temporal Dimensions of Child Care." *Signs* 5 (Spring):S242-47.
———. 1973. *The Place of Time in the Longitudinal Evaluation of Spatial Structures By Women*. Toronto:Center for Urban and Community Studies, University of Toronto.
Moen, Elizabeth et al. 1980. *Women and the Social Costs of Economic Development*. Boulder:Westview Press.
Popenoe, David. 1977. *The Suburban Environment*. Chicago:University of Chicago Press.
Rosaldo, Michele Zimbalist. 1974. "Women, Culture and Society: A Theoretical Overview." In *Women, Culture and Society*, edited by Michele Zimbalist Rosaldo and Louise Lamphere, pp.17-41. Stanford:Stanford University Press.
Rothblatt, Donald N., Daniel J. Garr, and Jo Sprague. 1979. *The Suburban Environment and Women*. New York:Praeger.

Saegert, Susan. 1982. "Toward the Androgynous City." In *Cities in the 21st Century*, edited by Gary Gappert and Richard V. Knight, pp.196–212. Beverly Hills: Sage.
———. 1980. "Masculine Cities and Feminine Suburbs: Polarized Ideas, Contradictory Realities." *Signs* 5 (Spring):S96–S110.
Slocum, Sally. 1975. "Woman the Gatherer:Male Bias in Anthropology." In *Toward an Anthropology of Women*, edited by Reyna Reiter, pp.36–50. New York: Monthly Review Press.
Stone, Clarence. 1980. "Systemic Power in Community Decision Making. A Restatement of Stratification Theory." *American Political Science Review* 74 (December):978–90.
Torre, Susan. 1981. "Space as a Matrix." *Heresies* 3:pp.51–52.
U.S. Department of Labor. 1984. *Women and Work*. Washington, D.C.: Government Printing Office.

11

ACCESS TO THE CITY MEANS MORE THAN CURB CUTS: THE DISABLED

Roberta Ann Johnson

It is politically useful for the disabled to argue that their demand for urban services is no more than an example of just another excluded group asking for access to the city. It is politically useful but misleading. The disabled are asking for changes more fundamental than finite programs such as bilingual ballots or city supported child care services. The underlying demand of the disabled is that their interests and needs be factored into every city decision without their even having to ask: when plans for subsidized housing are on the drawing board, that issues of physical access always be addressed; when plans for a public concert are being discussed, that a sign language interpreter be commissioned as a matter of course; when the old public transit system is being overhauled, that lifts and elevators be added as a natural part of the renovation; that churches, theaters, parks, libraries, restaurants, parking lots, and city halls always do what is necessary to make themselves accessible.

Access to the city means more than curb cuts for at least two reasons. First, it is not just physical barriers, like curbs, that block the entrance of the disabled to city life. A major block is attitudinal. Feelings which work against including the disabled range from reactions of mild discomfort to pity, upset, and disgust. Underlying these attitudes may even be a wish for the disabled just to go away and die, a theme raised by the drama, *Whose Life is This Anyway*, and the cases of Elizabeth Bouvia and Keri-Lynn (Baby Jane Doe).

Whose Life is This Anyway, a Broadway play and Hollywood movie, dramatized the story of a sculptor who was severely disabled in a car accident and wants the hospital to help him commit suicide; Elizabeth Bouvia is a 26-year-old severely disabled woman who checked herself into a hospital in 1984 and asked that she be made comfortable while she committed suicide by starving herself to death; and Keri-Lynn of Long Island was the multihandicapped "Baby Jane Doe" who, it was claimed, did not receive the life-saving medical treatment that a nonhandicapped child would have received. The common theme, that life is not worth living for a disabled person, runs through these cases.[1]

The second reason why disabled access to the city means more than curb cuts is that not all disabled people are in wheelchairs and need curb cuts. The disabled are a diverse group. It is a group that includes more than the pretty poster child and the brave veteran. With broad stroke, the Section 504 Regulations of the Vocational Rehabilitation Act of 1973 define "handicapped individual" as any person who (1) has a physical or mental impairment which substantially limits one or more major life activities, (2) has a record of such an impairment, or (3) is regarded as having such an impairment. This definition includes a wide range of disabled persons—deaf, blind, amputee, arthritic, individuals with cerebral palsy, those who have had polio, the scarred, asthmatic, paraplegic, the learning disabled and mentally retarded—and this short list just scratches the surface of group membership. Given the variety of disabilities and the potpourri of special needs, from deaf interpreters to special raised letter signs for the blind, a city must do much more than just cut curbs for wheelchair-users to make its services, its facilities, and its jobs accessible to the disabled.

Not only does the diversity of their needs and demands work against the disabled as a pressure group, the disabled have also been drastically undercounted. In 1980, the Census Bureau asked one out of four households, nationwide, if there was someone who had a physical, mental, or other health condition that has lasted for six or more months, and that limits the kind or amount of work the person can do or prevents employment altogether. Based on the responses to this question, the bureau reported that there were 12 million people in the United States, of working age, who did not work due to disability. But there are many more disabled people in the country who the Census Bureau did not count. There are those disabled persons under 16 and over 64 who do not work and, therefore, would not have been counted because the question is work-related; and there are those disabled who do not believe that their disability limits their work and thus would not have labeled themselves as disabled. For these and other reasons, the Census Bureau statistics have been criticized as a gross "undercount" by magazines such as *Mainstream* (Hammitt 1983) and *Disability Rag* (1984a). The best criticism of available statistics, however, was done by the U.S. Commission on Civil Rights. Quoting extensively from a report (Roistacher et al. 1981) produced by the Bureau of Social Science Research under contract with the National Institute of Handicapped Research, the commission concluded, "There is no single repository of adequate national data on the handicapped population" (U.S. Commission on Civil Rights 1983).

THE BERKELEY STORY

There are many reasons why the experience of the disabled in gaining access in Berkeley makes an interesting case study. As a city, Berkeley, California seems to contain all the ingredients which would lead it to full accessibility. Berkeley is a small city of approximately 100,000, with a strong commitment to fairness and affirmative action, and a tradition of responding to citizens' demands. Berkeley, too, was the residence of some of the best organized disabled advocates and the site of the first Center for Independent Living (CIL). Furthermore, Berkeley had a high percentage of disabled residents (18 percent) who, unlike those in most cities, were accurately counted by city officials (Berkeley 1978a). And yet the road to full accessibility for Berkeley was not a smooth one.

Berkeley began cutting curbs for its wheelchair-users in 1969. But the Berkeley story started before then, and it took over a decade after those first curb cuts for Berkeley's commitment to disabled access to expand and become routinized, inclusive, and bureaucratized. In the beginning, there were three major actors in the story: the University of California, the Center for Independent Living, and the city government. Like all good stories, this one has heroes.

Hale Zukas, disabled advocate and former member of the prestigious national Architectural and Transportation Barriers and Compliance Board [2], has chronicled the beginnings. The story started on the Berkeley campus in 1964, when Ed Roberts, a postpolio respiratory quadraplegic, was admitted to the University of California. Because he used an iron lung, he was assigned a room in Cowell Hospital, the campus student health service. By 1966, two more quadraplegics, Scott Sorenson and John Hessler, moved into Cowell; by 1969, there were 12 severely disabled students living there. They might have been bound even more tightly to their hospital residence had the City of Berkeley not responded to the students' urging to include ramping as part of the reconstruction already planned for a four-block area south of the university. The city included curb cuts in its renovation plan for this area in 1969-70.

In fall 1969, a combination of restrictive living conditions and impending graduation led most of the Cowell residents to organize, under the Group Studies Program, a university class called "Strategies of Independent Living." During the course of the class, the students shifted their focus from the goal of setting up a communal living arrangement to finding funding for the services they needed. They focused on getting U.S. Office of Education Special Service Program money to set up a campus Physically Disabled Students' Program (PDSP).

> [A]n attendant referral service, a provision for emergency attendant care, a wheelchair repair service, and an advocacy component were incorporated into the proposed program along with a component devoted to helping disabled students deal with the University-related matters.... (Zukas 1975)

PDSP was federally funded in July 1970. Immediate benefits were that the program employed the disabled (five of the nine staff members were severely disabled or blind) and it enabled disabled students to move out of Cowell and into the community yet still get the services they needed. An added by-product of the program was that the dropout rate among disabled university students went down. The program was a success, such a success in fact, that disabled nonstudents began to ask PDSP for help. After a year, (nonuniversity) community demand was so great that the program founders began to talk about creating a similar program out in the community.

In May 1971, meetings began which would result in the creation of the Center for Independent Living. Some of the same PDSP people were involved. By spring 1972, they incorporated CIL with the aid of a federal Rehabilitation Service Administration grant. In June 1973, when this grant was expiring and no new funds were forthcoming, Ed Roberts and PDSP Director John Hessler asked University of California Vice Chancellor Robert Kerley for help. A grant of $15,000 was made available through the university's Community Projects Office. In August, the City of Berkeley made a similar grant to cover CIL rent and utilities. By the next month, CIL was providing an attendant referral service, housing referral service, and transportation with a donated Volkswagon van. With city and university funding, CIL was now planted firmly in Berkeley as a resource/referral center for disabled Berkeley residents.

Thus, the City of Berkeley and the University of California, Berkeley, played key roles in the development of the first Center for Independent Living in the country (see Johnson 1982). And city funds continue to be part of the budgeting package CIL puts together each year. These city monies have, in turn, come from federal grant programs, including the Comprehensive Education and Training Act, Community Development Block Grants, and the Community Action Program (Berkeley 1980a).

CIVIL RIGHTS FOR THE DISABLED

About the same time that CIL was establishing itself in Berkeley, the U.S. Congress passed the Vocational Rehabilitation Act. Buried in this 1973 law was a civil rights provision that was to reap a revolution in the United States. The one-sentence provision simply prohibited discrimination on the basis of handicap. It was a promise that was to be implemented by the Section 504 regulations. During the next four years, while the Berkeley CIL flourished, providing needed services to the community, there were delays in implementing the 504 regulations.

> During 1975 and 1976, the Office of Civil Rights of the Department of Health, Education, and Welfare [HEW] delayed implementing Section 504 regulations, first with an inflationary impact study and then with countless meetings with groups across the country including ten town meetings held in May and June 1976. Even after HEW composed a final form for Section 504 "regs" ... the secretary of HEW did not sign them, ignoring a federal court order to do so.

Under the Carter administration, HEW did not move any faster. HEW Secretary Joseph Califano delayed signing the implementing regulations so that his staff could rewrite them. In February and March 1977, when it became clear that more than cosmetic changes were being considered by HEW, disabled groups started to plan action to prevent Califano from building "loopholes, waivers and exemptions" into the regulations (Johnson 1982, p.84).

In March 1977, the American Coalition of Citizens with Disabilities (ACCD), a Washington, D.C. umbrella lobbying group representing about 45 disability-related organizations, threatened political activities nationwide if HEW Secretary Joseph Califano did not sign the 504 Regulations by April 4, 1977. He did not, and there were demonstrations on April 5 at HEW buildings in ten different cities. At some sites, the demonstrations turned into sit-ins. In Washington, D.C. and Denver, the sit-ins lasted one day; in Los Angeles, it lasted three days, and in San Francisco, where the sit-in was spearheaded by the Berkeley Center for Independent Living, the 150 participants had enough community support to threaten to stay indefinitely. Food and other support was provided by the Salvation Army, the Black Panthers, a local Safeway, a Hispanic group called the Mission Rebels, an ex-prisoner organization called the Delancey Street Foundation, Werner Erhard of est, gay groups like the Butterfly Brigade, and labor organizations, including some AFL/CIO affiliated unions (Johnson 1982, pp.86–87). Twenty-four days after the San Francisco sit-in began, Califano signed the implementing regulations.

The signing of the regulations was seen as a direct result of the political pressure and political skill of Bay area disabled advocates and supporters, especially CIL, whose leadership had planned and orchestrated the successful sit-in. With the civil rights regulations in place, CIL could focus not just on services but on disability rights in Berkeley.

THE CITY RESISTS

Many advocates expected that Berkeley would be among the first cities to fully comply with the regulations to assure full accessibility. It was a small city with a liberal tradition and a large and visible disabled population. In fact, a Washington *Post* article dubbed the Berkeley area "the nation's capital for the handicapped" (Geyer 1977). By 1977, the Center for Independent Living had national prestige and had almost a million dollars worth of funding. Yet, a conflict between CIL and the City of Berkeley quickly emerged over the principle of affirmative action and who it included. When CIL, as a city contractor, was asked to comply with the City Council's Affirmative Action Resolution 46,913 protecting minorities, CIL responded with a heated letter wondering why the disabled were not also included as a protected class.

The CIL letter, dated February 13, 1978, read in part, "When an individual with a disability is refused employment it is not generally because of their ethnic background or their sex, rather the denial is based solely on the fact that they are disabled" (Center for Independent Living 1978). CIL was told by the city manager's office that the disabled "might" be recognized as a minority "in a month or two."

Meanwhile CIL was being asked to comply with the city's affirmative action program protecting other groups. Did this mean that CIL would have to meet the minority population parity goals in employment at the possible cost of not hiring the disabled? At that time, nearly 50 percent of CIL's staff was disabled. CIL raised this issue in their February 13 letter.

In this letter, CIL also asked to see the city's "self-evaluation and transition plan." A self-evaluation is basically just an assessment of buildings and programs as to their accessibility for disabled people; a transition plan, according to the regulations, was supposed to have been developed and made available for public inspection by December 1977, and is basically a calendar showing the dates by which the necessary architectural, structural, and programmatic changes to achieve accessibility would be made.

After numerous meetings with federal, state, and community groups, including representatives of CIL, the City of Berkeley formally responded to CIL's letter on May 11, 1978. The response was in the form of a memorandum from the City's Assistant Contract Compliance Officer, Sylvester Brooks, to the City Manager, Elijah Rogers, on "The Feasibility of an Employment Policy for the Disabled."

The city memo examined what Berkeley was obliged to do under Section 503, which related to affirmative action hiring practices, and under Section 504, which related to the self-evaluation and transition plan.

Section 503 of the act, administered by the U.S. Department of Labor, required government contractors and subcontractors to take affirmative action to employ qualified handicapped individuals. Brooks argued, "It is anticipated Section 503 of the act and implementing rules and regulations will minimally affect the City, since the City rarely has a direct contract with the Federal Government." Section 504, administered by HEW, required nondiscrimination on the basis of handicap in programs and activities receiving federal financial assistance. Because Berkeley was technically the recipient of "HEW financial assistance" due only to one program, a five-year grant from HEW to develop a community high blood pressure control program, Brooks argued that the City of Berkeley did not have to do a self-evaluation and develop a transition plan as required by the HEW implementing regulations. "Since the hypertension research project," Brooks wrote, "is not involved in service delivery, the project does not have to comply with the Section 504 regulation that requires the submission of the transition plan."

This narrow interpretation of the city's obligations under 504 proved erroneous. Later the city formally blamed the faulty legal reasoning on bad advice given to them by HEW. At the time, however, some disabled advocates blamed Brooks himself, and a source in the mayor's office blamed the city manager. The city did indeed have obligations under 503 and 504 but the opportunity to swiftly meet those obligations with a harmonic and historic effort was lost.

For the next five years, the city was reluctantly involved in developing a self-evaluation and transition plan. During this period the city bureaucracy resisted, defused, and finally absorbed access concerns as the city moved toward a commitment to full access. In July 1978, the City Manager's Office set up an Affirmative Action Task Force for the Disabled (Berkeley 1978b). But by 1979, the Task Force was no longer meeting. In December, letters from CIL, the Berkeley Outreach Recreational Program, the Physically Disabled Students Program, and the Disabled Students Union were received by the mayor and transmitted to the city council. Each organization sharply questioned the city's commitment to accessibility.

The letter from CIL was particularly critical and specific:

> We have a right to the services and job opportunities made available to non-disabled people in this City. We feel the day for "sensitivity training" is long gone. It is time for the City of Berkeley to live up to its moral and legal responsibility to meet the needs of its disabled residents.

The letter also complained that it took an hour-long discussion to get the city's Human Relations Commission to move a November meeting to an accessible site (Center for Independent Living 1979).

At this time, the effort looked like it was floundering, according to disabled advocate Eric Dibner.[3] Below the surface, however, there was activity, and Dibner was a moving force through these years. He himself was not disabled but came to the disability movement by "accident." As an undergraduate in architecture at the University of California in the mid-1960s, he answered an ad for a part-time job as an attendant. He became John Hessler's attendant and so got to know the original Cowell group. He became a friend and advocate to the movement and his professional expertise was just one of his many contributions.

In January 1980, the mayor formed, with council approval, another task force with the same name and purpose. And a self-evaluation and transition plan (without the timetables), the items originally asked for by CIL, began to be developed outside official city channels. The university became a participant again as students from the school's Architecture Field Studies Program were trained by CIL to do accessibility surveys. From October 1980 to February 1981, approximately 50 parks and 30 buildings were surveyed by university students with the assistance of the city's Department of Public Works. It was not a project mandated by the City Manager's Office, but it was done.

This architectural survey supplemented a 1978–79 survey of libraries and city office buildings done by a disabled advocates' network called Access

California. The two surveys were combined into a single report, divided into chapters which covered fire stations, parks and recreation facilities, health facilities, miscellaneous buildings, and libraries and city office buildings. The editors of the final city task force report (Berkeley 1982a) recommended giving priority attention to such things as signs and doorbells at fire stations, handrails at a senior center, and entrance access at the City Hall of Justice. Flyers publicizing a meeting to encourage community response and participation reported:

> The City Council will soon be deciding about the plans for complying with Section 504—what policies to change, what buildings to modify. The Mayor's Task Force on the Disabled has prepared written recommendations and surveys have been completed for parks and facilities. The *Community is invited to attend* this information-sharing and review of the City's plans. All persons wanting to have input on the rights of disabled people to use Berkeley programs should be at this workshop.

The city Department of Public Works, Engineering Division, provided cost estimates for all the recommended changes in February 1982.

After the formal community meeting held on February 8, the report listing architectural barriers was circulated throughout the disabled community to get the broadest possible response to help prioritize barrier removal. Then, on June 2, 1982, on behalf of CIL, Eric Dibner provided the Berkeley City Manager's Office with a prioritized list of sites for barrier removal and modification based on the principle of providing access for the most people at the least cost.

Not only was there movement on the architectural front, but the disabled community also helped stimulate progress on the city's self-evaluation of programs, the area which focused on the nonarchitectural aspects of accessibility. The Disability Law Resource Center (DLRC), a branch of CIL, contributed in a major way to that aspect of the city's self-evaluation. DLRC obtained from HEW's Office for Civil Rights a copy of the self-evaluation questions used by the County of San Mateo. With this document as a model, the Disabled Task Force adapted the questions for use in Berkeley and the questionnaire was sent to all the city departments in fall 1980.

In the memorandum accompanying the questionnaire sent by City Manager Wise Allen, Berkeley formally admitted its responsibility to do a 504 self-evaluation, calling the questionnaire being sent to all department heads "the beginning of a self-evaluation process by which [to] identify all barriers, both physical and programmatic, to the participation of disabled persons in all City programs, services and employment opportunities" (Berkeley 1980b). The 20-page questionnaire asked departments about their recruitment policies, grievance procedures, affirmative action efforts, physical barriers, use of readers, interpreters, tapes, auxiliary aids, and training programs.

It took nearly two years to sift through the department responses. At about the same time the architectural priorities were being presented to the city manager, the task force was making 70 programmatic recommendations to the City Manager's Office. The programmatic recommendations were reorganized into a categorical form and were submitted on December 7, 1982 to the mayor and to members of the city council (Berkeley 1982b). The city manager recommended that the council officially accept the report coming from the task force. The manager also recommended that the council direct the manager to return on January 25, 1983 with a report in response to the task force recommendations (Berkeley 1982c). An article in a local neighborhood newspaper, the *Montclarion* (Ewell 1982), described the task force recommendations as having come after "foot dragging by city staff" and quoted an advocate who called the recommendations, "too little, too late." If 70 recommendations seemed "too little" to some, imagine how disappointed many advocates were when a month later in his January 25, 1983 Report for Council Action, the city manager recommended action on only 11 items.

Once the task force recommendations had gone to the city council, the Mayor's Task Force on the Disabled was institutionalized as the Disability Subcommittee of the Berkeley Human Relations and Welfare Commission (HRWC). The subcommittee was itself divided into groups charged with implementing the 11 recommendations.

IMPLEMENTATION

Surprisingly, the city moved with dispatch in the implementation stage. Under a new city manager, Daniel Boggan Jr., a sense of accomplishment was felt by participants, especially the disabled advocates. Policies were changing. Responding to the manager's recommendations, the council immediately passed three resolutions: one establishing a policy of equal employment opportunity for disabled persons and a grievance process for disabled employees; another requiring that all contracts, subcontracts, and agreements contain nondiscrimination clauses prohibiting unlawful discrimination on the basis of disability; and a third, instituting a policy that all public informational materials containing telephone numbers must also include the deaf (TDD or TTY) telephone number. Several months later, in April 1983, the council approved a fourth resolution requiring that council, board, commission, and city-sponsored committee meetings be held in accessible locations.

It took another year for Berkeley to develop a comprehensive policy on communication access and even longer to deliver an awareness training workshop to 250 city employees. Both projects were well planned and worth the wait, however, and could be models for other cities. By 1984, Berkeley personnel had developed a draft proposal for a program of reasonable accommodation for qualified disabled employees and job applicants. The proposal was submitted to the Berkeley director of personnel from the city's senior personnel analyst. It committed the city to a policy of nondiscrimination in employment; committed the city to accommodate to the physical and mental limitations of qualified disabled applicants and employees; and proposed that funds be allocated to meet the city's reasonable accommodation needs (Berkeley 1984). Disability rights were being integrated into the bureaucracy.

One reason for this sense of "implementation success" surrounding disability issues was that a momentum was developing as goals were accomplished. Another explanation was the appointment of a 504 coordinator, Bill Castellanos, in 1983. He was able to coordinate the various activities of the subcommittees of the HRWC Subcommittee on the Disabled (for example the Affirmative Action Subcommittee, Reasonable Accommodation Subcommittee, Curb Ramping Working Subcommittee, and Self-evaluation and Employment Practices Subcommittee) by holding them responsible and providing oversight and continuity. While not disabled himself, Castellanos demonstrated a commitment which energized the advocates with whom he worked.

Ironically, although there was less conflict surrounding architectural barrier removal and the city construction projects were prioritized in 1982, it was not until 1984 that the city prepared construction specifications and drawings for bid to implement the first-year priority projects. According to Jack Pajoohandeh of the city Public Works Department, his department sought feedback on their specifications from the disabled community, a process that lengthened the preparation period. There may have been consensus on the project but there seemed to be no rush to spend the $88,550 earmarked for first year construction.[4]

Yet this was not the first time Berkeley had spent money on physical barrier removal. As already described, the city had cut curbs in 1969 to accommodate disabled university students. Then, starting in 1972, as a result of Council Resolution No. 44,866 N.S., the city appropriated $30,000 annually for curb cuts. This resolution committed the city to a policy in which streets, sidewalks, curbs, and railroad crossings are designed, constructed, or modified "to facilitate circulation by handicapped persons in the City of Berkeley." According to Herb Lotter, Senior Civil Engineer, Public Works Department, even the design of curb cuts was not a simple matter. Curb cuts had changed radically over the years, not only because the design and material had been improved but also because of the input of disabled people, including blind people who complained they had problems with ramping in crosswalks. Bureaucratic rules complicated the process. For example, the striping of crosswalks prescribed by the state architect was in conflict with the Department of Transportation Code.[5]

There are three things worth noting about the Berkeley curb-cut program. First, the Public Works Department worked smoothly with the disabled community. Second, the bureaucracy was so responsive that, until 1984, the location of curb cuts was decided on the basis of people calling and making personal requests. And third (as we have seen), even though curbs had been cut on-request since 1969, that did not make Berkeley an "accessible city."

The fact that accessibility means more than curb cuts was emphasized over and over again by the disabled advocates I interviewed. For example, according to Michael Winter, the Executive Director of CIL, Berkeley is succeeding in its major thrust for physical access, but it has failed in integrating the disabled socially and politically.[6] The exception that proves the rule is Kathy Pugh, a quadraplegic and former President of the Disabled Student Union at the University of California, who won a seat as a commissioner on the Rent Stabilization Board. Although she had a broad base of support and was elected by a wide margin, she still felt herself to be a "token candidate."[7] Even the mayor of Berkeley, Gus Newport, admitted, "We've got a long way to go."[8]

CONCLUSION

As we have seen, Berkeley struggled with the process of integrating access into the bureaucratic decision process. It was not a question of adopting finite programs as much as one of factoring into the very fabric of city decision making the interests and needs of the disabled. That is why the struggle for access in Berkeley took longer than one would have predicted.

The process was made easier for Berkeley, however, because of the large numbers of disabled city residents. For at least a decade, Berkeley officials assumed that approximately 18% of the city's population was disabled. Had Berkeley relied on 1980 Census data, however, fewer than 6% of the population would have been considered disabled. Most cities do not know with accuracy the number of disabled residents. An undercount usually means that cities will be less likely to respond to the demand for access. However, the visibility of the disabled in Berkeley, and the relative accuracy of their count, makes this city unique and also helps explain why Berkeley has responded to many disability-related issues.

The responsiveness of the city has not only resulted in things like wheelchair accessible police paddy wagons, but city responsiveness has also raised some fascinating new legal issues. For example, among the impairment cases heard by the Berkeley Police Review Commission is one that raised the interesting question of whether a wheelchair is a "motorized vehicle." If so, this would allow the user to be cited for violating the law against intoxicated driving![9]

Not only does city access raise new issues, it also sets the stage for a change in urban policy so fundamental that everyone would benefit. The disabled are actually asking for a wholesale "humanizing" of the city, a shift toward the interest of people when urban decisions are made. For example, the disabled are asking that instead of the individual accommodating to a job, that the job site provide reasonable accommodation for the individual. Think what this would be like if such a shift were generalized to the entire workforce. Instead of the person accommodating to a job, whatever the personal cost (for example high blood pressure, neglect of children), the job would accommodate to the individual's needs in scheduling and design. The disabled are asking for a shift in architectural design as well. Again, think what this would mean if it were generalized. Instead of buildings being monuments to some aesthetic god who demands uncomfortable chairs and level changes to suit the building "line" and "look," the building would be built to serve people, catering to their physical convenience and comfort.[10] All people would benefit from such a humanizing shift. And thus, access to the city means more than curb cuts for another reason. Access expresses a commitment to people; it may even reflect a basic shift in urban decision making that will humanize the experience of the city for everyone.

NOTES

1. The story line of *Whose Life Is This Anyway* revolved around the sculptor's desire to die and the hospital's final capitulation in the suicide. "Baby Jane Doe" was brought to national attention because her case sparked a conflict between the Department of Health and Human Services, Office for Civil Rights, and the medical profession over possible violations of her civil rights. (For one of the best general articles on this theme, see *Disability Rag*, Box 145, Louisville, Kentucky 40201, February-March 1984. Also see Jessica Scheer, "They Act Like It's Contagious: A Study of Mobility Impairment in a New York City Neighborhood," paper presented at the Annual Meeting of the Society for the Study of Chronic Illness, Impairment, and Disability, Western Social Science Association, April 27-30, 1983, Albuquerque.)

2. Section 502 of the Rehabilitation Act of 1973 (as amended in 1978) established the Architectural and Transportation Barriers Compliance Board. The 11 public members are appointed by the President; the remaining ten members are high executives or the heads of federal agencies.

3. Eric Dibner July 5, 1984: interview.

4. Jack Pajoohandeh October 11, 1984: interview. According to Pajoohandeh, the accessibility projects went out to bid in June 1984. There were no bids. His explanation was that contractors were busy during the summer season. They went out to bid again in November 1984.

5. Herb Lotter, Senior Civil Engineer, Berkeley Public Works Department July 31, 1984: interview.

6. Michael Winter, Executive Director, Center for Independent Living July 27, 1984: interview. Several months after the interview, Winter rolled down the aisle at the University of California's Newman Hall Chapel and married Atsuko Kuwana. The *Tribune*, the major East Bay daily newspaper, covered the event with a full-page story, which included large photos from the ceremony. This kind of coverage suggests a level of social integration which Winter had asserted was absent in Berkeley.

7. Kathy Pugh, Commissioner, Rent Stabilization Board August 7, 1984: interview.

8. Gus Newport, Mayor of Berkeley August 8, 1984: interview.

9. Eileen Luna Gordinier, Attorney and Chief Investigator for the Berkeley Police Review Commission July 31, 1984: interview.

10. The tension between the architect's commitment to an aesthetic ideal and the needs of the user was explored at the International Designed Environments for All People Conference, held at the United Nations, January 22-24, 1982. This theme was one of many discussed in an interview with Mary Lou Breslin, Executive Director, Disability Rights Education and Defense Fund (DREDF) and Steve Alwards, Urban Planner, June 21, 1984.

REFERENCES

Berkeley, California (city). 1984. Memorandum dated March 27. To: Dorothy Parrish, Director of Personnel; From: Beverly Lowe, Senior Personnel Analyst; Subject: Draft Proposal for "Reasonable Accommodation Program for Qualified Disabled Employees and Job Applicants."

———. 1982a. Supplemental Recommendations for Report on Accessibility of City Buildings and Parks: Priorities For Modification. June 2.

———. 1982b. For Council Action. December 7. To: Honorable Mayor and Members of the City Council; From: Mayor's Task Force on Disability; Subject: Report on Findings and Recommendations to Promote Equal Opportunity and Accessibility for Disabled Persons.

———. 1982c. For Council Action. December 7. To: Honorable Mayor and Members of the City Council; From: Daniel Boggan, Jr., City Manager; Subject: Report on Findings and Recommendations to Promote Equal Opportunity and Accessibility for Disabled Persons

———. 1980a. "Center for Independent Living, Inc. Government Grants and Contracts, 1972-1980," prepared by Grants and Contracts Office. January 25.

———. 1980b. Memorandum, dated October 14. To: Department Heads; From: Wise E. Allen, City Manager; Subject: City of Berkeley Self-Assessment Checklist for Section 504 of the 1973 Rehabilitation Act.

———. 1978a. Memorandum dated May 11. To: Elijah B. Rogers, City Manager; From: Sylvester Brooks, Assistant Contract Compliance Officer; Subject: Preliminary Status Report on Examining the Feasibility of an Employment Policy for the Disabled.

———. 1978b. Memorandum dated July 28. To: Center for Independent Living; From: Elijah B. Rogers, City Manager; Subject: Affirmative Action Task Force for the Disabled.

Center for Independent Living, Berkeley. 1979. Letter dated December 19 to Gus Newport, Mayor of Berkeley.

———. 1978. Letter dated February 13. To: Hon. Warren Widener, Mayor; From: Phil Draper, Executive Director; Judy Heumann, Sr. Deputy Director; and Guy Guber, Employment Rights Specialist, Center for Independent Living; Subject: Affirmative Action Compliance (Council Resolution 46,913).

Disability Rag. 1984a. Box 145, Louisville, Kentucky 40201. June.

———. 1984b. February-March.

Ewell, Miranada. 1982. "The Disabled: Task Force Report Called 'Too Little, Too Late.' " *Montclarion*, December 28, p. 1.

Geyer, Georgie Anne. 1977. "Moving Back Into Society." Washington *Post*, July 25, p. A21.

Hammitt, Jim. 1983. "We Got To Do It By the Numbers." *Mainstream*, March, p. 9.

Johnson, Roberta Ann. 1982. "The Mobilization of the Disabled." In *Social Movements of the Sixties and Seventies*, edited by Jo Freeman, pp. 82-100. New York: Longman.

Roistacher, Richard et al. 1981. *Toward a Comprehensive Data System on the Demographic and Epidemiological Characteristics of the Handicapped Population: Final Report*. Washington, D.C.: Bureau of Social Science Research, Inc.

Scheer, Jessica. 1983. "They Act Like It's Contagious: A Study of Mobility Impairment in a New York City Neighborhood." Paper presented at the Annual Meeting of the Society for the Study of Chronic Illness, Impairment, and Disability, Western Social Science Association, April 27-30, Albuquerque.

U.S. Commission on Civil Rights. 1983. *Accommodating the Spectrum of Individual Abilities*. Washington, D.C.: Government Printing Office.

Zukas, Hale. 1975. "Part I: C.I.L. History." Paper presented at the State of the Art in Independent Living Conference, October, Berkeley.

PART V
EQUALITY OF INFLUENCE, POWER, AND CONTROL

12

IS THERE A "GRAY PERIL"? THE AGING'S IMPACT UPON SUNBELT COMMUNITY TAXING AND SPENDING

James W. Button and Walter A. Rosenbaum

Much of the southern Sunbelt's political future is shaped by the sweep of demographic curves. The implications of many major changes in the southern population have already been explored: the impact of rising population immigration upon southern congressional strength; the transformations of traditional Democratic voting behavior by a new urban and suburban southern electorate; the changing policy priorities of southern governments faced with industrializing economies and better educated constituencies. But the political implications of the migrations of older Americans to the southern Sunbelt have rarely been examined. "Up to this time," recently observed sociologist Charles F. Longino, Jr., "the political consequences of retirement migration are not understood" (Longino 1980, p. 289). This reflects a broader lack of empirical information about the political behavior of the aging whose importance in U.S. civic life is expected to increase significantly in the next several decades.

In particular, the impact of a steadily growing older population upon the Sunbelt's state and local governmental budgets has been more discussed than researched. One common assertion—to many, an apprehension— is that the aged will become the Sunbelt's "Gray Peril," using their considerable voting strength to promote governmental services important to the aging while vigorously opposing increased spending for other programs and new taxes to underwrite other essential public services. Other commentators believe the aged will have a largely benign impact, if any at all, upon state and local budgets. Still others—aware of the growing proportion of younger, healthier individuals among the elderly moving to the Sunbelt—expect the full governmental impact to be felt years after the elderly relocate, when the once "young old" need more governmental services.

If there is a "Gray Peril," then the "cost" of an expanding older population in Sunbelt communities may often be a loss of community resources to younger constituencies and other economic and social interests. This raises important issues concerning which groups become winners or losers in the process and the equitability of the result. If the budgetary impacts of expanding older populations are likely to be felt in the future then the responsibility of local government to plan for these impacts, and the relative role of different social groups in providing resources to meet these anticipated impacts, become matters of urgent current importance to local governments. Thus, the "Gray Peril" hypothesis and its variations all imply a major consideration of what role the elderly do assume, and should assume, in the governmental allocation of community resources.

We have attempted to test some implications of the "Gray Peril" hypothesis by examining the budgetary impacts of rising older populations on local governmental spending in Florida's smaller cities over the last ten years. Our findings are preliminary because the data, available only recently, have not been subjected to time series analysis or more sophisticated statistical tests that can refine and clarify relationships. The relatively simple statistics presented here, however, do suggest several interesting conclusions about the validity of the "Gray Peril" argument. The conclusions can best be appreciated by first placing the study within the broader context of literature on public policy and the aging in the Sunbelt.

THE POLITICAL IMPORTANCE OF THE "OTHER" SUNBELT

The choice of Florida's smaller communities for examination is based upon important changes in the nation's retirement patterns over the last 20 years. Smaller governmental constituencies have become the political arenas where many of the public policy issues most important to the aging are now being resolved for a growing proportion of the older population. These civic settings provide a logical place for testing a multitude of assumptions about the political behavior of the aging.

In the mid-1980s, about one in five Americans over age 55 had moved across state lines to a new residence. More than half of these older Americans had moved to the Sunbelt states. Almost half of the older Americans now moving to the Sunbelt will live in Florida (Biggar 1979; Kraft and Osterbind 1981). Until recently, most of the Sunbelt's in-migrant aging moved to urban or suburban areas—Florida's St. Petersburg is the quintessential retirement haven in popular folklore—or bulldozed scrub oak forests and drained lowlands into geriatric suburbs like Sun City, Florida. Largely obscured by such images of Sunbelt retirement is what Glenn Fugitt and Stephen Tordella (1981) call the "nonmetropolitan turnabout" in Sunbelt immigration among the aging.

One of the most significant demographic trends within the Sunbelt over the last 20 years has been the slow but resolute rise in the number of retired Americans immigrating to the region's established smaller cities and predominantly rural counties—what we have clled the "other" Sunbelt. The national growth rate for older populations in nonmetropolitan areas first exceeded the urban growth rate in the 1960s. The number of aging moving to nonurban Sunbelt areas has grown steadily in the last 20 years. Although the number of elderly today living in nonmetropolitan Sunbelt areas has not been precisely estimated, almost all commentators believe it is a much higher proportion of the Sunbelt's older population than it was five years previously (Lee and Lassey 1980).

Not suprisingly, Florida leads the nation in the number of in-migrant elderly moving to nonmetropolitan areas and in its growth rates for older nonurban populations. The result has been a developmental "boom," sustained almost exclusively by an expanding older population in many small cities and counties. Between 1970 and 1980, for example, the average growth rate of the aged (over 60) population in Florida counties was about 69 percent, but 13 counties—a majority with populations under 75,000 at the decade's outset—more than doubled their older population in this period.

Political scientist Robert Hudson (1980, p. 154) has called the impact of expanding older populations on the Sunbelt's state and local governments "the first major question needing more explicit attention" in political gerontology. It might seem surprising that little research has been devoted to the political role of the older citizen in the local community and, most importantly, to the manner in which local public policy responds to older residents. Partially, as Henry Pratt (1979, pp. 155–68) has observed, this void exists because political scientists have only in recent years accorded to older age an important place in paradigms of political socialization, attitude development, issue concerns, and other aspects of political behavior. Neal Cutler (1977b, p. 1023) has argued that political scientists have been especially slow to perceive that generational trends, evidenced in the political behavior of the aging over the last 30 years, may invalidate many strongly held generalizations about political behavior.

The practical implication is that research on the politics of the aging in the nonurban Sunbelt ought to start with an examination of the most fundamental issues widely discussed in the relevant literature. The "Gray Peril" hypothesis, one of these issues, arises from a basic disagreement over the political sociology of the aging.

IS THERE A POLITICS OF AGE? THE "GRAY PERIL" ISSUE

Current discussions about a "Gray Peril" menacing state and local governmental budgets grow, like other speculations concerning the aging and public spending, from unresolved controversies over the probability that the nation's aged will become a politically mobilized, self-conscious interest active in promoting politics of age at all governmental levels.

The Political Mobilization Controversy

Many social scientists have predicted the U.S. citizens now reaching retirement age are likely to become an organized constituency with a political agenda and policy priorities dictated specifically by issue concerns relevant to the aging. This will be a far more politically active, broadly based, and persisting form of political participation among the aging than previously; it will be "an emerging politics of age" driven by a new sense of shared interests and common beliefs among the elderly. Many factors are cited to explain this phenomenon. Political scientists Neal Cutler (1977a) and Robert Hudson (1980) have suggested that political activism among the aged is likely to increase because those now at, or near, retirement age are generally better educated, more politically experienced and active, more prosperous, and more politically informed that prior generations of retired Americans; they "have been self-conscious in terms of age and public policy issues concerning age, for a much longer period of [their] life cycle than has previously been the case" (Cutler 1977a, p. 170).

Numerous gerontologists, like Ron Aday and Laurie Miles (1982, pp. 331–32), believe that growing political mobilization among the aging may be compelled by decreasing federal support for many programs important to the elderly and by the increased competition the elderly may feel, often for the first time, from other organized interests for state and local governmental services. Carroll Estes (1978, p. 47) has speculated that this mobilization may be abetted by "agencies for the aging" and other state or local bureaucracies serving older Americans. Gerontologists William and Norma Anderson (1978) have noted that retirement communities and other settlements almost exclusively populated by the aging are breeding "an emerging subculture of the aging" in which the elderly are becoming socially and politically self-conscious through their proximity and social interaction.

Other social analysts are skeptical about a new "politics of the aging." One common argument is that the aging are vulnerable to divisive social cleavages and differences of economic and political interest often more salient in shaping political behavior than shared opinions based upon age; there are, in effect, very few issues upon which most of the aging can be united in voting or policy preferences. "The heterogeneity of the elderly will continue to inhibit the development of a strong elderly voting block and the evolution of the elderly as a highly organized interest group" (Williamson, Evans, and Powell 1982, p. 256). Another frequent contention, as political scientists Dale Vineyard (1978) and Robert Binstock (1972) observe, is that historically the elderly have had to depend upon help from other groups in the "social welfare lobby," such as organized labor, to achieve significant victories for the aging and are unlikely to exert an independently strong influence on major policy issues. Finally, the aging risk a "backlash against the elderly," in the opinion of some observers, that will limit their influence in most governmental constituencies if they become too aggressive in promoting a politics of age.

The "Gray Peril" and City Hall

One place empirical investigation can clarify these arguments is the smaller Sunbelt communities where the aging are settling in growing numbers. Indeed, some observers believe that it is at the county and municipal level that this mobilization is most likely to occur first and where opportunities for its success are the greatest (Patrick 1980; Dobson 1983; Williamson, Evans, and Powell 1982). The "Gray Peril" hypothesis raises these issues very directly.

We state the hypothesis in a form that we believe defines more precisely and operationally a variety of closely related assumptions in the current literature of political gerontology. Broadly, the hypothesis asserts that:

> the rapid growth in the size of the aging population in smaller Sunbelt communities will be accompanied over relatively short periods of time by increases in local government expenditures for programs and services important to the elderly and by a significant decrease in the growth of local tax rates or revenues.

More precisely, the assertion is that the rapid expansion of an older population in smaller governmental constituencies can be expected to exert an independently significant influence upon the magnitude and substance of the local budget in the predicted manner. To make this proposition testable, it is necessary to create a model of the local budgetary process that identifies the major variables assumed important in determining local public taxing and spending and that places characteristics of the older population (collectively called here "the aging variables") within this context.

METHODOLOGY

Any attempt to explain local government expenditures is an ambitious undertaking. The range of responsibilities and prerogatives among local governmental units is often great. Different classes of government vary in service responsibilities and authority for taxing and borrowing. Often local governments are coterminous or overlapping. Nonetheless, a good deal of research by economists and political scientists suggests important relationships between various independent variables and local governmental budgets. A complete list of the dependent and independent variables, together with their data sources, is found in Table 12.1.

The Determinants of Taxing and Spending

Generally, socioeconomic conditions appear to influence local budgets much more than political, environmental, or other factors. Per capita income, for instance, is a major determinant of community expenditures: the higher the income, the greater the spending level, other things being equal. Local authorities, with a narrower tax base than federal or state officials, are severely limited in spending decisions. A manufacturing economy is likely to enhance greatly this tax base while creating heavy service demands for police and fire protection, roads, and utilities (Brazer 1959; Campbell and Sacks 1957; Lineberry and Sharkansky 1978; Wood 1961).

The literature on municipal economies also suggests that population size, density, and growth rates are important socioeconomic variables associated with city expenditures. Spending increases with population size and growth rates, presumably in respone to increased demands for urban servies. The effect of population density, for instance, is linked with more spending on law enforcement, fire protection, and sanitation but with lower expenditures for transportation. Finally, ethnicity—particularly race—is commonly found to be positively associated with both taxes and expenditures, because ethnic populations tend to have greater service needs (Clark 1968; Froman 1967; Weicher 1970).

Even so, some political variables do appear at least moderately significant in influencing local governmental expenditures. One factor is federal and state aid to local governments. A greater availability of aid normally means an increase in local spending, but it is less clear whether federal and state assistance has a stimulative or substitutive effect on most local budgets. The character of local government political structures also has a moderate bearing on taxing and spending; mayor-council cities with district elections tend to spend more than "reformed" cities with managers and elections at-large. This seems to vindicate the claim that municipal reforms promote governmental efficiency and less responsiveness to service demands, thus creating less taxing and spending (Lineberry and Sharkansky 1978).

TABLE 12.1. Inventory of Independent and Dependent Variables and Data Sources Used in Statistical Analysis

I. Independent Variables

Per capita income, 1970 and 1980 (*U.S. Census*)

Manufacturing firms per capita (1977 *U.S. Census of Manufacturers*)

Population 1970, 1980 (*U.S. Census*)

Population density (*Municipal Yearbook, 1976*)

Population Growth, 1970–1980 (*U.S. Census*)

Percentage Non-White, 1970, 1980 (*U.S. Census*)

Per capita intergovernmental aid (state and federal) 1970, 1980 (*Florida Local Government Financial Report*)

Degree of "reformed" government (*Municipal Yearbook, 1976*)

Size and percentage of population aged 55+, 1970 and 1980 (*U.S. Census*)

Size and percentage of population aged 65+, 1970, 1980 (*U.S. Census*)

Size and percentage of population aged 55–65, 1970 and 1980 (*U.S. Census*)

Size and percentage of population aged 65–75, 1970 and 1980 (*U.S. Census*)

Size and percentage of population aged 75+, 1970 and 1980 (*U.S. Census*)

Growth rate of aging population 1970 and 1980 (*U.S. Census*)

Presence, number of chapters, & length of time in community of AARP Chapter(s) (State Offices AARP, Sarasota, FL)

II. Dependent Variables

Per capita local taxes, 1972–81 (*Florida Local Government Financial Report*)
Per capita city expenditures, 1972–81 (*Florida Local Government Financial Report*)

- law enforcement
- fire protection
- physical environment
- transportation
- libraries
- parks and recreation
- housing

Source: Compiled by the authors.

This brief survey cannot exhaust the range of political and socioeconomic factors that may influence city budgets. Other less explored variables might be equally significant: the attitudes of community residents, the volume of local tourism, the nature of local political power structures and political cultures. We have chosen to focus upon the earlier variables because they are the most frequently mentioned in the relevant literature and afford a relatively well-tested set of factors to use in estimating the relative importance of an aging population among other common sources of influence on local governmental budgets.

Characterizing the Aging Population

We have noted the general lack of studies distinguishing empirically those population characteristics most likely to be associated with civic activism among the elderly at the local level and relating such findings to existing research on older populations. Nonetheless, the literature suggests many characteristics that merit examination.

Political gerontology suggests that the usual definition of the elderly as those aged 65 and above fails to distinguish between the more politically active "young-old" (ages 55 to 65) and those older. Also, the "old-old" (aged 75 and above) are assumed to be less politically active and more in need of governmental services, particularly health care, than younger individuals (Longino and Biggar 1982; Neugarten 1975; Cutler 1977b). Since these distinctions imply potentially significant differences in the impact of such populations on local budgets, we have defined three classes of age cohorts within the older population: the "young-old" (aged 55 to 65), the "old" (aged 65 to 75), and the "old-old" (aged 75 and older).

We have also attempted an indirect measure of political mobilization among older citizens in local communities. The most commonly used indicators of political activism, such as voter registration or voter turnout rates, are unavailable in Florida by age characteristics. One available measure that may be an indicator of the strength of political organization among the aging at the local level is the existence of a local chapter of the American Association of Retired Persons (AARP), the most common and familiar of the age-based organizations representing the elderly to government. While the political focus of AARP is often at state and national levels, many chapters are involved in local civic affairs as well.

The Local Governmental Budget

The major dependent variables in our city analysis are per capita local taxes (primarily personal property taxes), aggregate local expenditures per capita, and local expenditures per capita in specific policy categories. Program categories include law enforcement, fire protection, physical environment, transportation, housing, libraries, and parks and recreation. Almost all these services are provided exclusively by Florida muncipalities.

A common problem in using local governments as units of analysis for public expenditures is the variation across the United States in functional responsibilities between the same governmental levels. Some cities provide many services, others few; often special districts or counties provide services normally associated with cities. This problem is substantially eliminated when one confines analysis to municipalities in a single state. We also have omitted cities with more than 100,000 population and consolidated city-counties; both types typically provide more diverse services than the average city.

Inflation is also a consideration in describing local budgets. To control for the impact of inflation upon taxing and expenditure data, we have divided all budget variables by the appropriate "implicit price deflator" calculated in the annual *Economic Report of the President.* While these deflators are based on total services by all state and local governments (deflators are unavailable for individual municipalities), they remain the most reliable means available to control for inflationary distortion of our data.

The Communities

Our sample of municipalities includes all Florida cities with a population between 10,000 and 100,000 in 1980 (n = 85). This eliminates the six largest cities, for reasons explained earlier, and includes the smaller communities where aging populations have vigorously grown since 1970. It can be reasonably argued that the sample ought to include even smaller communities, but appropriate U.S. or state census data for these smaller municipalities are unavailable.

The Longitudinal Dimension

An important feature of our approach (See Table 12.1) is the time dimension: it deals with changes in dependent and independent variables over almost a decade (1972-81), in contrast to the more common cross-sectional analysis that isolates relationships in the local governmental budgetary process at a single time. One reason for selecting this particular period is that 1972/73 is the first year in which the state gathered municipal budget data and 1981/82 is the most recent year for which data are available. (These are state fiscal years running from July 1 to June 30.).

We examine the interaction of dependent and independent variables at three points in time: 1972/73, 1976/77, and 1981/82. Using the 1976/77 period allows a mid-decade check on budget variation over the nine-year interval and permits greater sensitivity to both short-term and long-term alterations in taxing and spending. Local budget data are available for the 1976/77 period; U.S. Bureau of the Census estimates for 1976/77 provide measures for many independent variables. Where population estimates are absent, 1980 census data are used to approximate 1977 figures.

Statistical Procedure

The relationships between independent and dependent variables were first examined for each of the three time periods by using simple bivariate correlations. The correlations indicated the absolute impact, or strength of association, between independent variables, including the character of older populations, and local governmental budgets. We then explored the relative impact of the aging variables through the use of stepwise linear regression. This enabled us to investigate the independent effects of the aging population characteristics when controlling for the effect of all significant independent variables. We expected the size of the beta coefficients to determine the ranking of the explanatory variables.

A common problem with this procedure is multicollinearity among independent variables. High intercorrelations between variables will often falsely inflate the beta coefficients in regression analysis and produce an invalid statistical interpretation of the relative importance among these variables (Bahl 1969). We used the zero-order correlation coefficients among all possible pairs of independent variables to check for multicollinearity. We also regressed all independent variables on each other to reveal any atypically high multiple correlation coefficients as an indicator of other significant correlations. If these tests implied some substantial collinearities, the variables were reduced by omitting proxy variables but keeping the aging variables.

FINDINGS

The results from our data analysis using simple correlations and beta coefficients to measure the strength of association between independent and dependent variables are presented in the aggregate in Tables 12.2, 12.3, and 12.4. Only correlations and coefficients of statistical significance have been reported (significance levels of .01 and .05, respectively). These data suggest several guarded conclusions about the "Gray Peril" hypothesis.

TABLE 12.2. Significant Bivariate Correlates and Beta Coefficients for Community and Aging Variables, City Taxing and Spending, 1972-73

Variable	Property Tax	Total Local Tax	Total Revenue	Law Enforcement	Fire Protection	Physical Environment	Transport
Population							
Per capita income	.98(.99)	.98(.99)	.98(.99)	.98(.99)			
Reformed government	.72	.73	.21				
Population					.47(.37)		
Mfg. per capita	.99(.84)	.99	.99	.99		(.39)	.99(.35)
Pop. density							
Black population							
Spanish population				.76(.36)	.35		
% Black							
% Spanish		.29			.22		
Aging							
Population 55+							
Population 65+	.29(.46)			.25	.32		
Population 75+	.27			.30	.34		
Population 55-65					.45		
Population 65-75	.28				.30		
% Age 55+							
% Age 65+	.26						
% Age 75+	.26						
% Age 55-65							
% Age 65-75							
% Change 55+	.26	.27	.27		-.26		
AARP chpt.				.32(.28)	.39(.26)		
No. AARP chapts.				.30	.39		
Yrs. of AARP chapt.					.37		
R =	.98	.98	.98	.98	.27	.15	.13

189

TABLE 12.2. Continued

Variable	Library	Housing	Parks and Recreation	Total Expenditure	Federal Aid	State Aid	Total Inter-governmental Aid
Population							
Per capita income							
Reformed government	(.29)		(−.27)	.27(−.28)	.24	.26	.32
Population					.27		.29
Mfg. per capita							
Pop. density				.21	.21		
Black population							
Spanish population	(.40)						
% Black					(.41)	(.32)	(.44)
% Spanish							
Aging							
Population 55+							
Population 65+	.33						
Population 75+	.39					.38(.38)	.29(.24)
Population 55-65							
Population 65-75	.25						
% Age 55+						.29	
% Age 65+						.31	
% Age 75+							
% Age 55-65							
% Age 65-75							
% Change 55+	.42(.46)					−.54(.39)	.25
AARP chpt.					.36	.26	.38
No. AARP chapts.					.34(.36)		.36(.34)
Yrs. of AARP chapt.						.26	.29
R =	.26	.07	.08	.13	.17	.15	.19

Note: Beta coefficents in parentheses.
Source: Compiled by the authors.

TABLE 12.3. Significant Bivariate Correlates and Beta Coefficients for Community and Aging Variables, City Taxing and Spending, 1976-77

Variable	Property Tax	Total Local Tax	Total Revenue	Law Enforcement	Fire Protection	Physical Environment	Transport
Population							
Per capita income	.98(.99)	(.91)	(.97)	.98(.99)			
Reformed government	−.23	−.27					
Population				.19	(.37)		
Mfg. per capita	.69(.84)	.71	.99			(.39)	(.35)
Pop. Density							
Black population							
Spanish population				(.36)			
% Black							
% Spanish		.29			.22		
Aging							
Population 55+							
Population 65+	.29(.46)			.25	.32		
Population 75+	.27			.30	.34		
Population 55-65					.28		
Population 65-75	.28				.30		
% Age 55+							
% Age 65+	.26						
% Age 75+	.26						
% Age 55-65							
% Age 65-75							
% Change 55+	(.22)	.27	.25		−.26		
AARP chpt.				.32(.28)	.32		
No. AARP chapts.				.30	.34		
Yrs. of AARP chapt.					.45(.45)		
R =	.70	.83	.94	.23	.20	.15	.13

TABLE 12.3. Continued

Variable	Library	Housing	Parks and Recreation	Total Expenditure	Federal Aid	State Aid	Total Intergovernmental Aid
Population							
Per capita income							
Reformed government	(.29)	-.25(-.27)		-.25(-.28)	.24	.29	.25
Population	.30						
Mfg. per capita							
Pop. Density				.21	.21		
Black population							
Spanish population	(.40)						
% Black					(.41)	(.32)	(.44)
% Spanish							
Aging							
Population 55+							
Population 65+	.33						
Population 75+	.39					.38(.38)	.29(.24)
Population 55-65							
Population 65-75	.25						
% Age 55+						.29	
% Age 65+							.31
% Age 75+							
% Age 55-65							
% Age 65-75							
% Change 55+	.42(.46)					-.54(.39)	.25
AARP chpt.					.36	.26	.38
No. AARP chapts.					.34(.36)		.36(.34)
Yrs. of AARP chapt.						.35(.26)	.29
R =	.16	.07	.08	.13	.17	.45	.19

Note: Beta coefficients in parentheses.
Source: Compiled by the authors.

TABLE 12.4. Significant Bivariate Correlates and Beta Coefficients for Community and Aging Variables, City Taxing and Spending, 1981-82

Variable	Property Tax	Total Local Tax	Total Revenue	Law Enforcement	Fire Protection	Physical Environment	Transport
Population							
Per capita income	.96(.96)		(.91) .98(.98)	(.99)			
Reformed government	.20	.20	.30	.25	.25	(.64)	
Population		.23			.23(.37)		
Mfg. per capita	(.84)					(.98)	(.37)
Pop. Density							
Black population				(.27)	.27		
Spanish population		.57	(.58)	.30(.36)		.25	
% Black		−.19				(−.58)	
% Spanish		.41		.36(.40)			
Aging							
Population 55+							
Population 65+	.29(.46)	.51		.24	.24		
Population 75+	.27	.51		.30	.34		
Population 55-65		.42		.25	.35		
Population 65-75	.28	.47		.24	.28		
% Age 55+							
% Age 65+	.26	.41		.32	.28		
% Age 75+	.26	.44		.28	.25		
% Age 55-65		.36(.38)		.37(.47)	.30(.35)		
% Age 65-75		.34		.31	.27		
% Change 55+	.24	.27	.24		−.26		
AARP chpt.				.32(.28)	.32		
No. AARP chapts.		.24		.30	.28		
Yrs. of AARP chapt.					.30		
R =	.91	.47	.96	.35	.12	.64	.14

TABLE 12.4. Continued

Variable	Library	Housing	Parks and Recreation	Total Expenditure	Federal Aid	State Aid	Total Intergovernmental Aid
Population							
Per capita income							(.95)
Reformed government	(.29)		.28(.27)	(.28)	.24	(.44)	.21
Population							
Mfg. per capita						(.73)	
Pop. Density				.21	.21		
Black population					.46	.26	
Spanish population	(.40)						
% Black					.51(.41)	.41(.32)	(.44)
% Spanish							
Aging							
Population 55+							
Population 65+	.33						
Population 75+	.39					.38(.38)	.29(.24)
Population 55-65							
Population 65-75	.25						
% Age 55+						(.30)	
% Age 65+		-.24				.31	
% Age 75+							
% Age 55-65		-.44					
% Age 65-75		-.33					
% Change 55+	.42(.46)				-.25	(.30)	.25
AARP chpt.		.28			.36	.26	.38
No. AARP chapts.					.34(.36)		.36(.34)
Yrs. of AARP chapt.						.29	.29
R =	.16	.23	.08	.13	.26	.48	.89

Note: Beta coefficents in parentheses.
Source: Compiled by the authors.

First, the aging appear to have had a very modest impact upon taxing and spending in the communities we have examined at each of the three time periods. Generally, significant associations between the "aging variables" and measures of local governmental taxing and spending, as described by the simple bivariate correlations shown in the tables, were not very frequent during any single time period nor, with a few exceptions, were they consistent between time periods. Even when the correlations did assume statistical significance (p > .01), the actual correlation values were usually very modest. The increasing frequency with which modest bivariate correlates appear over the time period studied does suggest that the impact of increasing populations of older residents in the communities studied may be growing and may become more pronounced in data from more recent years. Clearly, such a conclusion must await an examination of local community budgets through the 1980s and comparison with the 1970s data.

Second, most of the significant bivariate relationships become unimportant when stepwise regression is used to derive beta coefficients for independent and dependent variables during the three time periods. These coefficients are found in parentheses in the tables. This regression, which provides an indication of the contribution from individual "aging" variables to the total variability of each dependent variable, tends to reduce the significant relationship among "aging" variables on local governmental taxing and spending before 1981/82 virtually to insignificance. Even when beta weights remain relatively large (as in the 1981/82 relationship of changes in the population aged 55 to 65 with local spending on protective services and property taxes), the amount of public spending "explained" still remains very small. This tendency, stated differently, is an indication that the other urban characteristics we have included in the analysis—variables usually associated with levels of local governmental taxing and spending—make a much greater statistical contribution to explaining local public spending.

The impact of these other urban factors is apparent when the beta values for these socioeconomic variables are compared with the values for the "aging variables" during all the periods studied. Indeed, the fact that the communities we have examined were changing simultaneously in respect to a great many socioeconomic characteristics, in addition to those associated with aging, may have been ignored by those who tended to impute changes in local governmental budgets largely to such highly visible transformations as a growth in older populations.

Third, two categories in the bivariate analysis of local government spending—expenditures for law enforcement and fire protection—often appeared to vary concurrently with the growth of older populations and were increasingly associated with such change as the period progressed. Both services, of course, are of great (but not exclusive) importance to older community residents. These associations imply that the older population's impact upon these service categories may become increasingly evident in the future. The fact that, in general, simple bivariate correlations between the "aging variables" and other local governmental expenditures also seem to increase as one moves through the time period examined might lead to a similar conclusion about other governmental services.

It is also apparent that a modest but positive relationship generally persists between our "aging variables" and our measures of per capita community taxes and intergovernmental aid for all the periods we studied. This positive association is most apparent in per capita measures of state aid and total intergovernmental aid during this time. While the bivariate correlation and beta coefficient values are generally modest for all the periods, there is little in these data to support an argument that enlarging older populations have had a negative impact upon local governmental taxing; on the contrary, these data hint that rising older populations may be associated with rising per capita local taxes.

Finally, our data suggest, albeit very tentatively, that there may be substance to speculation that the "young-old" and organizations of the aging will strongly encourage the political mobilization of older Americans. During the period 1981/82 significant bivariate and beta coefficients appeared for the first time between several local government revenue and expenditure categories and a measure of growth in the "young-old" population of the communities surveyed. The tables also reveal significant bivariate and beta coefficient values for the relationship between the number of AARP chapters in a community and several categories of local government spending during all the periods examined. The data are far too fragmentary to be dignified as a trend, yet the appearance of these relationships emphasizes the importance of further investigation into the role of the "young-old" and organizations of the aging in the political mobilization of older Americans through the 1980s.

CONCLUSION

There is little in our data to lend credibility to the "Gray Peril" hypothesis or its variations. Almost without exception, the patterns of local governmental spending we have examined at three periods between 1972/73 and 1981/82 do not show a strong or consistent relationship between the growth of older populations in the communities studied and increases in functional categories of public spending. Nor, apparently, is this population change associated with decreased taxing. Instead, a modest but consistently positive relationship was observed between the growth of older populations and levels of local taxing. Stated differently, the data do not imply that the growth of older populations in the communities studied is likely to impose any distinctive economic burdens, or raise unique problems of equity, affecting other community interests with a stake in governmental budgets.

However, we believe these conclusions, as well as other implications of the present data, may be substantially altered when two deficiencies in the present data are remedied. In Florida, where counties usually assume the major responsibility for education and medical service delivery, it is also important to examine patterns of county-level taxing and spending in response to changing populations of older residents. Both programs are thought to be particularly sensitive to changes in the age composition of populations. We suspect these data may demonstrate with greater clarity the policy impacts of Florida's population changes than city data alone. Further, it is essential to project both city and county analysis into the 1980s.

As the 1980s progress, reductions in federal support for state and local governmental service programs, initiated under the Carter Administration and powerfully promoted by the Reagan Administration's "new federalism," may compel a much greater political mobilization of the elderly in local communities while provoking greater conflict between the elderly and other organized community interests. Many observers believe an especially important contributor to this growing politicization of older Americans will be the 1981 Omnibus Budget and Reconciliation Act and the 1981 Economic Recovery Tax Act. These budget bills substantially restructured Title XX of the Social Security Act by substituting new Social Service Block Grants (SSBG) for the Title XX programs; funding for social services important to the elderly was substantially reduced while greater discretion was given to state and local agencies for program definition and implementation. Well into the mid-1980s, many state and local governments were either experiencing their own fiscal crises or anticipating fiscally lean years. As a result, state and local social services for the elderly, once considered almost invulnerable to reduction, were now targets for possible administrative and budgetary cutbacks (Lindeman and Pardini 1983, pp. 135-67).

Some cutbacks in aging services were reported by as many as a third of local governmental officials surveyed by investigators in the early 1980s (Swan, Estes, and Wood 1983, p. 127). While these initial cutbacks were apparently modest, and most aging services were still considered priority programs for local governments in the early 1980s, a change has occurred in the political climate for aging services.

> Budgetary constraints and recent federal policy developments make it clear that the services and other hard-won benefits for the aged are not exempt from the consequences of shrinkage in the public service sector.... Even if benefits for the aged are the last to be cut, they nevertheless will be cut (Swan, Estes, and Wood 1983, p. 114).

In short, the aged can no longer count upon existing levels of public services nor upon existing public and private organizations to protect their future entitlements. Many observers believe that in this more threatening political environment, organizations of the aging, together with larger proportions of the aged themselves, will become more politically active to protect their service programs at state and local levels. They will also be exposed to greater competition with other organized constituencies for governmental services.

Whether the "new federalism" and other recent structural alterations in federal support for aging programs result in program cutbacks or arouse a new "politics of age" expressed in growing political activism among the aged in local communities are clearly important issues to which our data could be relevant when projected into the 1980s. We believe when this is done there will be much more substantial evidence of the aging's impact upon Florida's city and county service programs than we discovered in the 1970s. Our data hint at this. The tendency of the data to show increasing evidence of relationship between the growth of older populations and local spending and taxing at the beginning of the 1980s may be early evidence of an emergent trend in this decade. Thus, the 1980s may be the first decade to fully reveal the "politics of age" at local governmental levels, and Florida is likely to be the place where this will most clearly be discerned.

REFERENCES

Aday, Ron H. and Laurie H. Miles. 1982. "Long Term Impacts of Rural Migration of the Elderly." *Gerontologist* 22 (June):331-36.

Anderson, William A. and Norma D. Anderson. 1978. "The Politics of Age Exclusion." *Gerontologist* 18 (February):6-12.

Bahl, Robert W. 1969. *Metropolitan City Expenditures: A Comparative Analysis*. Lexington: University of Kentucky Press.

Biggar, Jeanne C. 1979. "The Sunning of America: Migration to the Sunbelt." *Population Bulletin* 34 (March):1-44.

Binstock, Robert H. 1972. "Interest Group Liberalism and the Politics of Aging." *Gerontologist* 12 (March):265-80.

Brazer, Harvey E. 1959. *City Expenditures In The United States*. New York: National Bureau of Economic Research.

Campbell, Angus K. and Seymour Sacks. 1957. *Metropolitan America: Fiscal Patterns and Governmental Systems*. New York: Free Press.

Clark, Terry N. 1968. "Community Structure, Decision-Making, Budget Expenditures and Urban Renewal in 51 American Communities." *American Sociological Review* 33 (August):576-94.

Cutler, Neal E. 1977a. "Population Policy: The Perspective of Political Gerontology." *Policy Studies Journal* 6 (January):167-74.

_____. 1977b. "Demographic, Socio-Psychological and Political Factors in the Politics of Aging." *American Political Science Review* 71 (September): 1011-25.

Dobson, Douglas. 1983. "The Elderly As A Political Force." In *Aging and Public Policy*, edited by William P. Browne and Laura Katz Olson, pp. 123-44. Westport, Conn.: Greenwood Press.

Estes, Carroll L. 1978. "Political Gerontology." *Society* 15 (June): 43-49.
Froman, Lewis A. 1967. "An Analysis of Public Choice in Cities." *Journal of Politics* 29 (February): 94-108.
Fugitt, Glenn V. and Stephen J. Tordella. 1981. "Elderly Net Migration: The New Trend of Nonmetropolitan Population Change." *Research on Aging* 3 (June): 191-204.
Hudson, Robert B. 1980. "Old-Age Politics in a Period of Change." In *Aging and Society*, edited by Edgar F. Borgetta and Neil G. McClusky, pp. 147-85. Beverly Hills: Sage.
Kraft, Joseph and Carter C. Osterbind. 1981. *Older People In Florida, 1980-81: A Statistical Abstract*. Gainesville: University of Florida Press.
Lee, Gary and Marie L. Lassey. 1980. "Rural-Urban Differences Among the Elderly," *Journal of Social Issues* 36 (June): 62-74.
Lineberry, Robert L. and Ira Sharkansky. 1978. *Urban Politics and Public Policy*. New York: Harper and Row.
Lindeman, David A. and Alan Pardini. 1983. "Social Services: The Impact of Fiscal Austerity." In *Fiscal Austerity and Aging*, edited by Carroll L. Estes, Robert J. Newcomer, and Associates, pp. 133-54. Beverly Hills: Sage.
Longino, Charles F., Jr. 1980. "The Retirement Community." In *The Dynamics of Aging*, edited by Forrest B. Berghorn and Donna E. Schafer, pp. 279-93. Boulder: Westview Press.
──── . and Jeanne C. Biggar. 1982. "The Impact of Population Redistribution on Service Delivery." *Gerontologist* 22 (August): 153-59.
Neugarten, Betrice L. 1975. "The Future of the Young-Old." *Gerontologist* 15 (February, Part II): 4-9.
Patrick, Clifford H. 1980. "Health and Migration." *Research on Aging* 2 (June): 233-41.
Pratt, Henry J. 1979. "The Politics of Aging: Political Science and the Study of Gerontology." *Research on Aging* 1 (June): 155-68.
Swan, James H., Carroll L. Estes, and Juanita B. Wood. 1983. "Fiscal Crisis: Economic and Fiscal Problems of State and Local Governments." In *Fiscal Austerity and Aging*, edited by Carroll Estes, Robert J. Newcomer, and Associates, pp. 113-32. Beverly Hills: Sage.
Vineyard, Dale. 1978. "The Rediscovery of the Elderly." *Society* 15 (June: 24-29.
Weicher, John C. 1970. "Determinants of Central City Expenditures: Some Overlooked Factors and Problems." *National Tax Journal* 23 (December): 379-95.
Williamson, John B., Linda Evans, and Lawrence A. Powell. 1982. *The Politics of Aging*. Springfield, Ill.: Charles C. Thomas.
Wood, Robert. 1961. *1600 Governments*. Garden City: Doubleday-Anchor.

13

RACE, POWER, AND POLITICAL CHANGE

Clarence N. Stone

In the past few decades, the politics of race has changed dramatically, and undoubtedly will continue to change in the years ahead. Minorities are a growing force in the electoral politics of U.S. cities. It is in order, then, to ask what changes in policy and political practice increased electoral strength might bring into play. This question is well worth considering for what it reveals about the nature of power in U.S. society. Is change in race relations evidence that the pluralist interpretation is valid after all? Or is there another interpretation that better fits the evolving pattern of race relations in our urban political communities?

The interwoven issues of race, power, and political change addressed here provide a way of examining the workings of democracy at the local level. On the basis of recent research on economic and community development in Atlanta, Georgia, I argue that pluralism is less appropriate than what I term "coalitional bias" as an interpretation of race and political change in urban communities. Atlanta's recent experience illustrates how a reconstituted "mobilization of bias" protects business influence in the face of black electoral power.

COMPETING SCHOOLS OF THOUGHT

Pluralism

Let us begin with a brief review of the pluralist position and how changing race relations might be seen from a pluralist perspective. For pluralists, two features stand out as shaping the character of urban politics. One is the Complexity of modern society; the other is the presence of universal suffrage.

The complexity of modern life, pluralists argue, produces a large number of group interests that crosscut divisions of class. According to Polsby (1980, p. 118), U.S. society is "fractured into a congeries of hundreds of small special interest groups, with incompletely overlapping memberships, widely differing power bases, and a multitude of techniques for exercising influence on decisions salient to them." So strong is the centrifugal force of complexity, pluralists argue, that any coalition is unstable. Polsby (1980, p. 137) suggested that "the larger the coalition, the more fragile it is and the more limited its political environment." Consequently in the pluralist view, localities are governed "by shifting coalitions of participants drawn from all areas of community life" (Merelman 1968, p. 451). Influence is particular to the issue and situation; those groups with the greatest immediate stake have the most say in any given decision arena.

Pluralists assume that one group of voters is about as important as another (see, for example, Dahl 1961, p. 75). Hence there is no particular affinity among sets of groups; those together on one issue are divided on another. Political entrepreneurs looking for a base of support, pluralists argue, have little incentive to favor one class over another. In this view of modern democracy, because political entrepreneurs are ever in search of a constituency, few groups are without a champion. As pluralists see it, those who are socially or economically disadvantaged find the electoral arena, with the equality of the ballot box, especially attractive (Dahl 1961, p. 293). Thus numbers supposedly counterbalance such elite characteristics as wealth and status. Because winning elections is ultimately the most important channel to power in a democracy, universal suffrage stands as a counterweight to any tendency toward cumulative inequality.

Numerous groups, fluidity of alignments, and the special usefulness of the electoral arena for those otherwise disadvantaged—these are key elements in the pluralist argument about governing coalitions. This argument recognizes no coalitional bias and, accordingly, assumes that if the disadvantaged continue to be disadvantaged under current policy, their disadvantage can be attributed to the difficulty of modifying a consensus. Veto groups supposedly find it easy to knock down proposals that depart very far from established practice. To the extent there is a bias, it is a bias toward the status quo. Yet change is possible.

Given that line of argument, pluralists naturally see the success of the civil rights movement in the 1960s as ample demonstration that power is dispersed, that inequalities are noncumulative, and that pluralism is vindicated. If blacks were powerful enough to achieve substantial change, they argue, then surely the system must be pluralistic. In a review of Floyd Hunter's *Community Power Succession* (1980), Joseph Gusfield (1982, p. 86) comments on the transformation of race relations in the urban South and asks, "If the power structure were so powerful, how did this happen?"

Coalitional Bias

Let us now turn to an alternative to the pluralist position, what is called here "coalitional bias." Before explaining what this term means, I want to lay to rest a couple of misconceptions and indicate why I am avoiding the more familiar term of "elitism."

In the above-mentioned review, Gusfield (1982, p. 86) observes that "the history of black-white relations since [Hunter's] first Atlanta study is as much a study of negotiated settlements as it is one-way monolithic use of power." The dichotomy between negotiation and one-way control, however, is not a useful distinction, though not an uncommon one. Critics of Hunter should put away the straw man of monolithic power. From Hunter on, no one has argued that business elites exercise total domination. What Hunter did describe is a situation in which an active and organized business community used its ample resources to manage the policy agenda in Atlanta.

While agenda management is different from monolithic control, Gusfield's example of race relations is still a telling one. In the 1960s, the business leadership of Atlanta was unable to prevent the opening of the agenda of public debate to a number of new concerns. Elite domination through a closed agenda did not survive the era of direct action. Yet, as we shall see, putting an issue on the agenda is not the same as being able to keep an issue on the agenda.

Some groups have more capacity to sustain issues than others do. Some groups encounter more resistance than others. Some groups are eagerly sought out as allies. Some are more formidable as opponents than others are. Because voting strength is only part of a very complicated picture, all groups are not equally attractive as coalition partners.

It helps to remember that important as elections are, governing is different from winning elections. As Stein Rokkan (1966, p. 106) once observed, "The vote potential constitutes only one among many different power resources. . . : what really counts is the capacity to hurt or to halt a system of highly interdependent activities." In a pithy subheading on policy making, Rokkan (1966, p. 105) offered, "Votes count but resources decide."

Elsewhere I have argued that urban officials are predisposed to cooperate with upper strata interests, disfavor lower strata interests, and sometimes to act in apparent disregard of the contours of electoral power. We have to face the fact that public officials act in a context in which a vast store of strategically important resources are both privately held and unevenly divided. Because this system leaves public officials situationally dependent on the upper strata interests, it is a factor in all they do. Consequently, system features lower the costs of exerting influence for some groups and raise them for others. Thus socioeconomic inequalities put various strata on different political footings, and these different footings represent a systemic dimension of power (Stone 1980).

Dependence on upper strata interests is, of course, not restricted to public officials. Other community actors are also predisposed to seek the cooperation of those who are economically, organizationally, and culturally well off. Lines of alliance, then, are not fully fluid.

Groups are not uniformly valued as partners in governance. Not all have an equal opportunity to become and remain part of the "shifting coalitions that govern communities." Indeed it seems that some governing coalitions are more durable and resilient than others. Once the political importance of the system of stratification is recognized, we can see the possibility that class position serves as a strong indication of attractiveness as a coalition member. Hence, instead of coalitions being fluid and heavily influenced by the immediate circumstances of an issue, they are a reflection of system biases.

The contrast between pluralism and coalition bias is therefore not one of rule-by-the-many versus rule-by-the-few. Instead, the contrast is over participation in the coalitions that govern communities. According to pluralism, rule—within the constraints of community consensus—is by those groups most substantially affected by the issues at stake. Where those immediately affected interests are in conflict, either compromise or impasse results. The latter possibility tilts decision making toward the status quo, and the overall process gives rise to disjointed incrementalism.

In a system of coalitional bias, some groups prevail consistently, though not totally. Over time, those that prevail do so in part because they enjoy a systemic advantage and are insiders in the governmental process. Other groups lose consistently, though not totally. Over time, those that lose do so in part because they suffer a systemic disadvantage and are outsiders in the governmental process.

Though the counter to pluralism offered here is not the stereotyped contrast between elitism and pluralism, the difference between coalitional bias and pluralism should nonetheless be unmistakable. Pluralism recognizes no particular constraints on participation in governing coalitions. For this school of thought, participation is a matter of motivation; and motivation comes usually from the immediacy of the issue. As an explanation of power and influence, coalitional bias suggests a different dynamic. It recognizes a bias in who is able to participate in governing coalitions and in the terms on which they participate. Because privately held resources are centrally important, that bias reflects the main features of the modern U.S. system of stratification.

RACE AND CLASS

Before looking at particular events in Atlanta, let us consider an additional general factor, namely the contemporary relationship between race and class. Although race and class are analytically separate, they are socially and politically connected in ways that are quite important (see Wilson 1980). For instance, while the civil rights movement was able to bring about important changes, it was greatly limited in its ability to deal with issues that had a class character.

To understand the civil rights movement, it is helpful to keep in mind what did and did not change. A significant transformation did occur. Blacks brought about the end of a Jim Crow system through which they had been relegated by custom and often by the law to an inferior status. Such change is testimony that significant social reform can be achieved in a democratic order, and the importance of this accomplishment of the civil rights movement should not be minimized. Moreover, all can agree that it belies any claim about monolithic control by an established elite.

Even so, it is well to remember that there is much the civil rights movement did not accomplish. For example, it was unable to alter the class character of such matters as residential location, education, health care, and the labor market. But why should a movement based in a concern with racial status also be concerned with class-based opportunities and benefits? The obvious answer is because blacks are disproportionately located toward the bottom of the economic ladder, and economic position has much to do with life chances.

There is, however, another and less obvious dimension to the connection between race and class; for many people race is a shorthand for class. Though it is not always done so consciously, "black" is often equated with lower class and "white" with middle class. Because blacks are poor in larger proportion than whites, statistical association leads to stereotypes, and these stereotypes are hard to displace because they are convenient for making decisions in situations of incomplete information. In many instances, decisions made on the basis of stereotypes are "efficient" for the decision-makers, even though highly unfair to the stereotyped population (see Aaron 1978, p. 47; Thurow 1981, pp. 180–81). The statistical association between race and class thus becomes fixed in mass conduct and has far-reaching consequences. As Schelling (1971, p. 89) argues, actions based on "minute shadings" of difference in perceived advantage or convenience can be transformed into collective results of which no one approves. Thus, while few people wish for race to continue to be a major factor in community life, it nevertheless is, because of its close association with class.

The great success the civil rights movement had in removing racial identity as a formal barrier to improved opportunity is compromised by the continuing informal barrier that is still in place. The picture is complicated. Ours is presumably an achievement-oriented society in which ascribed statuses such as race no longer have a place. After all, ascribed and achieved status are logically distinct, and race belongs to the former, while class supposedly has more to do with the latter. Yet, in social practice achieved and ascribed status are mixed. Even in an achievement-oriented society which gives wide sway to the workings of an impersonal market, the convenience of thinking in categories (for example, racial stereotypes) places all blacks under a disadvantage. As a collectivity—that is, as a category for convenient, quick labeling—blacks are regarded as a low-achievement and therefore lower-class group. A large-scale movement of blacks—even if most are middle class—into a school system, a center of employment, or a residential area gives a signal that the class character has changed. And that subliminal signal is extremely hard to counter publicly. Efforts to do so increase the visibility of the signal and may be self-defeating. Thus middle class blacks—whether as candidates for public office, potential employees in the private sector, home buyers, or clients for professional service—bear a degree of informal handicap through a subliminal association with lower class stereotypes.

Let us then consider how the intertwined character of race and class might affect the formation and maintenance of coalitions. Pluralism tends to discount the importance of class (see Polsby 1980, pp. 117-18). By contrast, the coalitional bias argument holds that those with low positions in the system of stratification will not be attractive allies for public officials as these officials confront the task of governance. (Since they may have significant voting power, they may be attractive as a source of electoral support, particularly if that support can be obtained by largely symbolic stances.) The result of this situation is that as political participants, lower strata groups face high opportunity costs—that is, their "demands" encounter strong resistance (cf. Harsanyi 1962). Consequently they have weak incentives to pursue broad, collective demands; and they have far stronger incentives to pursue particular and immediate benefits. Hence the representatives of lower strata groups are "ripe" for cooptation or for simply giving up the struggle (Stone 1982).

Coalition formation, of course, does not occur in a frictionless world in which information is perfect and past history of no consequence. Coalitional bias thus occurs through a process of learning about and adjusting to systemic factors. As pressures for change interact with systemic resistance, what kind of coalition building might we expect to emerge? The coalition-bias argument suggests that in the process of governing, public officials and others will gravitate toward alliance with upper strata groups. As officials seek to represent their constituents, even those who owe their election to black majorities have to respond to the inducements and constraints of privately controlled and unequally distributed resources. Moreover, although black middle and lower classes have important shared interests for the reasons discussed above, the system of social stratification puts a wedge into their cooperative relationship, as it does in any alliance that bridges class lines. (See, in particular, Chafe 1980 for a detailed account of the experience in Greensboro, North Carolina.)

RACE AND POLITICAL CHANGE IN ATLANTA

Coalitional Bias Before the Civil Rights "Revolution"

In the period right after World War II blacks in several southern cities, responding to the constitutional demise of the white primary and the signal of greater protection for voting rights, formed issue-oriented political organizations to make greater use of the ballot box as an instrument of influence. This was itself a period in which blacks sought to become part of the ruling coalition in their various communities. It was a period of black political activism as well as continuing caution (Chafe 1980, p. 29). But significantly it was a time in which black assertiveness was constrained by a variety of devices and considerations (cf. Matthews and Prothro 1966, pp. 137-46).

Most cities were characterized by a form of paternalism, in which blacks petitioned white benefactors with requests for aid or, in some cases, for approval of modest changes in racial practice. Standard procedure in Atlanta, for example, called for the white business and civic establishment to pass judgment on proposed major changes in community policy—it was this practice that informed Hunter's (1953) notion of community power structure. Typically negotiations between the races did not involve top business leaders as direct participants. Consistently they remained in the background. To illustrate, in Atlanta negotiations generally were between the mayor and the leadership of the Atlanta Negro Voters League or, on some policy issues, between the staff of white civic organizations and officials of the Urban League. Once negotiations at that level were completed, then the agreement was "cleared" with top leaders in the business community.

It should be emphasized that this was not an instance of monolithic control; established leaders did yield to a changing reality of black dissatisfaction, but only if it was not detrimental to collective business interests and the general commitment to economic growth. Further, business leaders did refuse requests.

Even before the college-age generation of the 1960s challenged this pattern of hierarchical decision making, blacks were dissatisfied. Threats of litigation and flexed electoral muscles were part of the negotiation process. But blacks clearly were not an autonomous power group. As Chafe (1980, p. 37) observes of Greensboro, "blacks had been viewed as dependent extensions of the white community, not recognized as independent people with an agenda of their own."

On what did the political subordination of blacks rest if they had voting power and significant legal protection? There was no single factor, but rather a mixture of material and attitudinal factors, regularized into an ongoing set of arrangements. White business leaders controlled great amounts of money, the major credit sources, and an extensive organizational network. In addition they enjoyed high civic status and favorable standing with the news media. Moreover, the whole of their power position was greater than the sum of its parts. Because the business elite represented an unmatched concentration of resources, subleaders, black and white, were deferential to them. To obtain their active support, many community actors believed, was to go far toward assuring success. To evoke their opposition was not only to run a risk of failure but a likelihood of sanctions. In some cases blacks were beholden to white officeholders, but as Hunter (1953) showed (and Banfield 1965 confirmed), the holders of public office were widely perceived to be subordinate to the business elite. And in those rare instances in which blacks were selected for public office, those who were elected were too constrained to be militant advocates (Chafe 1980, p. 36). Politics was therefore not a countervailing force against business leadership. It was either subordinate to the business elite or simply not forceful as a means through which blacks could exert pressure.

Black business and professional leaders also fell short of being a significant independent force, partly because blacks were direct recipients of favors from white business leaders. At the time that younger and more assertive black leaders were beginning to emerge, Jack Walker described the older generation of conservative black leaders in Atlanta this way:

> The conservatives feel that their position bars them from taking an active part in protest demonstrations because these public displays of discontent naturally cause bitterness and rancor and tend to destroy the cordial settled atmosphere which they feel is a necessary precondition to effective negotiations. They also worked hard to build institutions such as the Y.M.C.A., the Urban League and many churches which depend heavily on contributions from influential whites. . . . The businessmen among the conservatives have frequent dealings with influential whites in the city; both the bank and the savings and loan association operated by Negroes in Atlanta have very sizeable deposits from white customers. In fact, to a large extent, the power of the conservatives depends on their influence with the white community. They are spokesmen for the Negro community primarily because they have gained white recognition and favor, although their own achievements placed them in a position to be chosen for this role (Walker 1963, p. 116).

Why didn't dissatisfied black leaders go public before the student sit-ins of 1960? Why did they tolerate a situation in which whites largely chose who would represent the black community? It is hard now to recall just how repressive the racial climate was in the pre-1960 South. There was a pervasive fear of white violence, well based in historical fact. In understanding the pre-1960 era, it is important, then, to appreciate the extent to which the white business elite was seen to be a protective force in a hostile racial climate. They were touted as responsible leaders, and, indeed, as proponents and architects of economic growth, they presumably could be counted on to maintain an overall direction of orderly progress. Furthermore, they were not simply people with good intentions; they had the clout to act on their intentions and bring other "less responsible" elements into line.

Fearing that any race-related issue might arouse hostility among the white masses, old-line black leaders had great confidence in the process of quiet negotiations. The head of the Southern Regional Council observed, "Nearly always in Atlanta it's the manipulative adjustment of interests rather than the head-on clash" (quoted in Cater 1957, p. 18). In this system of quiet and manipulative adjustment, the white business establishment operated with several advantages. Not only did they control enormous resources, enjoy a patron-relationship to many black "clients," and stand in very good favor at city hall, but they were regarded as protectors of the public interest. They possessed a form of legitimacy that black leaders lacked.

No one described white business leaders as altruistic, but they were seen as hard-nosed realists—practitioners of "enlightened self-interest"—who had the best interest of the community at heart (cf. Clark 1969). Black leaders, by contrast, were perceived as pleaders of a special cause. They spoke for a factional interest, whereas white business leaders were regarded as representing the well-being of the whole community.

Much of the literature offering a pluralist view of power assumes that the presence of bargaining and negotiation is an indication of some kind of power balance. In one sense it is; power is never completely one-sided even in a "total institution" such as a prison or an asylum (Goffman 1961; Sykes 1958). However, what is important for our purposes is not the absence of complete one-sidedness (that is so universal as to be uninteresting), but the degree of imbalance. Bear in mind that we are not talking about different forms of pluralism—that obscures the issues. Rather our concern is with how much imbalance there is in the bases from which bargaining and negotiation take place. (For example, see Stone 1976, p. 74; Chafe 1980, p. 24).

The student sit-ins in 1960 were an effort to alter the terms under which bargaining and negotiation were conducted. As such, they were part of a political movement concerned with changing a coalitional bias. The civil rights movement sought to shift the position of blacks from that of being an indirect and subordinate member of governing coalitions to that of being a direct and coequal member. That is what the phrase, "Black Power," was explicitly about (Carmichael and Hamilton 1967).

The Civil Rights Movement as an Attack on Coalitional Bias

Coalitional bias proved to have multiple layers, and some layers were beyond the reach of direct action tactics. Let us now consider the impact of the civil rights movement as a frontal assault on the notion that the rights of black people could be guaranteed only by powerful white benefactors. Disdainful of the fears of "white backlash," civil rights activists deliberately made the position of blacks in America into a public issue (see Garrow 1978). In his "Letter from Birmingham Jail," Martin Luther King stated:

> I had hoped that the white moderate would understand that the present tension in the South is a necessary phase of the transition from an obnoxious negative peace, in which the Negro passively accepted his unjust plight, to a substantive and positive peace, in which all men will respect the dignity and worth of human personality. Actually, we who engage in nonviolent direct action are not the creators of tension. We merely bring to the surface the hidden tension that is already alive. We bring it out in the open, where it can be seen and dealt with. Like a boil that can never be cured so long as it is covered up but must be opened with all its ugliness to the natural medicines of air and light, injustice must be exposed, with all the tension its exposure creates, to the light of human conscience and the air of national opinion before it can be cured (King 1964, p. 85).

In Greensboro, where King had delivered a sermon credited with being a catalyst for the sit-ins (Chafe 1980, p. 113), student leaders announced that they would turn their case over to "the reasonable local bar of public opinion" (Chafe 1980, p. 127). The aim was not to bypass negotiations but to put them on a different footing. As King explained to his fellow ministers, negotiations were needed to resolve the crisis in race relations. Again quoting from his "Letter from Birmingham Jail":

> You are quite right in calling for negotiation. Indeed, this is the very purpose of direct action. Nonviolent direct action seeks to create such a crisis and foster such a tension that a community which has constantly refused to negotiate is forced to confront the issue. It seeks so to dramatize the issue that it can no longer be ignored (King 1964, p. 79).

But how did crisis generation produce a new bargaining lever? In what way was the bargaining situation different from the past? In its manifest form, the bargaining lever was often the threat of a mass demonstration, with its potential for disorder and a tarnished community image. In scores of cities, white business and political leaders were in fact concerned to prevent repeated demonstrations.

At a deeper level, however, direct action was a demonstration that racial exclusion could be maintained in public places only by "continuing coercion" and "massive repression" (Chafe 1980, pp. 99, 202). When blacks ceased to be compliant with a Jim Crow social order, the "private" decisions of business people to practice discrimination in public accomodations became a threat to community order. As Carmichael and Hamilton (1967, p. 53) argued, "There can be no social order without social justice."

The civil rights movement thus sought to change the bargaining ground in several ways. New leaders not beholden to white patrons moved to the forefront. Further, instead of retreating into passivity to avoid violence, blacks put the issue of race relations squarely into the public arena, calling for a just as well as an orderly resolution. In this way, they altered the terms of public debate. Moreover, the bugbear of "white backlash" was turned against the community's top political and business leaders. Whereas in the past the possibility of mass violence was used against blacks to urge them onto a path of caution, that same possibility came to be used against established white leaders to urge them into a course of activism.

As new leaders based on a new style of political activism emerged, they put forward a revised agenda of public debate focused on social reform. In contrast with the public passivity of the past, blacks openly sought a direct voice in community governance. What remained to be achieved was an institutionalized basis for such black participation. Protest politics can call attention to the need for change and prompt creative thinking about the need for new political arrangements, but protest politics is not itself a durable base of power (Lipsky 1970). Let us turn to the recent Atlanta experience in altering governing arrangements.

Atlanta and Neighborhood Activism

Atlanta, it is important to bear in mind, is a city with a substantial black middle class and numerous black business and educational institutions. Atlanta also has several significant political features. By 1970, the city had a black majority, and in 1973 elected its first black mayor, Maynard Jackson. After two terms, Jackson was succeeded as mayor by Andrew Young, the city's second black mayor.

Atlanta is the metropolis of the Southeast. Unlike many smaller cities, Atlanta is a place preoccupied with growth and change. Policies to encourage the enlargement and transformation of its central business district have engendered an ongoing conflict between downtown interests and the city's neighborhoods (Stone 1976; Grist, Abney, and Binford 1982; Henson and King 1982). Atlanta's development politics thus offers an opportunity to look at coalition formation in a situation in which several combinations are possible.

Atlanta's housing and redevelopment policy up into the protest era of the 1960s was heavily directed toward revitalization of the central business district and toward the deconcentration of lower-income families from around the center of the city into selected outlying areas. Neighborhood renewal was largely neglected, and residential stability had a lower priority.

In one ten-year period (1956–66), nearly one-seventh of the city's population was displaced by some form of governmental action. This policy was resisted vigorously at several stages over a period of years, but most intensely in the mid-1960s. City-wide black leaders and both black and white neighborhood groups protested this policy at various times and in the late 1960s era of civil disorder, succeeded for a brief period in committing the city to a new program of neighborhood renewal and improved housing opportunities.

After this brief period of responsiveness in the era of civil disorder, city hall backed away from a neighborhood-based housing and redevelopment policy. By 1969, the last year of his administration, Mayor Ivan Allen had lowered the priority given to his earlier announced slum eradication program and declined to pursue additional local funding for neighborhood improvements. This shift in policy occurred even before federal funding began to diminish. Moreover, Allen moved away from his earlier announced goal of providing new low- and moderate-income housing to a policy of "economic balance." Taking a cue from informal discussions in the business community, Mayor Allen became concerned that subsidized housing would be a "magnet for the poor," concentrating the lower-income population in the city.

Sam Massell succeeded Ivan Allen as mayor, but his electoral base was somewhat different from Allen's. Whereas Allen had come to the mayoralty through the presidency of the Chamber of Commerce and extensive involvement in civic affairs as a businessman, Massell had served as a vice-mayor and had a long history of association with and support by liberal elements in Atlanta's politics. In his mayoral campaign in fall 1969, Massell was opposed by Rodney Cook, a moderate Republican, who had served as chairman of the aldermanic Planning and Development Committee during Allen's mayoralty. Cook was endorsed by Allen, the newspapers, and the business community. Massell—liberal, white, and labor-backed—received strong support in the black community and was elected.

Under Massell, conditions seemed propitious for political restructuring. Instead, Massell made an early peace with the business community and centered his program on the development of a mass transit system oriented toward the central business district and funded by a bicounty sales tax acknowledged to be regressive. Neighborhood renewal stayed on the back burner. Massell's electoral base had little bearing on his strategies of governing.

The 1970 Census confirmed that Atlanta had become a black majority city, and Massell put some of his energies into an effort to expand Atlanta's boundaries. While he appointed a number of blacks to high level administrative posts, he also admonished black leaders to "think white" and to represent the general views of all portions of the city, not just those of the black community. During Massell's administration the city officially embraced Ivan Allen's earlier call for a redevelopment policy of "economic balance." As a result, the particular needs of black and low-income people were downplayed in favor of a rhetoric in which programs directed toward business-district growth were assumed to be uniformly beneficial (Stone 1976, p. 183; see also Peirce 1974, pp. 360-65).

As the era of direct action and civil disorder came to a close, neighborhood groups failed to gain institutionalized access to policy making, and their protest-based influence floundered. Though Sam Massell came into office in 1970 as a candidate opposed by the business establishment, he made no effort to bring together an alternative governing coalition. Even the rhetoric of city policy lost its neighborhood flavor and incorporated terms that were especially congenial to the Atlanta business community.

Atlanta: The Recent Period

While development policy underwent no fundamental alteration, race relations did. The city had a black majority and many of the traditional lines of racial separatism faded. Black business and professional people ceased to be excluded from the associational life of downtown Atlanta. Blacks became members of the Chamber of Commerce and various other civic organizations. Within the governmental sector, blacks began to hold more elective and appointed offices. Black-white relations were no longer mediated through a few restricted contacts, but had multiple channels—both public and private. One, the Action Forum, was almost exclusively private, and was formed to bring black and white business leaders together to discuss and act on community issues. Clearly the Jim Crow system had receded into history, and the black middle class had become part of Atlanta's civic life. But on what terms?

Race remained a central fact in the public life of the city. While appointing blacks to major posts, Mayor Massell, as we have seen, nevertheless urged leaders in the black community to "think white." Blacks were expected not to fill their positions in the city's civic life by being group advocates. Moreover, Massell associated "black" and "low income" and indicated that both were a source of difficulty for the city:

> The 1970 Census showed us that in the decade, 60,000 whites had moved out of the city of Atlanta, and 70,000 blacks had moved in. The average family income of the people who moved out was $13,000 a year; of those who moved in, under $9,000. This is intolerable for a city. It's getting more poor people, which means services have to increase (quoted in Peirce 1974, pp. 360-61).

In his reelection campaign, Massell warned of "white flight" should a "black takeover" occur, and he used the slogan: "Atlanta is too young to die" (Peirce 1974, p. 357). While Massell was defeated decisively, the concerns he voiced did not disappear. As Massell's successor in the office of mayor, Maynard Jackson was repeatedly urged by the news media and by white civic leaders to be chief executive to the whole community and not to be narrowly oriented toward the black community. In other words, group advocacy on behalf of the black community was unacceptable.

Business threats to leave the city if the climate became unfavorable served as a further constraint on city hall, and, at one point, representatives of the business community delivered a letter to Mayor Jackson detailing their concerns (see the account in Henson and King 1982, pp. 330-34). Subsequently Jackson arranged a series of "Pound Cake Summit" meetings with the business community. Cordiality between city hall and the business community did not resume, however, until Maynard Jackson was succeeded as mayor by Andrew Young. Young openly and vigorously courted business cooperation.

Given the friction between Maynard Jackson and white business leaders, one might argue that there is prima facie evidence of an alteration in the city's governing coalition—that what direct-action tactics did not achieve in the 1960s, electoral change achieved in the 1970s. Not only did a black mayor assume office in 1974, he did so under a new city charter that made significant change in the city's formal structure of government.

The new charter made substantial accommodations for neighborhood and black representation. Instead of city-wide elections for all council members, two-thirds (12 of 18) were elected by district. The new charter also provided for citizen participation in planning and zoning, and an implementing ordinance divided the city up into 24 Neighborhood Planning Units (NPUs) with hearings mandated in each. Minority business and employment opportunities also gained official recognition through the creation of an office of contract compliance and affirmative action, under the new strong executive administration structure (for a discussion of the previous governmental structure, see Stone 1976, pp. 27-30).

From outward appearances, city governance in the 1970s underwent a revolution, but appearances can be misleading. Let us, then, look at the main contours of development policy over the 1970s and early 1980s to see how various group interests have fared. What we find is as follows.

1. There has been no sustained program of neighborhood improvement. Neighborhoods have won some significant, high visibility victories, particularly in stopping expressways (Grist, Abney, and Binford 1982). But these are essentially defensive actions. Neighborhoods failed to gain a role in setting spending priorities and have encountered substantial resistance from the line agencies of the city (Grist, Abney, and Binford 1982; Stone and Whelan 1979). And neighborhood access to the Planning Department has eroded. The Division of Neighborhood Planning, which once provided planners for each of the NPUs,

has been replaced, and the number of neighborhood planners was steadily decreased during the Jackson mayoralty and virtually eliminated under Young.

2. There is no program of targeted employment for minorities or less skilled workers. The city has made efforts to see that business opportunities are provided blacks in construction, at the Atlanta airport, and at such events as the Piedmont Arts Festival. But despite an announced priority for black employment by Maynard Jackson during his mayoralty and despite Andrew Young's emphasis on economic development, neither administration launched a systematic program of targeting jobs. There is not even a study of the impact of development activities on the job market. Consequently there is no firm evidence on the employment effects of the city's economic development efforts. Jackson at one point touted the idea of a 20 percent guarantee of black employment, but the business community and the Atlanta Economic Development Corporation opposed such a formula on the ground that it would deter businesses from locating in Atlanta. Efforts to negotiate an employment guarantee for neighborhood residents in the redevelopment of the Bedford-Pine renewal area drew strong criticism, and the city failed to back the neighborhood committee on the issue. Further, in response to a study done by Central Atlanta Progress (the downtown business organization), the city changed land use in a section of the Bedford-Pine redevelopment project from light industrial to luxury housing and no one publicly questioned the employment impact of this decision. A job quota was debated for the proposed redevelopment of Underground Atlanta, but shelved in favor of a resolution "encouraging" the developer to reserve half of the construction jobs for Atlanta residents and give them preference in retail employment. Thus, while there is no shortage of rhetoric on the generation of jobs, concrete efforts to see such jobs are provided to those with the greatest employment needs are noteworthy for their absence (cf. Pressman and Wildavsky 1979, p. 25).

3. The city, in conjunction with the state and county, has sustained a multifaceted effort to promote central business district vitality and growth. An illustrative list of projects includes a business-district-centered system of mass transit, expansion of the complex of government office buildings around the southern portion of the business district (an area considered risky for private investment), expanded nonresidential development around Atlanta Stadium, modification of the agreement with the Bedford-Pine neighborhood to provide less subsidized housing and housing preservation, developing luxury housing in Bedford-Pine north of the civic center on the periphery of the business district, use of Community Development Block Grant funds for renewal in the central business district (the Fairlie-Poplar project), creating a historic preservation zone in the central business district in order to provide tax incentives for upgrading, construction of a new library and parks in the heart of the business district, raising the local sales tax in order to cut city property tax, providing bonds to finance economic development in the central business district, building and then expanding a World Congress Center (both state funded) to provide exhibit

space, launching an anticrime campaign of intensive police patrolling in the city's central business district to improve the city's image a a tourist and convention site, conducting an antipornography and antiprostitution campaign in the Midtown area just north of the central business district, and planning the redevelopment and expansion of Underground Atlanta. To be sure, business-backed ideas are not always embodied in policy action; for example, the idea of clearing Techwood Homes, the city's oldest public housing project, was entertained but not pursued. Yet, despite occasional setbacks, there is an overwhelming pattern of business success in seeing public authority and public funds mobilized behind an ongoing effort to promote the economic vitality of the central business district. In brief, the pattern of the 1950s and 1960s continues through the 1970s and into the 1980s.

Thus, despite a change in the electoral balance and the adoption of a new charter, the business community continues to be a major influence. While the black middle class is now a part of the city's governing coalition, neighborhood and lower-income interests enjoy no such favored position. Institutional rearrangements, such as district elections for city council and the creation of Neighborhood Planning Units, did not alter the class character of coalitional bias. It is in order, then, to ask how business influence is accommodated in a system in which electoral control lies with a black majority.

Let me first make explicit my assumption that business influence occurs in a situation of conflict. While it may be that, in the abstract, business district vitality is in the interest of the whole community (see Peterson 1981), concrete proposals involve trade-offs and competing priorities. Economic growth is not an all-benefit, no-cost policy (for example, see the various case studies in Fainstein et al. 1983). There are questions, then, about who will pay the social and other costs and who will garner what share of the benefits. Expressways and redevelopment displacement, tax burdens, spending priorities, targeted employment and housing opportunities, and the compatibility of land use are among specific issues over which the community has been divided. Promoting economic growth in the central business district is thus not a matter of consensual politics, nor one in which popular consent leaves no room for division. It is instead an arena of conflict and its management—an arena in which some contestants have a strong incentive to prevent what Schattschneider (1960) calls the socialization of conflict. Instead, the capacity of corporations to limit popular demands on their conduct is what Lindblom (1977) means by the "privileged position of business" (see also Elkin, 1982).

In Atlanta, in the case of economic development, we are dealing not just with the privileged position of individual business organizations but also with the privileged position of the business community. This position is achieved, at least in part, by conscious design. First of all, the major downtown businesses have created in the form of Central Atlanta Progress an organization that plans, acts, and lobbies on behalf of their collective stake in the business district. There are no other interest-group organizations that can match it in finances and professional staff; the one that comes closest is the Chamber of Commerce, another business organization. In addition, the business community has funded other organizations, such as Research Atlanta, that, because of their private sponsorship, would be able to conduct studies or execute projects without being subject to the "political" pressure of governmental agencies. (By "political" the business community means pressures that emanate from the city's electoral base; "nonpolitical" processes are therefore those which bypass popular control.)

There is, then, a rich network of business-supported organizations that can present themselves as nonpolitical and community minded. They are not departments within individual business enterprises, and they are not a direct part of the profit-seeking activities of any particular business. Consequently, they are not only presented as nonpolitical but also as nonprofit; thus they appear to be less self-serving than most of the organizational actors in city affairs. Their recommendations and actions are therefore not subject to the same kind of critical scrutiny as are the recommendations and actions of business enterprises and more explicitly political organizations.

As a further step toward insulating economic development activities from popular pressures, the business community lobbies for the creation of independent agencies of various kinds to carry on public functions (cf. Friedland 1983). Over time, these arrangements have become more elaborate. For example, during Ivan Allen's mayoralty, the Chamber of Commerce served as the city's economic development arm (and it still receives city money for promoting development). But under Maynard Jackson, the city created an Office of Economic Development. The business community responded to this step by lobbying successfully for replacing that office under the mayor's control with an independent Atlanta Economic Development Corporation, which is located, not in city hall, but in offices adjoining the Chamber of Commerce. The corporation board, of course, has heavy business representation.

A variation of this pattern of creating agencies occurred with the redevelopment of Bedford-Pine—the urban renewal area just east of the business district. In this case the connection to city hall was even more remote. The business community lobbied against having the Atlanta Housing Authority, the city's redevelopment agency at that time, deal directly with developers. Instead they called for the redevelopment of a large cleared area through a comprehensive plan controlled by one organization. Central Atlanta Progress, working with several banks, created a subsidiary called Park Central that served as that organization. With its subsidiary, Park Central, in control of redevelopment, Central Atlanta Progress was able to push ahead with its plan for luxury housing—a plan recommended by Central Atlanta Progress's own Task Force on Housing. In the face of neighborhood demands for the inclusion of subsidized housing, Park Central responded that they "did not want to give the impression to developers, lenders, investors, or particularly renters and homeowners that

Bedford-Pines was some sort of social experiment" (Henson and King 1982, p.324). By gaining control of land disposition through its subsidiary, Central Atlanta Progress "privatized" redevelopment and was able to describe it as an ordinary market transaction—hence not to be viewed as a "social experiment." Pushed into the background was the fact that the land had been acquired through eminent domain and the acquisition had involved the displacement of more than 1,000 low-income residents. At that time there had been a prolonged controversy with civil rights groups and a neighborhood committee that had an agreement with the city to rehouse residents in the area (see Stone 1976, pp.102-14, 153-64). But Park Central controlled the land disposition and outlasted neighborhood opposition (the Park Central phase is recounted in Henson and King 1982, pp.319-30).

The recently proposed redevelopment of Underground Atlanta provides a further example of conflict being confined by the city's role being obscured. The redevelopment of Underground is being promoted under the auspices of a task force representing multiple public and private entities. Because the funds involved are not exclusively city funds, the city council after considerable debate concluded that it could not require that a portion of the jobs be reserved for city residents.

In some cases, the insulation from popular pressure is not organizational. Business subsidies, such as development bonds and tax benefits from the historic-preservation designation, are "off-budget" expenditures. Because they don't come through an appropriations process, they don't compete directly with other expenditures. Moreover, they are not subject to the same kind of evaluation. Few officeholders question their impact, their cost-benefit ratio, or even count them as a form of public expenditure.

What can be said of individual phases of the effort to promote business-district vitality can be said with even greater force for the overall effort. Because the individual elements are frequently indirect, are not concentrated at any one time, often are highly technical, and have low visibility, the larger public is not aware of how many resources go into the effort. So, while there are continuing questions about priorities and uncertainties about benefits, in addition to opposition to specific actions, the conflict is too splintered to have much impact. In the meantime the business community has the organization, information, and economic resources to maintain a multifaceted drive to further its interests. And given business's systematic role as revenue provider as well as the amplitude of its resources, few groups including the mayor's office, are willing to go very far in resisting business influence. Some specific actions are opposed, but no issue is made of how business influence is an integral part of the governance of the community. And since that issue is not raised publicly, there is little opportunity to debate the consequences of business partnership in community governance and to frame questions about how the benefits and costs of business-guided economic development fall on various segments of the community.

Let us now return to our original inquiry about the accommodation between black electoral power and business influence. Inducements to officials to cooperate with business interests are substantial (see Stone 1980) and the risks in excluding them from city governance are great. And, as Maynard Jackson's experience illustrates, should the mayor not be fully attentive to these facts, the business community is quite willing to provide reminders.

The recent Atlanta experience is therefore especially instructive. Despite a shift in the balance of electoral power in favor of blacks and despite modifications in the formal structure of government, the old pattern of business dominance and flagging neighborhood influence reasserted itself. Institutionally this reassertion of business power has occurred through the devolution of planning responsibilities onto quasi-private entities insulated from popular pressure and substantially under the control of the business community.

Why would city officials allow public responsibilities to devolve to quasi-private organizations? Mainly because this was the price of business cooperation and business insisted on it. Seeking the cooperation of business could not be avoided. Prolonged conflict with business would be economically and politically costly, and almost sure to be a losing strategy for any set of local officials. Neighborhoods, especially nonaffluent ones, offer too few resources to provide, by themselves, a substantial base for governing the city. Public officials thus see little to be gained by courting such support at the expense of business disapproval. Hence the constraint on becoming group advocates of lower-class interests is effective. Lacking an alternative base of organizational and economic resources for running the city, public officeholders realize that they cannot govern through an adversary relation to business. Thus they accede to business insistence on working through quasi-private organizations, particularly in promoting economic development.

For its part, the business community is in a good position to play a protected role in governance. Working through a network of seemingly nonpolitical organizations and making use of informal contacts, business is able to remain part of the governing coalition. But it is a low-profile member of the coalition. Business influence is reconciled with black electoral power by the indirect character and low visibility of business influence and the limitations of popular control.

Atlanta Then and Now: A Comparison

Before offering a general conclusion on race and coalitional bias, let me make a brief comparison between Atlanta politics in the years after World War II and Atlanta politics as it took shape in the 1970s. While such matters as the growth of black electoral power and the shift to district elections for the city council are not inconsequential, they are not overridingly important. Consider how business influence has been maintained, while neighborhoods have failed to institutionalize their power. What is significant is how racial and class cleavages are so important in electoral politics but have so subdued a part in the governance of the city. In both the early and the recent period, many policy actions have been insulated from popular pressure and conflict has been scattered among a large number of particular, and usually short-lived, controversies.

I have suggested that, though this pattern represents no one's master plan for ruling Atlanta, it reflects the fact that the business community has worked assiduously to insulate its influence from popular pressure (often labeled as "politics"). While the system of conflict management that surrounds economic development policy has evolved incrementally, it nevertheless represents the superior power position of the business community. There is sufficient authority and control of resources in local government itself for black officeholders to be able to challenge the arrangements through which business protects its position. Black officeholders themselves are constrained to provide a favorable climate for business. To do that, they have to play down racial and class cleavages in the governance of the city. As junior members of the governing coalition, black officeholders find themselves in that classic position—"If you want to get along, go along."

As political officeholders, elected officials (of any race) and their appointees have little opportunity to engage in long-range restructuring. The reelection cycle leaves officials in a situation in which they not only have limited leverage, but they also have little time in which to use that leverage and make their mark. Inextricably officials are led to search for accommodations with established centers of organized power.

RACE, CLASS, AND COALITIONAL BIAS

Even though the Jim Crow system has faded into history, race continues to be a factor in the public life of the United States. Race is intertwined with class, and race is a major factor in public life because class is. While the ascriptive barrier of race is largely gone as an overt feature in public life, the tendency to equate race and class remains.

Middle class blacks face a dilemma. They can advance individually and secure those advances by associating themselves socially, politically, and economically with their class counterparts who are white. Thus there are strong inducements to become involved in the network of business and civic organizations in which white, upper-strata interests predominate. That is why racial segregation was legally and ethically indefensible in a society committed formally to the equality of citizens and informally to an achievement ethic. But the other side of the dilemma is that racial stereotyping continues, and, until the black community is perceived to be no different in class composition from the general population, blacks will be handicapped by an identification with lower-class status. Consequently blacks of all classes continue to share an interest in group advancement through racial solidarity.

Black political leaders find themselves cross-pressured by the electoral exigency of mobilizing a heavily lower-strata constituency at the same time they need the cooperation of upper-strata interests. Intense concerns with the collective interest of blacks are met with the charge from white business and civic leaders (including the news media) that this is special-interest advocacy. And, indeed in a real sense it is. However, it is worth remembering that a mayor with a business background, such as Ivan Allen, can promote the collective interest of business without encountering public criticism. Though Allen came to the mayor's office from the presidency of the Chamber of Commerce, he could work hard for business unity, "a favorable climate for business," and business well-being, and not be regarded as representing a special interest at the expense of the whole community.

Black political leaders lack the same kind of freedom to espouse group well-being. The black politician who works hard for black unity, "a favorable climate for blacks," and the collective well-being of blacks is accused of representing a special interest at some risk to the welfare of the "whole community." In Atlanta, Maynard Jackson encountered this accusation publicly and his leadership was restricted by it.

It might be argued that black political leaders should forego business cooperation and put together an alternative coalition. The left has long urged that class struggle be made manifest by a mobilization of have-nots on behalf of policies of redistribution. But such a strategy has crucial weaknesses. Most obviously, economic competition among cities places institutional constraints on those who would pursue redistribution (Peterson 1981). As we are frequently reminded, business and even nonprofit institutions can disinvest and relocate in other jurisdictions. Affluent individuals are also mobile.

For political leaders, the disincentive to pursue a strategy of redistribution is, however, not exclusively economic. After all, political leaders are not noted for making fine-tuned calculations about the long-term economic health of the jurisdictions they head. Presumably their dominant calculations are political. Let us then put ourselves in the position of a black elected official in a U.S. city.

To launch programs of wide public import and generate activities that can provide particular benefits of the kind that are so useful in coalition building, black political leaders have no place to turn except to white business and civic organizations. We return to Rokkan's phrase, "Votes count but resources decide." White business and civic leaders control the economic and organizational resources essential in undertaking major projects. While federal funds (now diminishing) have provided an alternative source of revenue, many federal programs entail substantial business involvement. It is not that public funds and public authority are inconsequential, but that they often serve as leverage in obtaining private resources for governmental objectives. Public officials have long recognized that efforts to do such things as expand employment, provide job training, and increase the supply of standard housing could be done on a large scale and in a short time period only in partnership with private business. Given a desire for visible action in the short time marked by the election cycle, elected officeholders have little choice but to come to terms with private business and the civic network of which business is an integral part. Class-based mobilization of have-nots on behalf of redistribution cuts off political leaders from economic and organizational resources they sorely need.

It cannot be said too often in the context of U.S. political science: voting strength is a limited base of power (see Keech 1968). Mobilization of mass support can achieve little if it is not connected to some set of arrangements through which social cooperation can be organized and sustained. Without such a set of arrangements, efforts to redistribute benefits will be seen by many people as merely confiscatory. Further, without an institutional base, redistribution efforts can offer at best only short-term gains. Thus leaders who head have-not coalitions and lack an institutional base are not only vulnerable to the charge that they represent special-interest advocacy, they are also unable to bring about substantial improvement in the collective well-being of the lower strata.

In the urban setting, potential leaders of redistributive coalitions thus face awesome barriers. They cannot simply embrace and enact a policy of redistribution. Rather they would have to restructure the associational life of the community and to do so on a time schedule that would not dissipate their support. Moreover, this would have to be done in the face of formidable opposition centered in the economic and organizational power of the business community. It is little wonder that there are few takers. Any major effort to lessen the inequalities of class carries with it all of the costs and risks of bringing about a deep-seated change in the social order itself. It is this stubborn fact that is the underlying foundation of coalitional bias.

What, then, can we say about race, power, and political change? In the civil rights activism of Atlanta and other cities, the politics of race underwent a significant change as blacks made a bid to become part of the governing coalition. By encouraging the neglect of black concerns and by imposing ascriptive considerations widely and blatantly, the Jim Crow system had effectively made all blacks politically subordinate. But not all blacks were "lower-strata" in all respects. In Atlanta blacks commanded significant economic, associational, and cultural resources, and it had a sizable black bourgeoisie. From this group came the vision of an ascription-free and more equal society—the dream of which Martin Luther King spoke so eloquently. That mobilizing vision did enable blacks to change the governing coalition in Atlanta as well as in many other communities. However, once blatant racial barriers were removed and the conflict focused more on class inequalities, the staying power of blacks as a mobilized political force weakened. As the resistance to class-oriented demands stiffened, the opportunity costs went up greatly, even in relation to expanded black political resources. Black unity and black activism gave way to a modified governing coalition in which the black middle class was a part. The price of that arrangement was the cessation of the advocacy of lower strata demands by middle class blacks (cf. Chafe 1980). "Economic balance" and biracial accommodation provided the terms for the inclusion of the black middle class in the governing coalition of Atlanta. Change has occurred, but coalitional bias did not disappear. The lower strata remain outside the governing circle.

REFERENCES

Aaron, Henry J. 1978 *Politics and the Professors*. Washington, D.C.: The Brookings Institution.
Banfield, Edward C. 1965. *Big City Politics*. New York: Random House.
Carmichael, Stokely and Charles V. Hamilton. 1967. *Black Power*. New York: Vintage Books.
Cater, Douglass. 1957. "Atlanta: Smart Politics and Good Race Relations." *Reporter* 11 (July):18-21.
Chafe, William H. 1980. *Civilities and Civil Rights*. New York: Oxford University Press.
Clark, Peter B. 1969. "Civic Leadership: The Symbols of Legitimacy." In *Democracy in Urban America*, 2nd ed., edited by Oliver P. Williams and Charles Press, pp. 350-66. Chicago: Rand McNally.
Dahl, Robert A. 1961. *Who Governs?* New Haven: Yale University Press.
Elkin, Stephen L. 1982. "Market and Politics and Liberal Democracy." *Ethics* 92 (July): 720-32.
Fainstein, Susan S. et al. 1983. *Restructuring the City: The Political Economy of Urban Redevelopment*. New York: Longman.
Friedland, Roger. 1983. *Power and Crisis in the City*. New York: Schocken Books.
Garrow, David J. 1978. *Protest at Selma*. New Haven: Yale University Press.
Goffman, Erving. 1961. *Asylums*. Garden City, N.Y.: Anchor Books.
Grist, Marilyn, Glenn Abney, and Michael Binford. 1982. "Neighborhood Groups: A Challenge to the Elite Theory of Atlanta Politics." Paper presented at the Annual Meeting of the Southern Political Science Association, October 18-30, Atlanta, Georgia.
Gusfield, Joseph R. 1982. Review of *Community Power Succession*, by Floyd Hunter. *Society* 19 (March/April):84-88.
Harsanyi, John C. 1962. "Measurement of Social Power, Opportunity Costs, and the Theory of Two-Person Bargaining Games." *Behavioral Science* 7 (January):67-75.
Henson, M. Dale and James King. 1982. "The Atlanta Public-Private Romance: An Abrupt Transformation." In *Public-Private Partnership in American Cities*, edited by R. Scott Fosler and Renee A. Berger, pp. 293-337. Lexington: D.C. Heath.
Hunter, Floyd. 1980. *Community Power Succession*. Chapel Hill: University of North Carolina Press.
———. 1953. *Community Power Structure*. Chapel Hill: University of North Carolina Press.

Keech, William R. 1968. *The Impact of Negro Voting*. Chicago: Rand McNally.
King, Martin Luther, Jr. 1964. *Why We Can't Wait*. New York: Harper & Row.
Lindblom, Charles E. 1977. *Politics and Markets*. New York: Basic Books.
Lipsky, Michael. 1970. *Protest in City Politics*. Chicago: Rand McNally.
Matthews, Donald R. and James W. Prothro. 1966. *Negroes and the New Southern Politics*. New York: Harcourt, Brace & World.
Merelman, Richard M. 1968. "On the Neo-Elitist Critique of Community Power." *American Political Science Review* 62 (June):451-60.
Peterson, Paul E. 1981. *City Limits*. Chicago: University of Chicago Press.
Peirce, Neal R. 1974. *The Deep South States of America: People, Politics, and Power in the Seven Deep South States*. New York: W.W. Norton.
Polsby, Nelson W. 1980. *Community Power and Political Theory: A Further Look at Problems of Evidence and Inference*. 2nd, enlarged edition. New Haven: Yale University Press.
Pressman, Jeffrey L. and Aaron Wildavsky. 1979. *Implementation*. 2nd ed. Berkeley: University of California Press.
Rokkan, Stein. 1966. "Norway: Numerical Democracy and Corporate Pluralism." In *Political Oppositions in Western Democracies*, edited by Robert A. Dahl, pp. 70-115. New Haven: Yale University Press.
Schattschneider, E.E. 1960. *The Semi-Sovereign People*. New York: Holt, Rinehart and Winston.
Schelling, Thomas C. 1971. "On the Ecology of Micromotives." *Public Interest* No. 25 (Fall):61-98.
Stone, Clarence N. 1982. "Social Stratification, Nondecision-Making, and the Study of Community Power." *American Politics Quarterly* 10 (July):275-302.
_____. 1980. "Systemic Power in Community Decision Making." *American Political Science Review* 74 (December):978-90.
_____. 1976. *Economic Growth and Neighborhood Discontent*. Chapel Hill: University of North Carolina Press.
_____ and Robert K. Whelan. 1979. "Post-Reform Politics: The Changing Context of Citizen Participation." *Midwest Quarterly* 220 (Spring): 300-15.
Sykes, Gresham M. 1958. *The Society of Captives*. Princeton: Princeton University Press.
Thurow, Lester C. 1981. *The Zero-Sum Society*. New York: Penguin Books.
Walker, Jack L. 1963. "Protest and Negotiation: A Case Study of Negro Leadership in Atlanta, Georgia." *Midwest Journal of Political Science* 7 (May):99-124.
Wilson, William Julius. 1980. *The Declining Significance of Race*. 2nd ed. Chicago: University of Chicago Press.

ABOUT THE EDITOR AND THE CONTRIBUTORS

JANET K. BOLES is an Assistant Professor of Political Science at Marquette University and the author of *The Politics of the Equal Rights Amendment*. Her articles on social policy, women and politics, neighborhoods, and urban fiscal stress have appeared in edited books and journals. She is currently researching the impact of the women's movement on the design of urban services.

CHARLES S. BULLOCK, III is the Richard Russell Professor of Political Science at the University of Georgia. He is the coauthor of *Implementation of Civil Rights Policy, Public Policy in the Eighties*, and *Public Policy and Politics in America*. His research on legislative politics and civil rights policy has appeared in numerous journals, including the *American Political Science Review, Journal of Politics, American Journal of Political Science,* and *Social Science Quarterly*.

JAMES W. BUTTON is an Associate Professor of Political Science at the University of Florida. He has been a consultant and expert witness for governmental agencies and private groups involved in community voting issues. His research focuses on the impact of federal legislation upon black and other minority participation in local politics.

JOYOTPAUL CHAUDHURI is an Associate Dean, College of Liberal Arts, and Professor of Political Science at Arizona State University. His research on democratic theory, American Indian policy and jurisprudence has appeared in monographs and journals, including *Ethics, American Journal of Political Science,* and *Social Science Journal*.

ROBERT F. CUERVO is an Assistant Professor of Political Science at St. John's University (Staten Island campus). He is a contributor to *A Public Philosophy Reader* and has published in the *Presidential Studies Quarterly*. His current research interests include normative political theory, the Presidency, urban history, and the history and politics of mass transit.

IRENE J. DABROWSKI is an Assistant Professor of Sociology at St. John's University (Staten Island campus). Her major research focuses on employment patterns and civic volunteerism of working-class women and has appeared in *Policy Studies Journal, Social Science Journal,* and *Western Sociological Review,* among others. She also is a contributor to *The Private Exercise of Public Function*.

RODOLFO O. DE LA GARZA is Executive Assistant to the Chancellor of the University of Texas System. He is coauthor of *The Chicano Political*

Experience and coeditor of a special issue of the *Social Science Quarterly* on the Mexican-origin population. His articles have also appeared in *Western Political Quarterly* and *Annals of the American Academy of Political Science.*

JOYCE GELB is Professor and Chair of the Department of Political Science at the City College of New York. She is coauthor of *The Politics of Social Change: A Reader for the 70's, Tradition and Change in American Party Politics,* and *Women and Public Policies.* Her numerous articles and monographs have appeared in scholarly journals and newspapers including *Polity, Urban Affairs Quarterly,* and the New York *Times.*

MARILYN GITTELL is Professor of Political Science at the Graduate School and University Center of the City University of New York. She has written extensively on both participation and the politics of education, including: *Community Control and the Urban School, Local Control in Education, Six Urban School Districts: A Comparative Study of Institutional Response* (coauthor), *Participants and Participation: A Study of School Policy in New York City,* and *Limits to Citizen Participation.*

ANTHONY L. HAYNOR is an Assistant Professor of Sociology at St. John's University (Staten Island campus). He has published in *Free Inquiry in Creative Contemporary Sociology* and the *Proceedings of the Society for General Systems Research.* His current research interests include the development of a system-based sociological perspective, and the relationship between personality and social structure in industrial societies.

BYRAN O. JACKSON is an Assistant Professor of Political Science and an Adjunct Assistant Professor of Urban Studies at Washington University, St. Louis. He has worked as a Social Science Research Analyst for the Department of Housing and Urban Development's Office of Policy Development and Research. His current research interests include citizen participation in urban revitalization and federal housing assistance policy.

ROBERTA ANN JOHNSON ia an Associate Professor of Government at the University of San Francisco. She is the author of *Puerto Rico: Commonwealth or Colony?* Her articles on Puerto Rico and minority rights have appeared in a number of journals and books, including *Polity* and *Journal of Black Studies.*

SUSAN A. MACMANUS is a Professor of Urban Affairs and Director of the Ph.D. Program in Urban Studies at Cleveland State University. She is the author of several books, including *Revenue Patterns in U.S. Cities and Suburbs, Federal Aid to Houston,* and *Governing a Changing America* (with Charles S. Bullock, III and Donald F. Freeman). Her numerous articles on urban politics and minorities appear in *American Journal of Political Science, Journal of Politics,* and *Western*

Political Quarterly, among others. She is currently working on a book on changing municipal expenditure priorities.

JILL NORGREN is an Associate Professor of Government at the John Jay College of Criminal Justice, the City University of New York. She is a contributor to *Women: A Feminist Perspective* and *Women, Power and Policy*, as well as to scholarly journals and popular periodicals. Currently she is working on a book on federal Indian law.

WALTER A. ROSENBAUM is a Professor of Political Science at the University of Florida. The author of numerous books and articles on public participation in governmental policy implementation, he is particularly interested in energy and environmental policy.

GRETA SALEM is an Associate Professor of Political Science at Alverno College and coauthor of *Fear of Crime: Incivility and the Production of a Social Problem*. She has published articles on community participation and the political science curriculum in a number of journals and edited books.

CLARENCE N. STONE is a Professor in the Department of Government and Politics and Institute for Urban Studies at the University of Maryland. His books include *Economic Growth and Neighborhood Discontent* and *Urban Policy and Politics in a Bureaucratic Age* (with Robert Whelan and William Murin). He is also the author of numerous articles on community power structure, urban leadership, policy implementation, and urban services.

DAVID J. THOMAS is an Associate Professor of Politics and a Fellow of Adlai E. Stevenson College at the University of California, Santa Cruz. He has published a number of scholarly articles on gay politics and has also written on gay affairs for newspapers and gay publications.

JANET WEAVER is a Research Associate at the Center for Mexican-American Studies, University of Texas. She is the coauthor of an article appearing in *Social Science Quarterly* and an Occasional Paper in the Center's "Mexican American Electorate" series. Her research focuses on Mexican-American political attitudes and behavior.

LIBRARY OF DAVIDSON COLLEGE